HARNESSING THE POWER OF
EQUINE ASSISTED COUNSELING

HARNESSING THE POWER OF
EQUINE ASSISTED COUNSELING

Adding Animal Assisted Therapy to Your Practice

KAY SUDEKUM TROTTER

Routledge
Taylor & Francis Group
New York London

Routledge
Taylor & Francis Group
711 Third Avenue
New York, NY 10017

Routledge
Taylor & Francis Group
27 Church Road
Hove, East Sussex BN3 2FA

© 2012 by Taylor & Francis Group, LLC
Routledge is an imprint of Taylor & Francis Group, an Informa business

Printed in the United States of America on acid-free paper
Version Date: 20110805

International Standard Book Number: 978-0-415-89841-6 (Hardback) 978-0-415-89842-3 (Paperback)

Library of Congress Cataloging-in-Publication Data

Harnessing the power of equine assisted counseling : adding animal assisted
    therapy to your practice / [edited by] Kay Trotter.
        p. ; cm.
    Includes bibliographical references and index.
    ISBN 978-0-415-89841-6 (hardback : alk. paper) -- ISBN 978-0-415-89842-3
    (pbk : alk. paper)
        1. Horses--Therapeutic use. 2. Horsemanship--Therapeutic use.
    3. Psychotherapy. 4. Horses--Psychological aspects. 5. Human-animal
    relationships. I. Trotter, Kay. II. Title.
        [DNLM: 1. Equine-Assisted Therapy. 2. Counseling--methods. WM
    450.5.A6]

    RC489.H67H37 2011
    615.8'51581--dc23   2011023050

Visit the Taylor & Francis Web site at
http://www.taylorandfrancis.com

and the Routledge Web site at
http://www.routledgementalhealth.com

CONTENTS

6   Techniques That Focus on Social Skills and Communication   151

INTRODUCTION

When I began my doctorate dissertation research on equine assisted counseling (EAC), I was studying at the University of North Texas to become a licensed professional counselor and knew little about horses. I had always been fascinated by the powerful animal–human bond and wanted to explore whether the anecdotal feel-good stories about horses helping people had any clinical validity. Under the guidance of Cynthia Chandler, developer and director of the Center for Animal Assisted Therapy, I compared the experiences of children and adolescents who participated in a 12-week EAC program with those who remained in a classroom for traditional guidance counseling. The results proved decisively that using a horse in counseling sessions gets clinically significant results in increasing positive behaviors while also decreasing negative behaviors in clients. My dissertation, The Efficacy of Group Equine Assisted Counseling With At-Risk Children and Adolescents, was summarized in the *Journal of Creativity in Mental Health*, a peer-reviewed publication of the American Counseling Association (Trotter, Chandler, Goodwin-Bond, & Casey, 2008).

Many of the youngsters in the study responded so positively and so quickly to the EAC intervention that I knew immediately, despite my previous lack of knowledge about horses, that I was definitely going to incorporate this powerful resource into my counseling practice. I also wanted to help make EAC accessible to other counselors, even those who, like me, had little previous equine experience.

This is why I worked with counselors, doctors, and other mental health professionals across the globe to create this book, which is designed to expand opportunities for licensed mental health practitioners to view, understand, respond to, and conceptualize treatment for clients through an EAC lens. This collection of EAC techniques was developed *by* counselors, *for* counselors, to help therapists add this cutting-edge and effective resource to their therapeutic toolbox.

Besides featuring step-by-step clinical protocols for incorporating EAC into any counselor's existing practice, this book also offers a unique look into EAC through the perspective of the horse by guest author Pat Parelli, who is the internationally respected creator of one of the top horsemanship programs in the world. His natural horse training is actually people training—educating others how to interact with horses in a positive, safe, and respectful manner. He shares the process of developing a relationship with a horse and the resulting journey of self-discovery that makes horses such an effective addition to the counseling dynamic.

☐ How to Use This Book

This book contains the information a mental health professional would need to begin an EAC program. It is intended to be an adjunct to your existing practice and to support you through a dynamic and clinically proven treatment modality. The material and techniques in this book are included for clients of a wide age range; however, developmental (cognitive, emotional, and social) needs must be taken into account at all times. Each section and chapter unit is created with its own topics and mix of techniques according to the needs and development of specific populations served or their clinical diagnoses. Though each chapter provides techniques and clinical processing suggestions, it is recommended that each counselor design his or her own opening and closing rituals and structure session check-ins. Adaptations may be necessary to fit the emerging needs of individuals or groups to accommodate the time, circumstances, and settings.

At any time during the session, the counselor may choose to intervene skillfully to facilitate problem solving, interpersonal communication, or personal growth. Skilled counselors will intuitively sense how to guide the group or individual toward awareness of one's process—that is, *what I did* and *how I did it.* Thus, as clients gain awareness of specific behaviors, they can choose to experiment with new ways of being. The role of the counselor will vary depending on the selections of therapeutic interventions.

In this book, I share techniques incorporating both ground and mounted therapies, and I use the term *equine assisted counseling* to indicate therapies requiring a licensed mental health provider working with clients and horses. I purposefully refer to this type of counseling as *equine assisted counseling* versus *equine assisted psychotherapy, equine facilitated psychotherapy,* or *equine therapy* because it strengthens and litigates the mental health focus of our work.

I feel the problem with using the term *equine therapy* to describe this type of work is twofold: (1) it is too generic in nature and (2) the general population assumes you are referring to using a horse for physical therapy work, such as *hippotherapy,* which is conducted by physical therapists who use the horse to accomplish treatment goals as specified by a physician's prescription. *Psychotherapy* and *counseling* are often used interchangeably. Although they are very similar, there are some subtle differences. I choose to use the term *equine assisted counseling* because to use the term counseling I am required to meet specific state and national licensing requirements. Unfortunately, there are no governing bodies that regulate titles such as *psychotherapist* and *therapist,* so anyone can claim these designations. The term counseling, when properly used, also refers to what occurs in a relationship between a client and a counselor and is generally used to denote a relatively brief treatment, primarily focused on behavior. Psychotherapy, on the other hand, is a longer-term treatment that focuses more on gaining insight into the root cause of chronic physical and emotional problems.

☐ **Reference**

Trotter, K.S., Chandler, C.K., Goodwin-Bond, D., & Casey, J. (2008). A comparative study of the efficacy of group equine assisted counseling with at-risk children and adolescents. *Journal of Creativity in Mental Health*, 3(3), 254–284.

ABOUT THE EDITOR

Kay Sudekum Trotter, PhD, LPC-S, RPT-S, NCC, is a licensed professional counselor and supervisor, a registered play therapist and supervisor, a national certified counselor, and a certified equine assisted counselor. She holds a doctoral degree from the University of North Texas, where she studied and practiced play therapy and equine assisted counseling and authored and presented on these topics.

In 2004, Trotter attempted to research empirical data from previous studies on the effectiveness of equine assisted counseling (EAC). To her surprise, there wasn't any. There was plenty of anecdotal evidence, but she could find no significant scientific research supporting the validity of using horses as an adjunct to traditional talk therapy. That discovery made her even more committed to conducting clinical trials to determine if horses could, indeed, make a positive therapeutic difference. At the end of her 12-week research study, the data were clear. Introducing horses into counseling sessions resulted in statistically significant improvements in increasing positive behaviors while also reducing negative behaviors. Trotter's groundbreaking research resulted in one of the first published studies on the clinical effectiveness of EAC and a frequently referenced cornerstone of the animal assisted therapy field.

Her work was published in the *Journal of Creativity in Mental Health*, a peer-reviewed publication of the American Counseling Association (ACA). The journal article written from Trotter's research, "A Comparative Study of the Efficacy of Group Equine Assisted Counseling With At-Risk Children and Adolescents," is available for free download from her website at www.kaytrotter.com/epic.htm.

In 2006, she founded Equine Partners in Counseling (EPIC) Enterprises to expand opportunities for licensed mental health practitioners to offer clients unique, clinically proven treatment with measurable results by providing a platform to view, understand, respond, and conceptualize clients through an EAC lens. Trotter is not the traditional girl who grew up loving horses, so over the years she's learned not only what horses can do in a therapeutic setting but also how to incorporate horses into the counseling arena. For Trotter, not being a horse person has actually proved beneficial when speaking to other counselors about equine therapy because she can let them know firsthand that they don't need to be professional wranglers to successfully use this resource with clients. To help other counselors new to equine therapy, Trotter has written the *EPIC Treatment Manual for At-Risk Youth* (available from www.kaytrotter.com/estore.htm).

Trotter is a board member of the Certification Board for Equine Interaction Professionals (CBEIP), an independent not-for-profit credentialing body for equine therapists. The organization is dedicated to promoting professional credibility through the establishment and monitoring of national certification and raising public awareness about the efficacy of equine assisted counseling.

Today, Trotter is in private practice in Flower Mound, Texas. In this countrified suburb of Dallas, she runs her own traditional counseling practice along with her equine assisted counseling practice, Mendin' Fences, where she provides unique counseling services to children, teenagers, and families with behavioral and mental health issues. Trotter specializes in child, adolescent, and adult survivors of childhood abuse and neglect. She also has extensive experience counseling individuals, families, and couples who are wrestling with abuse, trauma, grief, depression, and emotional and behavioral disorders.

☐ Fun Facts

Trotter is an avid organic gardener whose veggie and flower gardens provide her with a creative canvas to nurture her soul. She is a tree hugger who also enjoys refinishing furniture, cooking gourmet meals, and eating white bread, white rice, and white potatoes. She also regularly plays softball and tennis with her husband, daughter, and son-in-law. She has been married for more than 20 years and is looking forward to being a grandmother someday. You can follow Trotter on Facebook, Twitter, LinkedIn, and her blog (check her webpage for direct links to all of Kay's social media sites). Contact Trotter at 214-499-0396, kay@kaytrotter.com, or via www.kaytrotter.com.

ABOUT THE CONTRIBUTORS

Vallerie E. Coleman, PsyD, PhD, is the founder and clinical director of Stand InBalance LLC (standinbalance.com), which provides equine assisted psychotherapy and equine assisted growth and learning in Calabasas, California. As a clinical psychologist and psychoanalyst, Coleman specializes in helping individuals and couples improve their lives and relationships through relational and experiential therapies. She is certified by the Equine Assisted Growth and Learning Association, and her work is based in a combination of object relations theory, attachment theory, and sensorimotor psychotherapy. Coleman is passionate about horses and their ability to help humans embody their authentic selves. She is an accomplished presenter and has been on faculty at Loyola Marymount University and the Newport Psychoanalytic Institute. Coleman currently serves on the editorial board of the journal *Partner Abuse* and has published several articles on domestic violence. She can be contacted through email at drval@standinbalance.com or by phone at 310-450-8136.

Robert E. Dailey, PsyD, HSPP—horses, mules, and a headstrong boy in a hayfield are where it started. A 4-year-old boy roamed freely around, under horse and mule. Then one day a mule some 20 times bigger than the boy decided to extricate the nuisance with one kick. The boy saw insubordination on the part of the impotent equine. The kick missed, but the boy's did not: With a swift but short approach he landed a good one. No more revolt: The hierarchy was struck and behavior management and a base for research begun. Many years later, Dailey was approached to contribute to this pioneering equine therapy research suggesting a new venue for nonverbal intervention for individuals with severe limitations. The current research continued with Dailey's prior research interests in marital satisfaction, personality, and end-of-life research. You can contact Dailey at redassoc@hotmail.com.

Molly DePrekel, MA, LP, is the clinical director for Cairns Psychological Services. She is the cofounder of Minnesota Linking Individuals, Nature, and Critters. She uses the unique relationship people have with animals in therapy. She has practiced in hospitals and educational and mental health facilities and holds a certificate in sensorimotor (somatic) psychotherapy. DePrekel has also completed level-one eye movement desensitization and reprocessing (EMDR) training. She completed an internship at Green Chimneys. She is involved as past president of the Equine Facilitated Mental Health Association (EFMHA) and is an Epona-approved instructor. She has facilitated workshops and training nationally. Currently, DePrekel is a board member of the Certification Board for Equine Interaction Professionals, which promotes voluntary certification by examination for those who incorporate equines into their mental health or educational practice. Her website is www.mwtraumacenter.com, and she can be contacted at 952-934-2555 or molly@mwtraumacenter.com.

Sara D. Edwards, MA, LPC, has her master's and all-but-dissertation doctorate in clinical psychology from Duke University. Her clinical internship was completed at the University of Wisconsin Center for Health Sciences in the Department of Psychiatry. Edwards has worked as a psychological research specialist, psychological testing specialist (outpatient–inpatient), and psychological consultant. She has been a psychotherapist in private practice since 1989. Her therapeutic work is based on interpersonal theory and includes an equine program. Edwards worked as an animal behavior research specialist at the University of Wisconsin Primate Research Center, conducting independent research and assisting in animal behavior field and lab research. Work in the combined fields of animal behavior and clinical psychology has provided a unique perspective on equine assisted psychotherapy. She developed and practices the theoretical and clinical construct of Interpersonal Equine Therapy (IPET) and conducts seminars and training workshops using IPET as interpersonal therapy. She can be reached at 920-559-2278, sderiver@gmail.com, and www.interpersonalequinetherapy.com.

Steven B. Eller, MA, LPC-Intern, is a counselor for Abilene Christian University. He received his master's in marriage and family therapy from Abilene Christian University and is currently a licensed professional counselor intern working toward licensure in the state of Texas. He is a member of the American Association for Marriage and Family Therapy (AAMFT) and Equine Assisted Growth and Learning Association (EAGALA). Eller is an EAGALA certified equine assisted psychotherapist. He is currently serving on the EAGALA University/College Committee. Eller developed and directs the equine assisted psychotherapy and learning program at Abilene Christian University, which serves the students, faculty, staff, and dependents of the university. He allocates his time during the week with clients in both traditional counseling in the office and equine assisted psychotherapy in the arena. He can be contacted at steve.eller@acu.edu.

Tracie Faa-Thompson, MA, AASW, PDdipNDPT, DipC.hypno, is Equine Assisted Growth and Learning Association (EAGALA) certified, a specialist social worker in adoption, a nondirective play therapist, and a clinical hypnotherapist. She specializes in trauma, attachment, and relationship work with adoptive families. Rise Van Fleet and Faa-Thompson developed a specialist training course for play therapists using dogs and horses as cotherapists. Van Fleet and Faa-Thompson are currently cowriting various articles on the growing field of animal assisted therapy. Based near the Scottish border, she has a lifetime of working alongside horses and is a member of the Classical Riding Club. She is currently running an equine assisted research project for at-risk teenagers. She is a founding member of the attachment and resilience training consortium and has developed an experiential training course on life story work for social workers. Faa-Thompson can be contacted at mike.faathompson@virgin.net.

Deborah Goodwin-Bond, MS, LPC, has been practicing equine assisted counseling since 2001. She has been involved with horses for over 30 years. Currently, she owns two horses: an appendix quarter horse, Sugar Bart Smash, affectionately known as Boo; and an American Paint Horse Association (APHA) breeding stock gelding, Heza Smooth Brandy, affectionately known as Wally. Both horses have been involved in providing equine assisted counseling to hundreds of adolescents and adults. Goodwin-Bond can be contacted at dygb@aol.com.

Holly A. Hargreaves, MA, LCPC, NCC, is a doctoral student in the counseling program at George Washington University. She is a licensed clinical professional counselor as well as a nationally certified counselor with a master's degree in forensic psychology and a second master's in community counseling. She has published and conducted research studies on human–animal interaction, focusing on studies investigating the benefits of therapeutic riding programs with a research team of developmental psychologists, including Delores Westerman and Patricia Westerman, whose work began in 2005. She also serves as the codirector of training in the American Psychological Association's Section on Animal–Human Interaction: Research & Practice, of Division 17 on Counseling Psychology. Hargreaves may be reached at 703-717-2601 or at hollyhargreaves@hotmail.com.

Kristina Houser, PhD, LICDC, is a licensed psychologist and licensed independent chemical dependency counselor. She received her PhD in community counseling from Ohio University in Athens. Her interest in the impact of loss has led to service with populations with posttraumatic stress disorder (PTSD), adoption issues, and family dysfunction. She has made presentations to Tri-County Mental Health & Counseling, Inc., and Athens County Children Services. She is currently in private practice, serving individuals and families, in Athens, Ohio, and can be reached at 740-592-5689 and khouser@dishmail.net.

Holly Jedlicka, MSW, LISW, has been an equine professional for 15 years and spent her childhood learning, competing, and playing with her horses. Her vision is to give young people the great equine opportunities she had while growing up. Jedlicka is a registered instructor with the North American Riding for the Handicapped Association (NARHA) and holds an Equine Assisted Growth and Learning Association (EAGALA) certification. She spent 6 years coaching the dressage and combined training teams at Otterbein University and 2 years as the program director at a therapeutic riding center in central Ohio. Jedlicka graduated from The Ohio State University with her master's in social work and spent a year and a half working at the Buckeye Ranch. She cofounded and is the program director and lead mental health professional at PBJ Connections, Inc., in Pataskala, Ohio. She can be reached at hjedlicka@embarqmail.com.

Pamela Jeffers, MS, TRS, is an equine specialist and therapeutic recreation specialist. She received her BS in therapeutic recreation and her MS in recreation administration from Ohio University in Athens. She incorporated Natural Freedom, LLC, in Albany, Ohio, to serve populations who have experienced trauma. Her lifelong interest in equine behavior has led her to the practice of relationship-based equine assisted counseling. She serves families formed through foster care and adoption, veterans and their families, and individuals seeking improved relationships. She continues to develop her understanding of the equine's ability to teach humans about relationships and the mind, body, and spirit connection. Jeffers has 30 years of experience working with horses, including groundwork, training, instructing, coaching, and competing. She also has taught at Hocking College and has presented in The Ohio University College of Osteopathic Medicine and Meigs Cancer Initiative. She can be reached at 740-541-3053 or 740-698-6031 or jeffersfarms@yahoo.com. Her website is www.naturalfreedomohio.com.

Beverley Kane, MD, is on the clinical faculty at Stanford School of Medicine in Palo Alto, California, where she teaches both medicine and horsemanship and a class on maintenance of doctor–patient rapport during the use of the electronic medical record. Now in its sixth year at Stanford, medicine and horsemanship teaches communication and leadership skills to medical students and health-care professionals, including doctors, nurses, and therapists. Kane's private practice, Horsensei Equine-Assisted Learning and Therapy (HEALTH), additionally conducts programs for corporate groups and for those seeking psychospiritual growth and development. Horsensei's vision is to have medicine and horsemanship taught at additional medical centers. To this end, Kane wrote the *Manual of Medicine and Horsemanship* to enable anyone with an EAP or EAL practice to conduct programs for medical clientele. With the use of the manual, medicine and horsemanship is being taught across the United States and in Central America.

Mary Looman, PhD, is the executive director of Groundwork First Family Development Institute, a 501(c)3 organization that provides experiential growth and learning programs that develop and sustain well-functioning family practices and reduce family violence. She has a PhD in clinical psychology, a master's in counseling, and a master's in administration. She has been a licensed mental health professional in Oklahoma for over 15 years, a clinically certified forensic evaluator for 10 years, and a certified equine assisted psychotherapist, Level II, since 2008. She is a research practitioner in the area of human growth and potential and has been published in several professional journals. Her research on supervisor–trainee relationship synergy received an award for excellence in research. She can be contacted at groundworkfirst@yahoo.com or 405-326-2256.

Mari Louhi-Lehtiö, MSc, has a master's in clinical biochemistry, is a licensed teacher (grade 7 to professional education) specializing in special and alternative education and social emotional learning, is a certified supervisor and work counselor of groups and individuals, and is a certified riding instructor, Epona-approved instructor, and Equine Assisted Growth and Learning Association (EAGALA) Level 1. She is currently in solution-focused family therapy training and working on her PhD at University of Jyväskylä in the Department of Psychology. Her professional and research interests include the elements of efficacy and applications of experiential social emotional learning and ethical horsemanship based on bonding and stress control. She has been in the committees formulating

Equine Facilitated Mental Health Association (EFMHA) Code of Ethics and Standards for equine facilitated psychotherapy (EFP). She works with families weekly but also frequently lectures internationally on standards, ethics, and equine assisted social emotional learning (EASEL) and trains with her team of professionals in the EASEL methodology in Finland, Sweden, and continental Europe. She can be contacted via email at mari@cavesson.com or via her website, www.cavesson.com.

Erin Lucas, MA, is a licensed independent social worker. She received her undergraduate degree in biological sciences and Spanish and her master's in social work from Ohio University in Athens. Lucas serves a population of children and families formed through foster care and adoption. Her interest in the physiological basis for human behavior in response to trauma has prompted her use of equine assisted therapy, electroencephalogram (EEG) biofeedback and other relaxation techniques, narrative therapy, and other techniques based on attachment theory to facilitate healing. She has made presentations to The Ohio University School of Music, therapeutic foster care networks, and Athens County Children Services' foster and adoptive families and staff. She is a member of the Professional Association of Therapeutic Horsemanship International (PATH Intl.) and the National Association of Social Workers (NASW). She can be reached at 740-592-3091 or erinlucas97@yahoo.com.

Blair McKissock, MSEd, RTRI, a certified therapeutic riding instructor and wellness coach, has been certified by Equine Assisted Growth and Learning Association (EAGALA) Level 1, and has trained in many other equine assisted methods. She is the cofounder of ehorseeducation.com, which offers online and in-person professional development workshops. She is recognized for her curriculum created for the national Fatherhood Initiative. She is the Indianapolis horse writer for examiner.com and is the creator of Equi-Yo, a mounted yoga program. She is involved with the Professional Association of Therapeutic Horsemanship International (PATH Intl.) and has presented at three national conferences and several horse fairs. She has 20 years of experience working in animal assisted therapy and behavior change coaching. She holds a bachelor's degree in recreation therapy with an emphasis on animal assisted and experiential based interventions. She earned her master's in education studying the Black Stallion Literacy program and helped to create a certificate in animal assisted therapy at Purdue University.

Kay Neznik, LICSW, ACSW, has a private practice where she specializes in working with children, adolescents, and adults struggling from the trauma of sexual abuse. She also works with children and adolescents who have acted out sexually with others. She is level one–trained in eye movement desensitization and reprocessing (EMDR). She also specializes in therapy with children and teens who have Asperger's or high-functioning autism. She provides individual, family, group, and animal assisted therapy. She also works for an intermediate school district as a school social worker in programs for the mentally ill, for those with fetal alcohol syndrome, and for those on the autism spectrum. She has experience presenting and publishing articles. She can be reached at her private practice number, 651-642-1709, or kneznik411@hotmail.com.

Janet Nicholas, MA, LPC, LCDC, EAP, received her undergraduate degree in addiction studies from St. Edwards University and her graduate degree in clinical psychology from Sam Houston State University. Her training and certification for equine work have been acquired through Parelli methods and the Equine Assisted Growth and Learning Association (EAGALA) organizations. Her traditional counseling practice is located in The Woodlands, Texas. She operates her equine assisted counseling, learning, and team-building practice in Magnolia, Texas, and is a contributing writer for *Recovery Today Magazine* on equine assisted services. Nicholas often speaks in the community and church settings on a variety of issues. For more information about her areas of specialty, please visit her websites at www.janetnicholas.com and www.trails-less-traveled.com or contact her at janet@janetnicholas.com or 713-882-4268.

Joy Nussen, LMFT, has been a licensed marriage and family psychotherapist since 1991. She is a graduate of the University of California, Los Angeles, where she earned her BA in psychology. She subsequently completed graduate training in educational psychology at California State University at Northridge. Nussen has a wide range of experience from private practice to the hospital setting and in the corporate world; she has been studying horsemanship since adopting her mare in 2007, and equine assisted psychotherapy (EAP) has become her true passion. Nussen is the founder and executive director of EquineWorks and is Equine Assisted Growth and Learning Association (EAGALA) certified. Her website is www.equineworks.com, and she can be contacted at 949-422-6355 or joynussen@equineworks.com.

Pat Parelli founded the Parelli Program in 1981 and is a lifelong horseman and teacher. He combines in-depth equine psychology and common-sense communication techniques for the ultimate recipe to horse and rider success. The Parelli method allows horse owners at all levels of experience to achieve success without force, partnership without dominance, and harmony without coercion. Since coining the term *natural* *horsemanship* in 1991, Parelli and his wife and teaching partner, Linda, have worked tirelessly to perfect their at-home learning program with input from more than 200,000 students across 35 countries. As two of the world's preeminent equine behaviorists, the Parellis continue to tutor students and professionals of all disciplines, to advise Olympic and Paralympic medalists, and to captivate global audiences of recreational riders at sold-out venues worldwide. The popularity and success of the Parelli Program have allowed for significant changes in the equine industry, and the Parellis remain dedicated to improving the lives of horses and creating opportunities for the people who love them. In the future, Parelli is focused on developing youth programs, horse rescue initiatives, scholarships for talented and underprivileged students, and para-equestrian pursuits and Paralympic contenders. By using love, language, and leadership, Parelli is on a mission to help create a better world for horses and humans, working to inspire, empower, and educate through natural horsemanship. To learn more, visit www.parelli.com.

Judith S. Schneider, LISW, obtained her degree in social work from Boston University in 1986. Prior to moving to the Southwest, she worked with abused and neglected children, chronically mentally ill adults, polysubstance abusers, and military families facing deployment and suicide. While working as a probation and parole officer, she worked with female, violent, and sexual offenders. During the school year, she is a therapist in a rural school-based wellness center where she offers traditional and equine assisted counseling services to high-risk students who reside on the Navajo Reservation in New Mexico. It has been a lifelong goal of Schneider's to incorporate mental health services and horses. On May 2, 2007, she and her husband opened Healing Through Horses in Abiquiu, New Mexico, which offers equine assisted counseling to children, teens, adults, and families. In addition, it hosts day and overnight retreats for women. For more information, please visit www.healingthroughhorses.net.

Deirdre Stanton, MA/BC, CEIP-MH, CTRI, received her master's degree from Roosevelt University where she majored in clinical psychology and minored in both human and animal behavior. She has given presentations concerning program development and methodologies, most notably at a World Health Organization conference in Geneva, Switzerland. She has worked as a behavior consultant and behavioral services administrator for the past 7 years and as a certified NARHA registered therapeutic riding instructor since 2003. She is also a certified equine interaction professional–mental health (CEIP-MH). Stanton has developed curriculum and programming focused on human–equine interaction in behavioral methodologies. She is a canine behaviorist teaching a therapy dog class for VIPaws Therapy Dog Club and a certified American Kennel Club (AKC) Canine Good Citizen's evaluator. Stanton and her therapy dog, Brie, are also an Indiana K9 assisted crisis responder. You can reach her via email at dee4aat@yahoo.com.

Karen A. Tinsley, LPC, NCC, is a licensed professional counselor and national certified counselor in Ohio with special expertise in the area of deafness. As a Hard of Hearing alumna of Gallaudet University's mental health counseling program and a certified interpreter from the Registry of Interpreters for the Deaf (RID), she has worked as a case manager, therapist, and interpreter throughout a broad spectrum of environments. She has published in the RID newsletter on issues of educational interpreting and has presented at two breakout conferences regarding mental health services for the deaf. She is currently working as a contracted therapist through PBJ Connections, Inc., (www.pbjconnections.org) and serves on the board of Last Chance Corral (www.lastchancecorral.org), a nonprofit equine rescue facility in Athens, Ohio. Tinsley can be reached via email at ktinsley@insight.rr.com.

Melissa Verge, MA, graduated from George Washington University in 2010 with a master's in education and human development specializing in instruction for children with emotional and behavioral disorders. She is certified to teach special education (K–12) in both Washington, DC, and Virginia and is currently an in-home applied behavior analysis (ABA) therapist completing additional coursework to become a board certified behavior analyst (BCBA). Verge seeks to integrate theories from the fields of psychology, education, and behavior analysis to help children with autism experience feelings of self-efficacy, to learn how to communicate their wants and needs, to engage with others, and to increase appropriate behaviors. She first became interested in working with special needs populations while volunteering at a therapeutic horseback riding center as an undergraduate student and seeing the impact the human–animal bond has on empathy and verbal behavior in children with autism. Verge may be reached at melverge@yahoo.com or at 571-294-6149.

Tanya Welsch, MSW, LICSW, is a licensed social worker, licensed school social worker, and director and founder of the nonprofit Natural Connections Learning Center. For close to 20 years, she has partnered with domestic and farm animals in mental health and social–emotional-learning programs for youths, adults, and families. She provides consultation, training, and program development in the field of animal assisted interactions (AAI) for agencies, schools, and professionals as well as specific training in equine- and canine-based youth services. She has presented extensively at local, national, and international conferences, cofacilitates a graduate course in AAI at the University of Minnesota, is a Pet Partners team evaluator with the Delta Society, is a practitioner-in-training in the Tellington-TTouch Method for horses, and is a graduate advisor and adjunct faculty for the master of arts in education with an emphasis in equine assisted learning (EAL) through Prescott College. Welsch can be reached at 651-307-0981 or tanya.welsch@gmail.com. The NCLC's website is naturalconnectionslc.org.

Delores Westerman, PhD, graduated from the Catholic University of America with a PhD in educational psychology. She had a postdoctoral fellowship at the Army Research Institute in Alexandria, Virginia. For the following 18 years, she taught undergraduate and graduate level courses at Marymount University in Arlington before retiring in 2007. Many of the courses she taught involved lifespan development, adolescent development, and moral and ethical development. Being a lifelong animal lover, she became interested in equine assisted therapy when she got her first horse. For many years she served on the board of directors for an equine therapy program for children and adults. Westerman may be reached at 301-349-5234 or deloreswes@aol.com.

Patricia Westerman, PhD, is a tenured associate professor of psychology and director of the Center for Excellence in Teaching and Learning at Bowie State University. She earned her PhD in human development from the Catholic University of America in 1996. Westerman teaches undergraduate courses in the areas of child, cognitive, social, and sport psychology. Her primary research interest consists of the use of animal assisted activities, including horseback riding, to enhance self-efficacy, resiliency, and hope in children. She has served on the board of directors for a therapeutic riding program for 7 years. Westerman may be reached at pwesterman@bowiestate.edu or at 301-860-3264.

Judy Weston-Thompson, MA, LMFT, CEFIP-MH, is a certified equine interactive professional–mental health (CEIP-MH) and marriage and family therapist (CA license #MFC 23268), licensed for 23 years. Her equine clinical background includes training in intuitive horsemanship, horse-power equine facilitated psychotherapy training, certified horsemanship Level 1, and North American Riding for the Handicapped Association (NARHA) registered instructor. Her horse experience consists of extensive training in Western, English, and dressage schooling as well as a summer spent as a trail guide and wrangler at Eaton's Ranch, Wyoming. Weston-Thompson and her cofacilitators,

Caesar and Star, work with children and adult individuals and groups in her equine facilitated private practice in San Rafael, California. She specializes in attention deficit disorder (ADD)/attention deficit hyper-activity disorder (ADHD), anxiety disorders, depression, addiction, and learning disorders and facilitates groups for psychotherapists. Weston-Thompson is a staunch believer in the inherent wisdom and unfailing intuition and honesty of the horse. She can be contacted through her website, www.equineinsight.net.

CHAPTER

Equine Assisted Interventions in Mental Health

Kay Sudekum Trotter

☐ Defining Equine Assisted Interventions

"The field of animal-assisted interventions currently lacks a unified, widely accepted, or empirically supported theoretical framework for explaining how and why relationships between humans and animals are potentially therapeutic" (Kruger & Serpell, 2006, pp. 25–26). In the field of equine assisted interventions, there is movement toward establishing a national certification or credentialing process similar to that of the National Board of Certified Counselors (CBNN) and that proves to the public and employers that the counselor has met the national standards set by the counseling profession. Two primary models or theoretical frameworks currently dominate this growing field and may be referenced in this book by various authors. This book does not endorse any specific model of *equine therapy*. References to any treatment or therapy model or to any program, service, or treatment are solely the views and opinions of authors. In this book, we use the term *equine assisted counseling* (EAC) to indicate therapies requiring a licensed mental health provider working with the clients and equines. We will also share techniques incorporating both ground and mounted therapies. However, we felt it important to offer a quick overview of the prominent models of equine assisted interventions dominating the equine therapy field today: Certification Board for Equine Interaction Professionals (CBEIP); Equine Assisted Growth and Learning Association (EAGALA), and Professional Association of Therapeutic Horsemanship International (PATH Intl).

☐ Certification Board for Equine Interaction Professionals

CBEIP is a not-for-profit, tax-exempt organization started by professionals in the field who feel a credential for equine facilitated professionals is needed to identify the body of knowledge and those who practice in the field. The vision of the group is to promote professional credibility and to achieve public confidence in the transformative value of equine–human interaction. Their mission is to offer a credentialing process for equine interaction professionals grounded in a foundation of knowledge and experience that supports safe, humane, and ethical practice. Integrity, compassion, excellence, respect, and collaboration are the stated values of the organization.

CBEIP promotes the concept of voluntary certification by examination for those who incorporate equines into their mental health or education practice. Certification is just one part of a process called *credentialing* and focuses specifically on the individual. The designation from CBEIP is one indication of current competence in the specialized field. Certification of equine interaction mental health and education professionals provides formal recognition of basic knowledge in this field. Certification by the CBEIP indicates licensed mental health professionals that have complied with the following criteria:

1. Provided documented evidence that they have been examined by an independent professional certifying organization and found to possess a certain level of basic knowledge about the specialized field of equine interaction mental health or education

2. Established a level of knowledge required for certification of equine interaction mental health or education professionals

3. Provided encouragement for continued personal and professional growth in the field

4. Provided a standard of knowledge requisite for certification, thereby assisting clients, students, the public, and members of the profession in assessment of equine interaction mental health or education professionals

5. Provided a direction and focus for new professionals in the field seeking to increase their knowledge and skill levels

6. Protected the public

7. Increased the credibility of the field of equine interaction, education, and learning

☐ PATH International

Professional Association of Therapeutic Horsemanship International (PATH Intl), formerly North American Riding for the Handicapped Association (NARHA) is a professional organization that promotes equine-assisted activities and therapies for individuals with special needs. PATH Intl calls its model "equine facilitated psychotherapy (EFP)." This experiential psychotherapy includes equines and may incorporate a number of mutually respectful equine activities, such as handling, grooming, lunging, riding, driving, and vaulting. A licensed mental health professional must work with a PATH Intl certified equine specialist in mental health during all EFP sessions (PATH Intl, 2011b).

According to PATH Intl, the mental health professional must met the criteria to legally and independently provide mental health counseling in the state (or country) in which the services are being delivered, and must maintain current professional liability insurance. The mental health professional must also have additional training, education, and supervision in EFP. If the mental health professional is an intern or graduate student, he or she must be supervised by a licensed mental health professional (PATH Intl, 2011b). The equine specialist must be certified by PATH Intl as an Equine Specialist in Mental Health, thereby insuring that the equine specialist possesses the professionalism, experience and skills necessary to act as the horse handler in a PATH Intl un-mounted mental health session. Additional PATH Intl certification in riding, vaulting and/or driving is needed by the equine specialist to include mounted activities in EFP sessions The mental health professional may also be dually credentialed as a PATH Intl equine specialist (PATH Intl, 2011a).

PATH Intl also allows for equine facilitated psychotherapy assistants (EFP-assistants) or volunteers to be present during mental heath sessions. PATH Intl requiries that the EFP-assistants receive very specific training in client behaviors, treatment plans and confidentiality policies, treatment goals, behavioral modification programs, early signs of behavioral escalation, medication side effects, and appropriate personal boundaries, in order to provide stability of treatment to the clients (PATH Intl, 2011b).

☐ Equine Assisted Growth and Learning Association

The EAGALA Model of Equine Assisted Psychotherapy and Learning requires a cofacilitating team that must include an EAGALA-certified mental health professional and an EAGLA-certified equine specialist in all sessions. EAGALA also specifies all session activity must be performed with the client remaining on the ground and never mounting the horse. The mental health professional needs to have college-level educational training and a degree in the mental health field. The mental health professional also needs to be under a governing board for ethical or scope of practice violations relating to mental health practice. The equine specialist must have 6,000 hours (approximately 3 years of full-time work) of hands-on experience with horses and must have completed at least 100 hours of continuing education in the equine field. EAGALA offers two levels of certification: EAGALA certification and EAGALA advanced certification. The certification is valid for 2 years and thereafter must be renewed. The certification process is experiential and hands-on during a 4-day weekend (EAGALA, 2010).

☐ Equine Assisted Interventions in Mental Health Theoretical Foundations

Animal–Human Bond

The interaction between animals and humans has endured since the beginning of time (Hirschman, 1994; Levinson, 1972; Serpell, 2000).

The two schools of thought on the development of the animal–human bond reflect either the evolution theory or the social cultural perspective. The innate essence of our relationship with animals, and our predisposition to interact with certain species that provide valuable services (such as being alerted to danger by dogs barking), became part of the *collective consciousness* that was passed down from generation to generation and reflects the evolutional theory perspective on the animal–human bond. The other school of thought comes from the social cultural perspective, which believes the animal–human bond has to be viewed throughout the cultural environment where individuals learn at an early age to negatively or positively regard certain animals (Graham, 2000).

The role of animal–human interactions has been postulated to promote wellness and prevent illness (Beck & Katcher, 2003; Garrity & Stallones, 1998; Graham, 2000) similar to maintaining a healthy diet and exercising to promote overall general well-being. A large component of the animal–human bond stems from the social support that individuals receive from animals that translates into positive health effects (Beck & Katcher, 2003). The social support that animals provide humans, such as love and acceptance, which is not dependent on appearance, social, or economic status (Chandler, 2005), often fills a void that otherwise would remain empty. In contrast to human relationships, which may be complex, confusing, and at times painful, bonds with animals are inherently relaxed and intimate. The need for animals to be cared for on a daily basis fulfills the human need to be needed, to nurture, and to love (Hirschman, 1994).

Animals play a symbolic role in society, influencing the psychological and physiological domain (Beck & Katcher, 2003). Animals can serve as a client's substitute to which tenderness and protection can be given. The raising and caring for animals provides individuals the opportunity to learn about themselves and can serve to prepare couples for parenthood (Levinson, 1972). As friends, animals provide unconditional love and loyalty—they are often seen as a faithful intimate companion. Hirschman (1994) found that the intimate relationship that exists between humans and animals was a "mutual evolving relationship that defines their lives together. They find they can communicate in subtle, nonverbal ways grounded on mutual understanding and experiences. Much like long-term human friends, they 'grow into' one another's lives through daily rituals and habits of behavior" (p. 620).

Development and the Animal–Human Bond

Animals play an important role in shaping child development (Carey, 1985; Levinson, 1972; Melson, 2003; Myers, 1998) because learning can be stimulated by the presence of animals. Learning occurs because the interaction with animals teaches in a concrete experiential manner the needs of the animal, thus providing individuals with the opportunity to apply this newly developed knowledge with others (Carey, 1985). Furthermore, interacting with animals for some can be a powerful motivator for learning, according to Vygotsky (1978), for two well-established reasons: (1) learning is retained more when individuals are emotionally invested; and (2) learning is maximized when it occurs within significant relationships.

The individual's sense of self and ability to trust are directly influenced by the animal–human bond (Levinson, 1972; Melson, 1998; Myers, 1998). The ever-faithful responsiveness of an animal in an individual's life and the individual's attachment to the animal serves to reinforce and reassure the individual by providing the basic elements of developing trust and building healthy attachments (Melson, 1998). Another developmental task that animals contribute to is the individual's sense of self. This is accomplished through many modalities, such as the individual assuming responsibility for the animal or through the unconditional acceptance offered by the animal or by the emotional support provided by the animal. Furthermore, because animals do not disappoint or make excuses or demands on individuals, the animal–human interaction provides the individual the ability to disregard other hurts and disappointments in his or her life (Levinson, 1972; Melson, 1998). In addition, the opportunity to interact and learn with an animal provides an opportunity to develop a sense of identity. According to Levinson (1972), "When a child has a pet with which he works and toward which he expresses a wide range of feelings, he can get a better understanding of what he is like and what his strengths and limitations are" (p. 49).

☐ Animal Assisted Therapy

The recognition of the value of the animal–human bond has encompassed the period from the 1960s to present day. The first to publish about the therapeutic power of the animal–human bond was Boris Levinson (1962). Animal assisted therapy (AAT) built on this animal–human bond to create a therapeutic goal—directed counseling intervention. Chandler (2005) describes animal assisted therapy as an adjunct to therapy, where a therapist can incorporate the animal into whatever professional style of therapy the therapist already uses. Animal assisted therapy can be directive or nondirective in its approach. Animal assisted therapy sessions can be integrated into individual or group therapy and used with a very wide range of age groups and persons with varying abilities. Animal assisted therapy is a practice modality and not an independent profession. Mental health professionals that provide AAT must have the proper training and credentials for their professional practice (Chandler, 2005). Since animal assisted therapy was first viewed as a justifiable adjunct to traditional counseling techniques in the late 1970s and 1980s, national therapeutic programs have been established, training courses have been developed, international professional organizations have been formed, conferences have been established, and a dramatic increase in AAT literature has surfaced (Burch, 2000).

Counseling interventions that use animals tend to create opportunities for healing, learning, stimulation, curiosity, and attachment. The presence of an animal in therapy gives the client the opportunity to develop personal and social identity, to strengthen self-concept and self-esteem (Chandler, 2005), and to elicit a wide range of emotions from joy to sorrow. The physical touching of an animal promotes comfort and safety (Fine, 2000) and helps the clients understand their behavior as well as the behavior of others more accurately (Katcher & Wilkins, 1998). Fine (2000) reported that many therapists observed that the presence of an animal reduced client stress, and the therapist is perceived as less threatening and therefore is seen as more approachable by the client. Plus, the presence of an animal seemed to help clients overcome anxiety related to therapy. The therapeutic relationship between the client and the animal added an element of safety and freedom to the counseling session.

The Delta Society

In the mid 1970s, seven veterinarians and a psychiatrist created the Delta Foundation to scientifically research the positive effects animals have on people's lives. The name of the organization was changed to the Delta Society in 1981 to reflect the growing interest on the part of researchers and medical practitioners in both human and animal fields.

The Delta Society's ongoing clinical research reflects the fact that having an animal in one's life helps reduce blood pressure, lower stress and anxiety levels, and stimulate the release of endorphins (Delta Society, 2006).

The Delta Society (1996, pp. 2–3) outlined 10 mental health applications of animal assisted therapy:

Emotional safety: When an animal is included in the therapy session, the environment of power has changed. The therapist is seen as more approachable and likable. The presence of an animal opens a pathway through the client's psychosis or resistance. Clients also tend to project their experiences and feelings onto the animal.

Relationships: An animal can be a source of love and companionship. For clients who do not relate well with other people, an animal can become the object to which they can direct their own love and compassion.

Limit setting and consequences: Clients learn that there are limits and parameters they must behave within around animals and, consequently, within the world. An animal's quick response to a client's behavior can be generalized to others and provides an opportunity to process the client's feelings toward the animal's response.

Attachment: An animal can offer the isolated client a healthy attachment, one that is less threatening than with people.

Grief and loss: The first experience of loss for many clients centers on the loss of their pet, and that grief primarily remains unresolved. Tearfulness and feelings of loss and abandonment are frequently experienced in therapy sessions when an animal is present, providing an opportunity to explore and work through unresolved losses.

Reality orientation: An animal can act as a link between a client's internal fantasies and external reality. The client can live in the here-and-now and enjoy it.

Pleasure, affection, and appropriate touch: It is socially acceptable for men as well as women to touch, caress, and hug an animal. Touching an animal is safe and nonthreatening. Clients also learn new ways of touching, with gentleness, nurturance, and concern for the animals' well-being.

Socialization: The safety of an animal provides the catalyst toward social interactions and connections for interpersonal communication.

Play and laughter: People often laugh and are playful when interacting with animals. This playful expression can be associated with the well-being of joy and happiness.

Anxiety: An animal can divert clients' attention away from their internal anxiety, allowing the therapist to nurture alternative functional responses to anxiety. An animal can reduce a client's discomfort (physical or emotional), acting as a distraction, shutting out reactions to aversive stimuli.

☐ Equine Assisted Counseling

The emergence of EAC has developed as an outgrowth of the healing bond that can develop between animals and humans. This type of animal assisted therapy is in its infancy in terms of research, theory, and practice, and, as with any newly developing counseling field, the literature on qualitative observations and case studies is greater than empirical-based quantitative research and theory exploration.

With EAC, both individuals and groups interact with horses to facilitate the prevention or resolution of emotional and behavioral difficulties with themselves and others. This type of counseling provides a safe and secure environment that nurtures inner healing and encourages optimal growth and development (Trotter, Chandler, Goodwin-Bond, & Casey, 2008). This is achieved with traditional counseling processing and equine activities designed to teach individuals about themselves, to allow recognition of dysfunctional patterns of behavior, and to help define healthy relationships.

EAC is based on experiential work that uses equines to increase clients' awareness of their thoughts, words, and actions. This type of counseling also provides tools for individuals to better manage their lives and foster positive relationships while also teaching problem-solving communication and social skills. The risk-taking activities associated with working with horses are a conscious decision by clients—a decision that is physical as well as emotional in nature. Through the process of risk-taking, clients can test and improve their abilities to control self and their surroundings. This risk-taking behavior tends to produce deeper therapy than working in a traditional counseling setting (Trotter et al., 2008).

EAC addresses a variety of mental health conditions and human development needs, including behavior issues, attention deficit disorder, substance abuse, eating disorders, abuse issues, depression, anxiety, relationship problems, and communication needs. Equine assisted counseling promotes both personal exploration and clinical interpretation of feelings and behaviors.

Horses are used in a counseling session because the animals are much more effective at confronting behaviors and attitudes than people are, partly because of their honesty but also because of their ability to observe and respond to nonverbal communication (Irwin & Weber, 2001). The horse provides the vehicle for the projection of the client's unconscious worries or fears. This provides the client the opportunity to look at what works, what does not work, and whose needs are being met while offering the client the opportunity to take responsibility for recognizing how personal actions affect others. Psychoanalysts and social anthropologists have long recognized the symbolic meanings associated with horses that individuals use to represent strong emotions and feelings that are both difficult to describe and prone to repression (Kruger, Trachtenberg, & Serpell, 2004).

Because all horses are different, they each require different treatment from participants to successfully complete tasks. Through their experience with the horses, individuals learn to observe and respond to behaviors of the horse instead of staying stuck in their current patterns of behavior. Traditional counseling processing techniques used by the counselor during and after every session facilitate clients' ability to relate personal insight into their own lives (Chandler, 2005). Personal insight for an addictions client could result in learning about their attitudes toward their temptations or addictions, and, as a result, they can identify the behaviors that can lead to relapse. They can learn new ways to handle frustration, challenges, and fears while also learning healthy communication, problem-solving skills, and solution-oriented behaviors. According to Chandler, "The skill of the group process leaders is the key to the success of the program for the participants" (p. 112).

☐ Theoretical Foundations of Equine Assisted Counseling

EAC, like any AAT, is considered an adjunct to existing therapy, where therapists can incorporate the use of a horse into their own professional theoretical orientation (Chandler, 2005). However, EAC tends to draw more heavily from some philosophy and principles of four major counseling theories: (1) brief therapy; (2) Gestalt therapy; (3) reality therapy; and (4) Adlerian therapy.

Brief Therapy

EAC uses a brief therapy problem-solving model of change, which follows two basic philosophies of change: (1) the focus on visible behavioral interactions; and (2) the use of purposeful interventions to change the visible pattern of undesirable behavior (as cited in Williams, 1999). Brief therapy, like EAC, focuses on action versus insight—new actions produce change. Expectancy is another principle of both brief therapy and

EAC, which focuses on disrupting client's negative expectancies and creating the positive expectation that change is possible (Williams, 1999). Although the client's problem developed in the past, both brief therapy and EAC focus on how the problem or negative behavior is maintained and experienced in the present. In the brief therapy approach to counseling, the therapist is an active participant and shares responsibility with the client for initiating therapeutic movement and creating context in which change can take place (Williams, 1999). This philosophy is also a tenet of EAC. That is, in both approaches to counseling, the therapist may invite or confront clients to grow and change by creating a context in which change can occur. Underlining principles of both brief therapy and EAC are action-oriented viewpoints that respect the client and emphasize the client's strengths.

Gestalt Therapy

EAC also has strong underpinnings to Gestalt therapy, which is grounded in the assumption that meaning is best derived and understood by considering the individual's interpretation of immediate experience. Like Gestalt therapy, EAC emphasizes the immediate experience—what is happening in the here-and-now—and explores all aspects of the individual's present perception. Perls emphasized *immediate* experience because this is the experience that is present and can be attuned to and impacted, where the client and counselor explore the individual's current perceptions (Fall, Holden, & Marquis, 2004). The client's role in Gestalt therapy and EAC is active and focused on the present. The client plays a very important role in the therapeutic process that leads to greater awareness of the reality of oneself and how one interacts with one's surroundings, including people, animals, and contact with one's natural environment. This awareness facilitates natural and spontaneous change.

Reality Therapy

EAC also uses principles from reality therapy, both of which use directive techniques. The therapist is an active participant in the counseling process, and both have an education-oriented focus. Glasser's focus on the central importance of love and belonging needs (Fall et al., 2004) is facilitated through the relationship clients establish with the horse during therapy. Reality theory also emphasizes the importance of doing and thinking behavior (Fall et al., 2004), which mirrors EAC focus on what clients are doing in the present and correlating the here-and-now experience into opportunities for them to understand and discover themselves.

Adlerian Therapy

The Adlerian therapy of counseling also is applicable to EAC, specifically his tenet that all individuals move from feelings of inferiority toward a feeling of significance. According to Adler, striving for significance can be broken down into four categories: physical, intellectual, psychological, and social (Fall et al., 2004). EAC, unlike other counseling modalities, requires that participants be in a physical relationship with the horse and the other group members. Because EAC usually takes place out-of-doors, the outdoor environment demands greater physical responsiveness from the participants. As with the Adlerian psychological aspect of striving for significance, not enough can be said about the power individuals feel when they are successful in getting a 1,200-pound horse that could easily overpower them to respond to them. Adler's striving for significance in the social content is also applicable with EAC activities that are designed to build teamwork and group cohesion to be successful. EAC activities are designed to recreate potentially troubling life situations the participant may be experiencing. Thus, the group provides an arena for the client to discover and work through social difficulties or issues the client might be avoiding, repressing, or deflecting.

☐ The Nature Connection

Implications for Conducting Counseling Outdoors

There is something unique about the natural setting that requires examination; perhaps it is the interplay between experiencing life in communion with nature and the essence of human existence. Time spent in the natural environment reading a book, participating in activities, riding a bike, or perhaps just enjoying the gentle breeze blowing against your face with the scent of freshness and sunshine—just being in nature—nurtures the soul. Nature provides a special place for the human adventure of body, mind, and spirit—it provides an opportunity for mindful ways of being, for reflection, for peace. Time spent in the natural environment contributes to an individual's sense of well-being and creates connections and a sense of belonging between the self and the world.

The natural environment provides a potentially powerful adjunct to the mental health of both the client and the treatment providers. Nature stimuli have been shown to elicit positive emotional states, behavioral relaxation, and reduction in stress levels (Kahn, 1997; White & Heerwagen, 1998). As a counseling modality that takes place in the out-of-doors, EAC can only benefit from the powerful psychological and physical connection clients experience from being in the natural outdoor environment.

Once the counseling session steps outside the traditional four walls of the counseling room to the wide expanse of the great outdoors, the very act of counseling undergoes a delicate shift that is hard to define but is quite real. This phenomenon holds true if the counseling session takes place in a horse arena, on the side of a mountain, or sitting on a bench in a beautiful garden. Being outdoors demands greater client responsiveness, which influences the holistic development of the client because the outdoor environment offers the stimulation of hands-on learning and experiencing and sometimes an atmosphere of greater risk. The outdoors is a natural place that creates unique opportunities that change the nature of clients' reactions to relationships with themselves, with others, with animals, and with their world. Counseling in the outdoors also creates situations in which the counselor and client are more attuned to the relational elements of the counseling process. This is partly due to the spontaneous reactions to unpredictable moments that can occur while counseling outdoors.

Being in a place that is a little unfamiliar or uncomfortable and that requires natural reactions to unpredictable moments produces pure engagement—a heightened emotional state the counselor can gently guide the client through while creating an intense connection between the client and the counselor without the four walls and the staleness of the traditional counseling room. Outdoor counseling also requires counselors to allow direct experience to take over; this is possible when the counselor creates an environment of trust and support. There is no denying that outdoor counseling is challenging. At times it is counseling in the realm of the unpredictable. Confronting challenging situations, predicaments, and difficulties are powerful adjuncts to the counseling process. How a counselor guides a client through those moments and supports them during that time is what defines the power of EAC in the natural environment (Foran, 2005).

As more research emerges scientifically proving the healing properties of connecting with nature, at the time this book is going to press I am in the process of creating Green Therapies and Research Institute in the

Dallas area. This non-profit organization will change the way therapists interact with their clients and the natural world. Repairing the relationship between people and nature will center them in their lives, allowing them to heal and fully express their potential.

Green Therapies and Research Institute will be a counseling and research oasis that utilizes the integrative wellness model of treating the body, mind, and spirit through a therapeutic framework involving the direct and creative dialogue humans have with nature and animals. Green Therapies and Research Institute expands the classical concept of "mental health" while developing concepts and methods that place nature and animals as partners in the healing therapeutic process.

Both research and application are crucial to the development of effective therapeutic modalities that can be taught to mental health professionals and used in every type of community. I will chronicle the development of this integrated wellness center through blogs and my website, www.kaytrotter.com.

☐ References

Beck, A.M., & Katcher, A.H. (2003). Future directions in human–animal bond research. *American Behavioral Scientist, 47*(1), 79–93.

Burch, M.R. (2000). Program evaluation and quality assurance in animal-assisted therapy. In A.H. Fine (Ed.), *Animal-assisted therapy* (pp. 129–149). San Diego, CA: Academic Press.

Carey, S. (1985). *Conceptual changes in childhood*. Cambridge, MA: MIT Press.

Chandler, C.K. (2005). *Animal assisted therapy in counseling*. New York: Routledge.

Delta Society. (1996). *Animal-assisted therapy: Therapeutic interventions*. Renton, WA: Delta Society.

Delta Society. (2006). *About Delta Society*. Retrieved from: http://www.deltasociety. org

Equine Assisted Growth and Learning Association (EAGALA). (2010). Retrieved from: http://www.eagala.org/Certification_Program

Equine Facilitated Mental Health Association (EFMHA). (2010). Retrieved from: http://www.narha.org

Fall, K.A., Holden, J.M., & Marquis, A. (2004). *Theoretical models of counseling and psychotherapy*. New York: Brunner-Routledge.

Fine, A.H. (2000). Animals and therapists: Incorporating animals in outpatient psychotherapy. In A.H. Fine (Ed.), *Animal-assisted therapy* (pp. 179–211). San Diego, CA: Academic Press.

Foran, A. (2005). The experience of Pedagogic intensity in outdoor education. *Journal of Experiential Education, 28*(2), 147–163.

Garrity, T.F., & Stallones, L. (1998). Effect of pet contact on human well-being. In Wilson & Turner (Eds.), *Companion animals in human health* (pp. 3–22). Thousand Oaks, CA: Sage Publications, Inc.

Graham, B. (2000). *Creature comfort*. Amherst, NY: Prometheus Books.

Hirschman, E.C. (1994). Consumers and their animal companions. *Journal of Consumer Research, 20,* 616–632.

Irwin, C., & Weber, B. (2001). *Horses don't lie: What horses teach us about our natural capacity for awareness, confidence, courage, and trust*. New York: Marlow & Company.

Kahn, P.H. (1997). Developmental psychology and the Biophilia hypothesis: Children's affiliation with nature. *Developmental Review, 17,* 1–16.

Katcher, A., & Wilkins, G. (1998). Animal-assisted therapy in the treatment of disruptive behavior disorders in children. In Lundberg (Eds.), *The environment and mental health* (pp. 193–204). Mahwah, NJ: Lawrence Erlbaum Associates, Publishers.

Kruger, K., & Serpell, J. (2006). Animal-assisted interventions in mental health: Definitions and theoretical foundations. In A. Fine (Ed.), *Animal-assisted therapy: Theoretical foundations and guidelines for practice* (pp. 21–38). San Diego, CA: Academic Press.

Kruger, K.A., Trachtenberg, S.W., & Serpell, J.A. (2004). *Can animals help humans heal? Animal-assisted interventions in adolescent mental health*. Center of the Interaction of Animals and Society (CIAS), University of Pennsylvania School of Veterinary Medicine.

Levinson, B.M. (1962). The dog as co-therapist. *Mental Hygiene, 46,* 59–65.

Levinson, B.M. (1972). *Pets and human development*. Springfield, IL: Charles C. Thomas Publisher.

Melson, G.F. (1998). The role of companion animals in human development. In C.C. Wilson & D.C. Turner (Eds.), *Companion animals and human health* (pp. 219–266). Thousand Oaks, CA: Sage Publications.

Melson, G.F. (2003). Child development and the human-companion animal bond. *American Behavioral Scientist, 47*(1), 31–39.

Myers, G. (1998). *Children & animals*. Boulder, CO: Westview Press.

PATH International (2011a). *Equine specialist in mental health: PATH international certification booklet*. Denver, CO.

PATH International (2011b). *PATH international standards for certification and accreditation* (pp. 30–34). Denver, CO.

Serpell, J.A. (2000). Animal companions and human well-being: An historical exploration of the value of human–animal relationships. In A. Fine (Ed.), *Animal-assisted therapy* (pp. 3–19). San Diego, CA: Academic Press.

Trotter, K.S., Chandler, C.K., Goodwin-Bond, D., & Casey, J. (2008). A comparative study of the efficacy of group equine assisted counseling with at-risk children and adolescents. *Journal of Creativity in Mental Health, 3*(3), 254–284.

White, R., & Heerwagen, J. (1998). Nature and mental health: Biophilia and Biophobia. In Lundberg (Ed.), *The environment and mental health* (pp. 175–192). Mahwah, NJ: Lawrence Erlbaum Associates, Publishers.

Williams, J.M. (1999). Brief therapy: A problem solving model of change. *Counselor, 29*–32.

Vygotsky, L. (1978). *Mind in society*. Cambridge, MA: Harvard University Press.

Looking at Equine Assisted Counseling From the Horse's Perspective*

Pat Parelli with Linda Parelli

☐ How to Assure the Safety and Comfort of the Horse in a Counseling Session

For a counselor who wants to include a horse in a therapy session, start with a horse that is already pretty healthy—physically, emotionally, and mentally—and that has been played with enough that the equine specialist (ES) has a real sense of the horse's *horsenality*, a term I came up with to describe the horse's *druthers* and its likely response in any situation.

The *dead-broke/bomb-proof* horse is not a good choice for this kind of work, as it is likely dead-broke/bomb-proof to the way the *normal* (as opposed to natural) world interacts with the horse, which can be quite different from how equine assisted counseling clients will interact with

---

* Special thanks to Shannon and Richard Knapp of Horse Sense of the Carolinas, www.HorseSenseOtc.com.

them. This way the treatment team will know which clients are a good potential fit and which ones may be outside the realm of that particular horse's abilities.

As much as possible, sessions should be conducted in an area with enough space for the horse and humans to get away from each other and stand comfortably. Ideally, the horse should not feel restricted or confined at all.

If working on-line, consider using a 12-foot lead to give the horse *drift* room if needed and a rope halter to allow the client or the ES to communicate quickly and effectively with the horse without the horse feeling *muffled* by a traditional web halter. Ultimately, make sure the horse has choices in the session, such as whether it wants to participate in a particular exercise, so the horse can offer honest feedback cleanly and without interference.

☐ How to Select Horses Appropriate for Equine Assisted Counseling

Ideally, the equine assisted counseling horse is physically sound and healthy. Although some equine health issues may be opportunities for therapeutic work with clients, that occurs usually more due to synchronicity rather than as a sought-after goal. For instance, maybe a horse that was rescued from an abusive situation where it was malnourished would be a very effective addition to a session with a person dealing with eating disorders. Mouthy horses or horses who are prone to kicking may be counterindicated or be used in session as a deliberate, specific intervention, not as a matter of everyday session work.

As mentioned previously, dead-broke horses tend to be those whose natural instincts have been specifically and deliberately squelched, making them inappropriate for work that centers on the natural responses of the horse. Virtually any horse can be a part of equine assisted counseling, as long as the equine specialist and the counselor are mindful of the treatment goals and what the horse brings to each and every session.

Since riding is not always a part of equine assisted counseling, counselors should be looking for horses that don't have severe or extreme reactions to most situations. It's important for the ES to know when any of the herd of equine assisted counseling horses is stressed and what the default response of each horse is likely to be. Then the ES can ask: Is that response OK in *this* session with *this* client? Is it a potential danger to the client, team, or horses?

Overall, a varied herd to choose from is best with a variety of sizes, colors, breeds, and horsenalities. But being solid in mind, body, and spirit with their natural instincts intact are the most important qualities in selecting appropriate equine assisted counseling horses.

☐ Potential Risks and Stresses to the Horses Used in Counseling

Some risks and stresses to the horses used in counseling sessions come from the clients, some come from the way the horses are used in session, and some from the way they are cared for outside of the session. In regards to the potential risks and stresses from clients, the horse theoretically could always be in danger of abuse from clients, although if precautions regarding confinement and restraint of horses are observed, that can minimize the possibility.

Like other professionals in the healing and therapeutic fields, some horses can suffer negative effects from being in the midst of the chaos and emotional turmoil presented by clients. In general, though, horses are much better at shedding emotional stress than humans are. Mitigate potential *burnout* by having regular playtime with your herd during which you attend to their needs, whether that be through challenging them, stimulating them, building their confidence, or providing unstructured time.

How horses are used in session also impacts their well-being. Regarding the horse in session solely as a tool without sentience, opinion, and feedback negatively affect both the session and the horses. I teach that the dignity of the horse must be maintained in and out of session.

Finally, how horses are cared for outside of session impacts their fitness for this work. When horses are turned out in herds as much as possible and cared for as naturally as possible, they'll be much less stressed. Most importantly, remember that horses are great at taking care of themselves as long as they are given space and permission to do so.

☐ The Best Way for a Counselor Inexperienced With Horses to First Approach and Connect With the Horse

Horses have trouble when people approach them head on. The first approach can set up the session for success—or difficulty—so counselors need to understand that horses need to be approached slowly and a little from the side. Because they're prey animals, they need to be able to observe what's happening all around them at all times. We talk about people having personal bubbles—well, so do horses.

When you approach a horse slowly you can feel for that bubble and then slow down even more, softly reaching in to make contact by leaning forward with an outstretched hand for them to sniff as opposed to walking right into the horse's personal space and patting it. I think it would be important and advantageous for counselors to learn basic horse behavior before working with clients and horses together.

Meeting the horses well before the session and being familiar with Parelli Horsenalities and the Seven Games can only set counselors up for success in their initial encounter with horses. Putting yourself in the position to be a student of the horse, before the stress of having to be a *professional* with horses in session, will allow the counselor to have already gotten comfortable with the horse in session.

If the counselor is nervous, anxious, or uncomfortable during a session because of the presence of a horse, that will draw the horse "off point" from the focus on the client. Taking clinics with Parelli professionals to improve horse-reading skills and overall understanding of horse psychology can serve counselors on many different levels.

In the moment of the first encounter, letting the horse approach the counselor instead of the other way around is a good start. Although horses are prey animals and humans are predators (or mixtures of predator and prey), thinking of approaching the horse the way you might a client is a useful practice.

☐ Parelli Natural Horsemanship Four Key Points: Relationship, Understanding, Communication, and Trust

Relationship

Horses are prey animals. What is important to them is the opposite of what is important to people. They need safety, comfort, play, and food—in that order. Conversely, humans (as a predator species) value praise, recognition, and material things, and this is where they disconnect with horses. Calling horses by name, patting them, or giving them treats will not help a horse relate better to the human. It won't make him feel safe or comfortable, but a horse that already feels that way will surely enjoy the treats. When in Horseville, do as horses do, and they will be more drawn to you. We need to understand what is important to horses, and using the Horsenality tool (see it at www.parellinaturalhorsetraining. com) will help enormously when working individually with horses.

Understanding

I feel communication is two-way: One asks the horse to do something and then waits to see the response. If the horse responds, all is well. If she hesitates, we need to wait rather than push forward or we destroy trust. We encourage the horse to "ask questions" when we wait for the horse to express herself. A *question* can be recognized when the horse looks at you with both ears forward. This demonstrates that she is waiting for further direction.

A lot of people learn to behave differently in their interpersonal relationships from the way we treat horses; it invites participation rather than just being ordered around. This is how horses maintain their dignity and how horses and humans can form extraordinary relationships and partnerships.

Communication

When we put the relationship first with horses, it means understanding things from their perspective and modifying our behavior to communicate with them. Horses don't speak English, and even though they can learn to understand a number of words this is not how communication can occur between horse and human.

We have to learn their language, which is primarily expressed through body language (rather than sounds) and a definite hierarchy of leadership. Horses befriend and dominate each other, vying for leadership. The same can happen between horse and human once the horse is no longer afraid. Confidence can lead to pushy behavior because in Horseville, horses push each other around.

Through the Parelli Seven Games you learn how to exert leadership in a natural way, the way horses do with each other, because these are the seven moves they make when getting to know each other and then playing dominance games to see who will be the alpha. Horses need that, and when they don't get to play with each other they will play with the human—and not always in ways that are safe. The Seven Games will solve these problems and keep things in balance between horse and human.

Trust

Earning the trust of a horse is not easy. Fearful horses take a lot of convincing and a lot of *retreat* on the behalf of the human. The more direct or demanding your approach, the more skeptical the horse will be. By using reverse psychology we learn to cause it to be the horse's idea, but only by understanding what its ideas and needs are first. Because horses know we are a predator species, they are on the lookout for any sign that could mean danger, such as fast movements, forceful techniques, or making them feel trapped or cornered.

I teach you how to do the opposite of all the things that elicit these reactions in horses, keeping everyone safe and progressively earning the trust of the horse. Going slower and using repetition until relaxation becomes evident helps tense horses to become more confident.

Trust and respect need to go hand in hand, and through the model I developed, one can learn quickly where the horse is coming from and what its individual character and needs are. This gives counselors a huge leg up when it comes to better understanding and reading horses for use in therapy and particularly in helping to select the right horses for the job.

☐ How to Read a Horse's Emotional State

Here are a few basic keys to reading body language that can be very helpful.

- Body language that indicates unease, tension, loss of confidence, fear, aggression:

  - Head up

  - Looking strongly away, especially in the direction of the gate

  - Neck tight and bulging on the underside

- Ears tight (out to the side or pinned back)

- Eyes staring (not blinking)

- Nostrils flared

- Tail swishing or clamped tight or held high over back

- Inability to stand still

- Rapid or shallow breathing

- Tense body

- Foot stomping

- Body language that indicates relaxation, friendliness, confidence:

  - Head level with body

  - Muscles loose

  - Ears soft or pointed at you

  - Eyes blinking, soft expression

  - Quiet tail

  - Standing quietly, one hind leg cocked

  - Regular, rhythmic breathing

  - More "with" you and present

☐ Core Ethical Guidelines in Working With Horses

In the equine assisted counseling field, there is often talk of being congruent, of having the insides match the outsides, which horses do so well without effort. Congruency is also important in the treatment and care of horses for equine assisted counseling, as incongruent treatment of the horse outside of session has a way of showing up in session and damaging the impact of equine assisted counseling. Doing everything possible to restore all horses to a sound mind, body, and spirit is incumbent on every equine assisted counseling program.

Overall, avoiding restraint and confinement in session is desirable and, as much as possible, treating and caring for them naturally is equally important. Avoid the use of force, fear, and intimidation tactics with horses, as one would certainly avoid treating clients in this way.

I always say I don't do anything with a horse I'd be uncomfortable having my mom watch me do. I suggest you don't do anything with horses, whether or not there are clients there, that you'd feel uncomfortable having abused and traumatized clients watch you do.

How Do Horses Process Information?

Horses are highly perceptive animals and very emotionally connected to other horses and even humans. For example, if another horse is agitated or a human is nervous, most horses are affected by that unless they have learned to be more self-confident. This is why horses are so good for personal development because they tend to reflect the emotional state of the human. It's like instant biofeedback. Horses also change when the human changes, which is once again a powerful element for equine assisted counseling.

Horses are rapid learners, and one-time learning experiences tend to shape their behavior because as prey animals this is a key to survival. Some people think that horses learn slowly but learn the bad things quickly. We do not agree with that thought; instead we acknowledge that horses are phenomenal learners when in a *left-brain* state.

In our system, left brain means calm, confident, and trusting. Horses in a *right-brain* state are alarmed, disturbed, fearful, and not in a learning frame of mind—at least for the things a human wants to teach them. Instead, they will learn to tense up, resist, and escape, and these behaviors can be quickly triggered in a distrustful horse if handled in a way that is disturbing for them.

I have a saying that I think is really helpful: Horses never forget and often forgive. As humans get better in their relationship skills with horses, they bring out the best in the horse by accessing the best in themselves.

☐ What Should Counselors Know About Natural Horsemanship?

My method of natural horsemanship is driven by understanding equine psychology and horse behavior. We seek to put the relationship—friendship—first when training and interacting with horses, and we use communication, understanding, and psychology instead of mechanics, fear, and intimidation.

Understanding the nature of horses shapes our way of being with them and helps us learn their language and causes them to want to be our partners. By playing with horses on the ground, we get to know them and to read their body language and horsenality.

☐ How Can Understanding Horsenality Help Facilitate Positive Sessions?

Not all horses are the same. Just as humans have individual personalities, horses have individual horsenalities that are shaped by innate characteristics, learned behavior, and spirit. The Parelli Horsenality™ Profile I developed helps people to quickly analyze the behavioral characteristics of a horse, to notice the patterns, and to plot their profile as either extrovert or introvert and either right-brain (more fearful) or left-brain (more dominant). Through this understanding of horsenality we learn how to approach horses as individuals—slowing down for introverts, speeding up for extroverts, retreating and using reverse psychology with right-brain horses, and being more progressive with left-brain horses.

I don't think there is one horsenality more suited to equine assisted counseling than another, but I would advise you to choose fairly low-spirited horses. Spirit amplifies a horse's tendencies, whether positive or negative, and this can be the difference between a horse that is easier to work with and one that is hard to handle. It is interesting, too, that people tend to be attracted to horses whose horsenality is similar to their own personality, and in this way they not only understand the horse better than someone else might but also may start to understand more about themselves.

Understanding horsenalities and the appropriate leadership strategies for each horsenality has an enormous impact on the choices an ES makes in overall horse selection for the herd and in session with clients.

If a client is shy and nervous around horses, picking a few predominantly extroverted, spirited, playful horses might be too much for a first session, yet having that same client encounter a high-spirited horse at the end of the treatment process might be incredibly beneficial.

Understanding the patterns of different horsenalities will help the ES make good choices for horses and clients and will help the ES make decisions about appropriate actions to take in session. Ultimately, having a mix of horsenalities in the herd for clients to choose from is ideal.

☐ Other Tidbits of Information and Advice

I think horses are incredible partners for humans; they make us better people by learning to put relationship first, grow a solid foundation, and dedicate ourselves to never-ending self-improvement. I have received letters and feedback from all over the world as to how natural horsemanship has mended relationships, has saved lives, and has given people hope. I can include myself in this because of how horses have helped my own son.

Caton was born with so much brain damage that doctors said he would never walk or talk if he lived through the night. I know that my horses have played an incredible part in his healing. Now in his 20s, Caton walks, runs, talks, drives, and even competes in Western horsemanship events against able-bodied people.

My wife, Linda, and I are passionate about our cause in helping the world become a better place for horses and humans, and to that end our Parelli Horsemanship Fund has been established to help serve four areas: (1) children and youths; (2) educational scholarships for the educators of the future; (3) horse rescues; and (4) therapeutic riding.

3

Techniques That Address Trauma

☐ Reclaiming Boundaries Through Equine Assisted Counseling

Vallerie E. Coleman

Introduction

At Stand InBalance Equine Assisted Growth & Learning we have developed a unique program to help women overcome the effects of domestic violence. For survivors, the trauma of domestic violence leaves deep, long-lasting emotional and neurophysiological wounds that affect their daily lives long after the abuse has ended. The case I will discuss demonstrates how working with horses provides profound opportunities for healing and empowerment. Through interaction with horses, clients learn to trust themselves and are empowered in ways that can't be accomplished solely through talking. A key element of our work with domestic violence survivors is a focus on reclaiming boundaries. This chapter illustrates the ways an activity regarding space can produce powerful metaphors that lead to change.

Rationale

Statistics show that one in four women will be the victim of intimate male or female partner violence in her lifetime (Tjaden & Thoennes, 2000). Battered individuals experience numerous boundary violations—physical, sexual, and emotional—that frequently generate long-term effects such as fear, anxiety, depression, chronic pain, dissociative states, hypervigilance, somatization, shame, and poor self-esteem (van der Kolk, 2003; Walker, 1994). Survivors often have difficulty "attending to their own inner sensations and perceptions" (van der Kolk, 2006, p. xxv) and identifying their emotional reactions. Similarly, they often have difficulty accurately reading the nonverbal and emotional cues of others. This is evident in the significant confusion battered women tend to have about the difference between assertion and aggression.

When women are unable to control their batterer's violent outbursts they typically find themselves feeling powerless, helpless, and hopeless—resulting in learned helplessness (Burman, 2003). As identified by van der Kolk (2003) this leaves them "vulnerable to develop 'emotion focused coping,' a style in which the goal is to alter one's emotional state, rather than the circumstances which give rise to those emotional states" (p. 170). This can manifest in a variety of ways, including substance abuse, and often leads the survivor to adapt by emotionally and physically shaping around others (Benson, 2003; Lisa Guerin, personal communication, December 17, 2008; Lutes, 2003) rather than holding her own shape and boundaries.

Equine assisted counseling (EAC) provides an opportunity for trauma survivors to increase self-awareness and self-regulation while developing new ways of being in the world. As noted by van der Kolk (2006), trauma results in past experience becoming

> embodied in present physiological states and action tendencies: The trauma is reenacted in breath, gestures, sensory perceptions, movement, emotion, and thought. The role of the therapist is to facilitate self-awareness and self-regulation, rather than to witness and interpret the trauma. Therapy involves working with sensations and action tendencies in order to discover new ways of orienting and moving through the world. (p. xxiv)

Although van der Kolk is referring to the role of sensorimotor psychotherapy (Ogden, Minton, & Pain, 2006), the same concepts apply to EAC. Horses serve as nonjudgmental mirrors that help clients learn about themselves and their energy. To effectively partner with a horse, clients must learn to tune in to their own sensations and engage in new action tendencies.

As prey animals, horses are constantly aware of their surroundings and use their animal wisdom—keen sense of smell, hearing, body awareness, and vigilance—to keep themselves safe. As June Gunter (2007) notes, they are "relaxed and ready" (p. 20). Their survival depends on their ability to sense any underlying emotional current in their environment, yet they are also able to graze and be relaxed. This provides domestic violence survivors with a powerful model for living. To be "relaxed and ready," women must be aware of their sensations and learn to self-regulate.

Description

Overview

The Equine Assisted Healing™ Program developed at Stand InBalance is based on the nine key principles of survivor therapy identified by Lenore Walker (1994): safety, empowerment, validation, emphasis on strengths, education, expanding alternatives, restoring clarity in judgment, understanding oppression, and making one's own decisions (p. 303). At Stand InBalance we provide both group and customized individual sessions for survivors of domestic violence. Our 8-week group program consists of education, discussion, and experiential exercises that address the sequelae of domestic violence; topics include emotional intelligence, self-awareness, embodiment of focus and intention, assertiveness, problem solving, communication, and relationships.

One key component of our program is the focus on reclaiming and reestablishing boundaries. Women's struggle to maintain their authentic shape (core self) is complicated by the fact that girls, in contrast to boys, are socialized to define themselves in relation to others (Chodorow, 1978). Although this serves to enhance women's capacity for intimate relating and identification with others, it can make it difficult for them to feel entitled to have and set clear boundaries. For domestic violence survivors, abuse and continued violation of their boundaries by the batterer makes it even harder for them to feel entitled to boundaries and a sense of self. Working with horses offers a unique opportunity for women to regain their sense of self and differentiate between passive, assertive, and aggressive communication. Moreover, it provides an opportunity to experience setting and holding their boundaries in an assertive, effective manner—thus gaining an embodied sense of empowerment.

Boundaries and Communication

Following a discussion on boundaries and the impact of boundary violations, we give clients a handout that differentiates between passive, aggressive, and assertive communication (Appendix A). We then go over the handout and have each client take a few minutes to circle the types of communication that best describe them. They then highlight the communication skill they would like to focus on for the session. We have also developed a handout that depicts horses in passive, assertive, and aggressive interactions (Appendix B). Most remarkable is the photo of a miniature horse asserting her boundaries with a quarter horse. After exploring the clients' assumptions and beliefs about the horses' communication we move into the arena.

My Space—Individual Version (Within the Group)

One of my favorite activities for the topic of boundaries is an adaptation of My World (Cramer, Knapp, Jacoby, and Anthony, 2007, pp. 32–34) that we call "My Space." We use the concept of space because it is an apt metaphor for one's internal and external world. This exercise offers clients an opportunity to create their personal space and identify what is precious to them. It reveals participants' dynamics around boundaries and helps them learn to assert their boundaries.

Although the My Space activity generally uses food as a temptation for the horses, we have had sessions with clients where just keeping the horses out of their Space, without the temptation of food, was a major accomplishment. Thus, when deciding the parameters of the exercise it is important for staff to consider the capacities of the clients and introduce food only when appropriate. In addition, it is essential that the equine specialist be cognizant of using horses that are curious and interested in pushing the boundaries but that are not food aggressive.

Setup

As described by Cramer et al. (2007, pp. 32–35), the activity takes place in an arena where building materials are available, such as cones, PVC poles, hula hoops, barrels, and upright poles. You will also need:

- At least three horses, ready to bring into the arena

- One bucket of grain for each client, ready to bring into the arena

- Tape to label buckets and horses

- A pen

Directions

The clients are given up to 10 minutes to build their own *space* inside the arena using any props or items in the arena. They must build their spaces separate from each other. Sometimes we ask the clients to build a *safe space*. Each woman's space can be as symbolic or complex as she desires but must have a physical boundary that defines its perimeters.

After the spaces are built, we ask all clients to describe their space—what they built and what it represents for them. They are then asked to name the most precious thing for them in their lives. This is then written on the tape and affixed to their bucket of grain. Clients then name the biggest threat to what they have identified as precious. These threats are written on tape to be affixed on the horses. Ideally, clients choose what horse represents which threat; the tape is then put on the respective horses.

The women are then asked to take what is precious to them (bucket of grain) into their space. They must stay inside their space and protect their bucket. The horses cannot enter their space or eat out of the bucket. The horses are then let loose; the staff determines how many additional horses should be let loose and at what intervals. The clients must protect their space and what is precious to them for 10 minutes.

Discussion

Topics for discussion include

- How effective were the clients in protecting their spaces and asserting their boundaries?

- Whose spaces were violated and which precious valuables were eaten by which threats?

- How did the clients handle having their space or valuables being violated by the horses?

- How does this mirror dynamics in their lives?

- In what ways did they take care of themselves?

- Did they ask for any help?

- When was it easiest? When was it most challenging?

- What strengths did they use to effectively assert their boundaries?

- Were they able to practice using the skill they identified on the handout?

My Space—Group Version

My Space (adapted from My World; Cramer et al., 2007) can be done in either individual or group sessions. As described by Cramer et al., one way to make this a group exercise is to have the clients first build their own individual spaces and then do a second round of the exercise where they all work together to create one larger space. This group version gives the women an opportunity to explore how they use their support systems and to experience teamwork while simultaneously addressing boundaries.

If the group exercise follows the individual version, the horses and buckets of grain are removed from the arena; the labels remain intact, and buckets of grain are refilled as needed. The clients are then asked to take apart their individual spaces and are given 5 minutes to rebuild one space for the group. They follow the same rules described in the individual version (Cramer et al., 2007, p. 34). The clients all enter their community space and are given their buckets of grain. The horses are released, and the clients must keep the horses out of the space and away from what is precious to them (buckets of grain) for 10 minutes.

Discussion

Topics for discussion include

- How effective were they as a group in protecting their one space?

- How effective were they at asserting their boundaries?

- Was the space violated by any of the threats (horses), and were any valuables eaten?

- What worked well, and what didn't work?

- How did the women take care of themselves?

- Did they work together as a team?

- Which version of My Space went the smoothest, and what was the difference?

- Did they practice their identified target skill?

- What did they learn about themselves, and how does that apply in their lives?

Application

My Space can be adapted in a number of ways and is appropriate for just about any population where boundaries need to be addressed. It can be used as a form of assessment or for a focused treatment goal. As an assessment tool, My Space functions to identify what is precious for the client, what the threats are, and how their dynamics around setting boundaries play out. When conducted as a team version it also provides significant information about how each client relates with others and how the group functions together. This exercise can be used with both children and adults and is effective for family work. Areas to explore and address when working with families, as well as other groups, include

- What kind of space they build

- What they identify as precious

- Who takes the lead

- How the different family and group roles play out

- How they work together (or not)

- What strengths they have as a family and group

- How they communicate

As a treatment tool, My Space offers the facilitation team a range of options. It is a useful exercise for a variety of diagnostic categories and related challenges. For instance, My Space can be used with clients who are struggling with depression, anxiety, trauma, attention-deficit/hyperactivity disorders, or conduct-related disorders. It provides an opportunity for clients to practice being calm and assertive, setting clear boundaries, protecting oneself, problem solving, asking for help, and staying focused even when things become chaotic. Through learning to effectively protect themselves and their space clients learn about their energy and how to communicate in a clear, congruent manner.

Case Example

Sandra, a 37-year-old Caucasian woman, came to Stand InBalance after leaving her abusive husband of 15 years. She had two children, ages 7 and 10. Sandra reported that she had lost her "sense of herself" and her confidence. She felt tremendous shame and suffered from depression and anxiety related to the abuse. Sandra tearfully described needing to move on with her life but not knowing how to do so. She was very conflicted about having left her husband, and at the same time knew that being with him was not good for either her or the children.

For the first several sessions my human cofacilitator, equine specialist Amy Pulitzer, and I focused on helping Sandra learn to tune into herself and the horses while she began to develop trust and confidence in herself. Sandra was very confused about how to assert herself effectively and to have her needs met without feeling abusive. For example, in one session Sandra was instructed to connect with a horse and bring it to us; although she went over to one of the horses in the arena, she couldn't figure out how to move it. Upon exploring what had drawn her to the horse she chose to work with, Sandra reported that the horse reminded her of herself because it was standing alone and looked sad. She did not want to use a halter because she stated it would "be a way of controlling and trapping the horse." However, she found that she couldn't get the horse to follow her without using some sort of a lead. She eventually threw the rope around the horse's neck and tied it in a slipknot; she then tossed the other end of the rope around her own neck and shoulders. We called a time-out to explore how she had unconsciously set herself and the horse up in a situation where they could both be choked. For Sandra, being connected meant endangering herself or others. After some time, Sandra was able to halter "Sandra" (the horse) and explore the ways that connection (the halter) could be used to facilitate healthy relating and shared leadership. These were entirely new concepts for her and it was beautiful to see her and the horse learn how to walk together in partnership.

For the module on boundaries, Sandra chose to work on standing up for herself and making direct requests of others without making excuses or feeling bad (see Communication Styles Handout, Appendix A). When doing the My Space exercise, she initially created a space that was triangular, sparse, and very small. When naming what was precious for her, Sandra was torn between her children and her self-esteem. She decided to go with her *self-esteem* as she felt that was what she needed most to keep herself and her children safe. We decided to have her label two threats (horses)—she chose her *husband* and *self-doubt*. We told Sandra that she could use anything in the *community* (arena) as a resource. She took her bucket to her space, and we let the horses loose one at a time. Sandra initially tried to hide the bucket, but this didn't work for long. As both *self-doubt* and her *husband* moved in, Sandra found herself giving mixed messages—petting the horses, particularly her *husband*, while at the same time trying to push them away. First her *husband* violated the boundaries of her space, followed by *self-doubt,* and Sandra found herself backed into the corner and up against the fence (she had placed her space against the fence line).

In processing the experience, Sandra had not been aware she had been sending mixed messages to the horses, nor had she been fully aware of how she ended up backed into the corner against the fence. She then stated that she had felt bad for the horses. Exploration revealed Sandra's fear that if she really stood her ground the horses (especially her *husband*) would get mad. This led to a discussion about how she could tell if a horse was getting mad and what she could do to protect herself. Sandra then decided that she wanted to try the exercise again. When asked if there was anything she wanted to change about her space, Sandra decided to make it bigger and added some Hula-Hoops. This time, she caught herself as she started to give mixed messages, and she became firmer about pushing both the horses out; however, it was clear that she still didn't fully trust that she could own her space and use her energy to say, "Keep out!" Interestingly, while focusing on keeping her *husband* out, *self-doubt* snuck in and grabbed a bite from the bucket. This metaphor of how much the abuse had affected her sense of self and how self-doubt now crept in when she tried to assert herself was very powerful for Sandra.

When Sandra came back for the next session, she reported that she had actually become angry that self-doubt had been able to sneak in and stated that she didn't want to let self-doubt rob her of her self-esteem anymore. Before we moved into the arena with the horses, I did a little work with Sandra around her sense of self and her energy—helping her increase her somatic awareness and connect with her empowered self. Sandra then did the My Space exercise one more time.

This time the way Sandra built her space was different. Her attention was much more focused, and she created sturdier boundaries by using more materials, including cones and a couple of barrels. We brought out the labels from the prior session and asked Sandra if she wanted to make any changes: "Nope. I want to go with those same things; they are really where my issues are." When she picked up her bucket of *self-esteem,* Sandra carried it with the energy of "this is mine and you can't take it from me." In response, the horses (husband and self-doubt)—while inquisitive and clearly interested—were more respectful. She even used a Hula-Hoop at one point as an extension of herself and her energy and managed to keep them both out for a full 10 minutes. This was a huge accomplishment, and the smile on her face was radiant.

The work that Sandra did in the My Space exercise helped her move through her ambivalence and guilt about leaving her husband. Though she'd had an intellectual awareness of this, getting it on a somatosensory level in the moment created a shift. Sandra was also able to generalize her ability to set boundaries with the horses to setting clear and loving boundaries with her children and friends. Her experience of keeping herself safe while also keeping two 1,200-pound animals from taking a bite out of her self-esteem created an amazing sense of confidence for Sandra that continues to empower her on her healing journey.

Summary

Domestic violence shatters the lives of its victims and their loved ones. As demonstrated by our work with Sandra, EAC provides an opportunity for battered women to work through trauma to achieve a sense of empowerment. This type of healing enables women to take back their shape and break free from the vulnerability that often perpetuates a cycle of returning to the abuser. Horses have a remarkable ability to help humans regain confidence, freedom, and a sense of security. Through interaction with them we can learn to connect with our natural wisdom and ultimately become better, more emotionally intelligent human beings. It is a powerful and moving experience to collaborate with horses in providing women an opportunity to reconnect with themselves and to witness them develop newfound levels of self-worth, self-confidence, and self-respect.

Appendix A. Communication Styles Handout

TABLE 3.1. Three Basic Communication Styles

Passive	Assertive	Aggressive
Objective is to avoid confrontation	Objective is to get needs met and share ideas	Objective is to always be right and win
Don't directly express feelings, thoughts, needs, and desires; don't say what you mean	Make direct statements regarding thoughts, feelings, wants, and needs	Capable of stating how you feel, what you want, and what you think but often demanding and at the expense of others' rights and feelings (intrusive boundaries)
Tend to smile a lot and subordinate your needs to others (poor boundaries)	Stand up for your rights and also consider the rights and feelings of others	Tend to humiliate others by using sarcasm or humorous put-downs
Find it difficult to make requests of others	Open to negotiation and compromise, but not at the expense of your own dignity	Can't tolerate criticism and likely to go on the attack when you don't get your way
Say yes to others when you want or need to say no, or you make excuses	You can make direct requests of others and say no to others without making mistakes or feeling bad	Stir up guilt and resentment in others by pointing the finger of blame

TABLE 3.1 *(Continued).* Three Basic Communication Styles

Passive	Assertive	Aggressive
Soft, weak, or wavering voice	Listen attentively to others and let others know you have heard them	Tend not to hear or acknowledge the needs or feelings of others; sentences often begin with "you…" followed by an attack or negative label
Pauses and hesitations are common	Can start and stop a conversation (healthy boundaries)	Use absolute terms such as *always* and *never*
Rely on others to guess what you want or need	Can deal with criticism without becoming hostile and defensive	Describe things in a way that implies you are always right
Posture is often slouched or you lean on something for support	Convey an air of assured strength and empathy	Posture is that of a solid rock, rigid, and intimidating
Eye contact is difficult; tend to look down or away	Voice tone is relaxed but firm; comfortable with direct eye contact, and eyes communicate openness and honesty	Mostly talk; often won't listen and don't hear others

Appendix B. Depiction of Three Basic Styles

FIGURE 3.1 Assertive, aggressive, and passive communication. Courtesy of Stand InBalance.

References

Benson, D. (2003). Coming home to the body: A journey for adolescents. In R. Strozzi-Heckler (Ed.), *Being human at work* (pp. 167–173). Berkeley, CA: North Atlantic Books.

Burman, S. (2003). Battered women: Stages of change and other treatment models that instigate and sustain leaving. *Brief Treatment and Crisis Intervention, 3*(1), 83–98. Retrieved from: http://btci.edina.clockss.org/cgi/reprint/3/1/83.pdf

Chodorow, N. (1978). *The reproduction of mothering: Psychoanalysis and the sociology of gender.* Berkeley: University of California Press.

Cramer, K., Knapp, S., Jacoby, R., & Anthony, L. (2007). *Girls rule: An 8-week EAP group for adolescent girls ages 11–15.* Marshall, NC: Horse Sense of the Carolinas, Inc.

Gunter, J. (2007). *Teaching horse: Rediscovering leadership.* Bloomington, IN: Author House.

Lutes, T. (2003). Wringing out an old sponge: Where personal dysfunction meets the pretense of corporate caring. In R. Strozzi-Heckler (Ed.), *Being human at work* (pp. 75–88). Berkeley, CA: North Atlantic Books.

Ogden, P., Minton, K., & Pain, C. (Eds.). (2006). *Trauma and the body.* New York: W.W. Norton & Company.

Tjaden, P., & Thoennes, N. (2000). *Full report of the prevalence, incidence and consequences of violence against women.* Office of Justice Programs, National Institute of Justice. Retrieved from: http://www.ncjrs.gov/pdffiles1/nij/183781.pdf

van der Kolk, B. A. (2003). Posttraumatic stress disorder and the nature of trauma. In M.F. Solomon & D.J. Siegel (Eds.), *Healing trauma: Attachment, mind, body, and brain* (pp. 168–195). New York: W.W. Norton & Company.

van der Kolk, B. A. (2006). Foreword. In P. Ogden, K. Minton, & C. Pain (Eds.), *Trauma and the body* (pp. xvii–xxvi). New York: W.W. Norton & Company.

Walker, L. (1994). *Abused women and survivor therapy: A practical guide for the psychotherapist.* Washington, DC: American Psychological Association.

Animal Assisted Group Interventions for the Treatment of Trauma

Molly DePrekel and Kay Neznik

Introduction

As a licensed clinical psychologist and social worker working with clients who are survivors of trauma, we believe therapeutic interactions with animals have value in their healing process. According to Perry (2006), "Beginning the recovery process for relational neglect can start with animals" (p. 38). As a part of this recovery process, our equine assisted or facilitated psychotherapy sessions provide clients with a safe environment to begin to deal with the traumatic events, or series of events, that have shaken their ability to function or to feel by creating negative belief systems about their self, others, and the world.

Our equine partners help bring our clients, usually young women who have experienced sexual trauma, out of their shells. They motivate them to talk while at the same time soothing them. Adolescents, in particular, often find it awkward to connect with group facilitators. However, in the process of developing a relationship with an equine partner, an adolescent is often better able to move beyond initial discomfort and build trusting relationships. Clients grow in confidence and gain a more positive sense of power in a world where they have historically felt powerless.

In our work, we are always cognizant of how the human–animal connection acts as a catalyst for communication, insight, and change. Through their body language, equines give immediate feedback to clients on how they are functioning and handling their feelings. This feedback helps clients learn how to pay better attention to the connection between their body and mind so they can inhabit their body in a new way. Processing this feedback also offers clients insights, which assist them in a more productive and healthier expression of their emotions.

Rationale

In one session, for instance, a group member grew quite frustrated when she could not get her equine to follow her without a lead. She became visibly agitated, so we asked her to take a minute and relax before she tried again. As soon as she let out a breath of air and relaxed her body, the equine came up to her and nuzzled her. This gave her immediate feedback on how she processes tension in her body when she gets stressed. Because the equine responded positively to her physical calming *out-breath* response, the client was able to reorganize what she did. This gave her and the group a different approach to talk about how she deals with daily frustration and ways that might work better for her.

Description

Training and Preparation

In working with equine assisted group therapy, it is important that the therapeutic team have training and experience in therapeutically relevant skills for working with trauma clients and that sessions remain safe for all parties. Because therapy may trigger intense stressful or traumatic reactions from the client, the therapist must be able to understand the client's process and help manage feelings as they surface.

Sessions should also include an equine specialist to monitor the animal's well-being during sessions. For individual sessions, the clinician and equine specialist may be dually trained and function in both roles; however, it is critical to have two or more treatment team members present with groups. The treatment team-to-client ratio in a group is based on the number of clients and equines as well as the expertise and cross-training of the facilitators. A main component for successful equine assisted therapy (EAT) group sessions is an appropriate equine facility. It is recommended that the location include a private area conducive to safe expression of potentially strong emotions and check-in spaces. There should be room to meet in a circle and for other experiential activities. It is also imperative that either the facility or treatment team has equine liability insurance, that the treatment team also carry personal malpractice and liability insurance, and of course that all clients complete appropriate paperwork. In addition to the normal mental health forms, EAT-specific forms include a hold-harmless agreement and an emergency consent form to obtain medical treatment. It is recommended that treatment teams work either with trauma survivors or offenders exclusively until they become highly skilled with both populations. In preparing for EAT group work, it is important to

- Decide how to market sessions and what billing procedures will be used

- Identify the size and length of the group.

- Decide whether the group will be ongoing or time limited, closed or open, and mixed sex or gender specific

- Determine their roles

- Choose a developed curriculum to use as a guide or develop their own, bearing in mind that properly developing a curriculum is very time-consuming and requires a lot of concentration and research

- Plan the goals, outcomes, and content of each group in written form, especially in the beginning stages so the staff is able to maintain the group's structure and stay focused or otherwise clients may become "off task" and not reach the planned goals

- Run practice or mock groups with other staff who are willing to give feedback on the group's content and process

- Take care of marketing and billing

Our experience has taught us that marketing is most efficiently done through word of mouth and by sending flyers to other clinicians, treatment programs, schools, and families. Many times, individual clinical therapists will refer clients, and often the clinician cofacilitating this group has appropriate referrals that are ready for a group process. Work closely with outpatient treatment programs for sexual abuse; local child protection, county probation, and human services groups; social workers; and other referral sources to create a network. Prepare flyers to send, and in marketing meetings be ready to talk about your group's goals, content, and the potential client benefits.

Decide if your services will be insurance reimbursable, private pay, or both. Will they be funded by the county or a grant? Will a center raise funds to fully or partially cover clients' costs? Note that insurance companies or other funders may require that one or both of the facilitators be licensed to practice mental health.

Group Rules

In beginning group work, we first go over four preestablished ground rules adapted from *The Four Agreements* by Don Miguel Ruiz (1997):

1. Don't take things personally.

2. Always do your best.

3. Don't make assumptions.

4. Be impeccable to your word.

These ground rules are important because they give clients four simple, yet profound, principles to strive for, and they also help define boundaries within the group. We ask group members to continue to put these agreements into practice throughout the group process, which demonstrates how they could practice these ground rules in other areas of their life.

Body Awareness Techniques

The treatment team can engage clients in this type of work in many ways. Our treatment involves not only understanding how trauma plays out in cognitive beliefs but also how trauma is carried in the body. We believe that being in motion, practicing mindfulness, and breathing and understanding how our bodies can carry trauma is critical in resolving trauma. Clients seem to listen better and are able to incorporate more of the feedback with less resistance if they can have a hands-on experience and be in motion in their body during sessions. Our therapy incorporates somatic (body) awareness, some sensorimotor psychotherapy techniques based on the work of Odgen (2010), and Tellington TTouch for Your Horse exercises (Tellington-Jones, 2010).

TTouch is a system of gentle circular touches, lifts, and slides that works at the cellular level to activate the body's potential. We incorporate it as a way to teach clients relaxation and self-soothing skills and connect better with the animals. Not only does it benefit equines in equine assisted psychotherapy (EAP) or equine facilitated psychotherapy (EFP), but also it can create deeper rapport between the equine and client. This relational connection develops through an understanding of each other and facilitates more effective communication. We always stress to clients that TTouch should be done only on the equines or themselves and not on each other. TTouch ground exercises can also be beneficial. "Using a variety of obstacles and ground poles, TTouch exercises result in self-control, focus, self-confidence, cooperation, balance and coordination" (Tellington-Jones, 2010).

During and after the sessions, we give clients feedback about how their behavior, individually and as a team, impacts the equine's behavior and willingness to do what is asked. This can be a powerful technique as it is observable behavior occurring in the moment. Research has found this works better than traditional talk therapy group in an office setting. In Krawetz's (1992) study that measured self-esteem involving teens in an equine social and emotional learning program, focus group comments by participants included

> "They have ways to talk back to you. Like if you look at them straight in the eyes, or you, like, listen to their breathing, sometimes it sounds like they're talking to you. I just, sometimes, listen or stare them in the eyes... You can hear a story in their eyes and stuff." Another comment goes on to say, "You can tell them stories, tell your problems even though they don't give you an answer. Because sometimes lately I go home crying, because people make fun of me because I don't wear what they're wearing. I'm different. Everyone's different in their own way, and horses are too. You can tell them a secret. Things that you would not tell even, even a priest because they're so private.... I feel I can talk to horses. They don't give you an answer, but they always make me feel better." Yet another participant states, "I learned to cooperate more with other people. People who are with me, I think they accept me." (pp. 26–27)

This gives some insight into the theory that young people with emotional and behavioral issues can develop relationships with animals rather than people because they are less threatening and provide less opportunity for rejection (Okoniewski, 1984). Using the Behavioral Assessment System for Children (BASC), improvement on the Behavioral Symptom Index, which reflects an overall reduction in problem behaviors, indicates that after children and adolescents received equine assisted counseling their ability to cope and adapt to new situations increased, whereas overall maladaptive behaviors decreased (Trotter, Chandler, Goodwin-Bond, & Casey, 2008).

Expressive Art Techniques

For some groups, we choose to integrate expressive arts to work on the expression of feelings and issues that surround these feelings. This also provides a rainy day option during inclement weather. Examples include

- Making an equine braid for bookmark or other keepsake as a transitional object (an object to take with them that represents their time in group)

- Designing a "who am I" poster of personality using pictures from magazines of equines and words chosen to describe self

- Designing group posters with half of the pictures showing positive examples and other half negative examples (i.e., positive boundaries, poor boundaries)

- Painting a shirt or using an iron-on equine patch; designing a logo to represent yourself or painting your own coat of arms

Working in the Moment

In our work with clients, topics are introduced in a meaningful manner. We use the idea of incrementally *increased perceived risk* not only with our equine activities but also with the verbal sharing and discussions. As comfort is established, we increase the expectation for clients to share more about themselves and their trauma stories. It is important as clients share traumatic past issues for the therapist to help them understand the ways they have survived and thrived. Clients can then begin to state competency-based reframes of survival. For example, when a client is asked to take a safe and perceived risk with the equine, it may be to ride the equine with her arms extended outward or to close her eyes while on the equine or to lead an equine through a challenge course. Clients are asked what they need to do to complete this task to feel safe. Clients may ask for side walkers or a staff to be with them. When they have completed the exercise, the staff, and at times the group members, comment on their ability. "Wow, you really took a risk, but you were able to keep yourself safe and ask for help, while working with an equine. This is quite a success. If you can do that with this large animal how can you use these skills in your everyday life?" Without directly saying it, clients are able to see how they shared power with an animal and that asking for help met their needs directly. There are risks that you can take in life and still be in control and safe.

At the same time, it is important to understand that group therapy is dynamic and fluid. As the group process progresses, it is important, at times, to be flexible and move away from the planned activities and deal with immediate topics and issues that arise (e.g., revictimization, sexual harassment at school or work, sexual acting out). These "in-the-moment" group shifts can create powerful metaphors for the client's process as a direct result of their work with the equines. Opportunities for growth and therapeutic transformation occur in every moment. Therefore, group facilitators need to be able to shift focus quickly and move into new reframes that will benefit the clients and sometimes the equines.

Closure

Working with trauma clients with a history of sexual abuse can be both very stressful and rewarding. The clients develop very close relationships with the equines and therapeutic team. Ending the group can be a very painful process for some of the clients. As the group progresses, some members may continue in the group, and others may leave. As part of the therapy, we work on closure rituals to allow members to learn appropriate ways to say good-bye and, if the group is offered again, the ability to make decisions regarding continuing or terminating the treatment process. This can empower clients, giving them a sense of control over their lives and offering them another chance to have a choice or say in their lives.

Again, we need to stress the importance of having a therapeutic team that is clinically skilled in the areas of sexual abuse and perpetration. Clinicians can never predict what will be revealed in the group. Therefore, they must be able to handle the issues and provide a safe environment for the clients and equines so that this experience is positive and provides growth for the clients rather than more traumas.

Application

These techniques and therapeutic tools can be used with persons of any age who have experienced trauma in their lives. The curriculum in our manual *Animal Assisted Group Interventions for the Treatment of Trauma** can be adapted for other sorts of trauma and does not necessarily have to focus on sex-specific trauma. Trauma may look different for various people. It is up to clients to determine their level of trauma and what their needs are in relation to this trauma. Equine assisted therapy works with the client with a hands-on approach. It is especially beneficial to clients who have difficulty expressing their emotions verbally or directly with a therapist. This is why it is especially beneficial to adolescents who may show resistance to being in therapy; this process does not have the stigma associated with one-on-one therapy. Clients may perceive that going to the farm and working with horses is tolerable and not so invasive. Equine assisted therapy incorporates the body and brain to help move clients' trauma to a place where it can be managed in their daily lives.

These techniques can be used in a group or one-on-one format. We have found that the group format is the preferable mode of therapy, but many clients are not able to work in a group situation. Applying these

---

* This manual is available for order by contacting Molly@mwtraumacenter.com.

techniques in one-on-one therapy or pair therapy can also be beneficial to the client.

References

DePrekel, M., & Neznik, M.K. (2008). *Manual: Animal assisted therapeutic group interventions for survivors of trauma.*

Krawetz, N. (1992). *The effect of riding horses on self esteem in adolescent girls.* Unpublished master's dissertation, University of Minnesota.

Perry, B. D. (2006). Applying principles of neurodevelopment to clinical work with maltreated and traumatized children. In N. Boyd Webb (Ed.), *Working with traumatized youth in child welfare* (p. 38). New York: Gilford Press.

Ogden, P. (2010). *Sensorimotor Psychotherapy Institute professional training for psychotherapists.* Retrieved from: http://www.sensorimotorpsychotherapy.org

Okoniewski, L. (1984). A comparison of human–human and human–animal relationships. In R. Anderson, B. Hart, and L. Hart (Eds.), *The pet connection: Its influences on our health and quality of life.* St. Paul, MN: Globe Publishing Co.

Ruiz, M. A. (1997). *The four agreements: A practical guide to personal freedom.* Carlsbad, CA: Hay House.

Tellington-Jones, L. (2010). *Tellington TTouch for your horse.* Retrieved from: http://www.ttouch.com

Trotter, K.S., Chandler, C.K., Goodwin-Bond, D., & Casey, J. (2008). A comparative study of the efficacy of group equine assisted counseling with at-risk children and adolescents. *Journal of Creativity in Mental Health, 3*(3), 254–284.

☐ The Magic Room

Joy Nussen

Introduction

The *magic room* is an equine assisted counseling (EAC) technique I created for children and adolescents while working in a residential treatment program. This technique centers on creating and experiencing an emotionally safe space, practicing leadership, an opportunity for expression of feelings through verbal and nonverbal communication, teamwork and sharing, and time to create and imagine.

The youth at this facility came from abusive histories, so issues around safety and trust were my focus. Within the arena, I offered building props (e.g., PVC piping, cones, barrels, logs) and opened a physical space for the child to design a special place where these issues could be addressed. The horse added the element of a nonjudgmental friend who could navigate this new world with them. A bonus could include self-empowerment for the child, particularly when leading the powerful equine into the created space.

Rationale

Horses are motivated toward basic needs. Because of this very specific motivation, horses keep themselves very focused, healthy, safe, and happy. In contrast, children who have not had their basic needs met are easily distracted; do not feel safe; are depressed, angry, or otherwise emotionally disturbed; and are often physically unhealthy. Partnering with a live being who is a positive role model is an ideal solution.

The large size of a horse offers a perfect opportunity for a client to overcome fear and develop confidence. Plus, just like us, horses experience a large variety of emotions and are intuitive and social animals with distinct personalities, attitudes, and moods. They have defined roles within their herds comparable to human dynamics. Because of these similarities, horses can demonstrate and teach self-awareness, honest communication, trust, healthy boundaries, leadership, patience, assertiveness, play, affection, nurturance, and more.

An essential tenet of EAC states: "If you have a better understanding of your body language, you have a better understanding of yourself." Horses have the ability to mirror exactly what human body language is telling them and therefore provide us with metaphors and lessons about ourselves to help facilitate change. I observed shifts in physical body posture of the children as they gained confidence in leading this large majestic creature around the arena. I also witnessed changes in facial expression as fear melted away and the joy of the partnership between the child and the horse developed.

The philosophy of the Equine Assisted Growth and Learning Association (EAGALA) includes believing that clients have the best solutions for themselves and stepping out of the way so they can discover those solutions (Kersten & Thomas, 2005). In the created space of the magic room, the children felt safe to tell their silent, nonjudgmental friend about their life struggles, or for a few precious moments, just allowed themselves the chance to relax in the company of a natural leader.

Description

The group builds a magic room together from a variety of materials available to them in the arena. The definition of *magic room* is decided on by the group (e.g., if the counselor is asked what a magic room is, children are told that it is up to them to define what that means). Children choose a horse (may or may not be haltered already) and then take turns entering the room by themselves with their horse. They are told they can stay as long as they want in the room and that if they choose, they can talk privately to their horse. The remaining group methods who are waiting their turn to enter the room go for a walk around the arena with their horses. Depending on the number of participants in the activity, groups of two can walk with one horse, taking turns leading. When participants in the room state that they are ready to exit the room, they change places with one of the clients walking a horse around the arena. A period of time is offered at the conclusion of the session for those who want to share any of their experiences during the activity. The number of horses used for the magic room depends on group size. This activity may need to be carried over to multiple sessions to enable each participant to be in the magic room. Children may decide to change horses at times, and that can also be an interesting topic to discuss as many children have a difficult time sharing "their" horse.

Meaningful Questions to Ask

- How did you decide to build the magic room?

- Was there a leader?

- How did you decide to choose the horse you did?

- What makes the room magic?

- How would it have been different if you didn't have the horse in the room with you?

- Did you choose to speak to your horse? Would you like to share anything about your conversation?

- How would it have been different if you had a person instead of a horse in the room with you?

- Is there anyone you know you would like to be in the special room with you?

- How did you decide when you were ready to leave the room?

- When you were in the magic room, what was it like to have someone else waiting to go in?

- What was it like waiting your turn to go into the room?

- When is there a time you feel you would like a safe, special space of your own?

- Is there a safe place you can go? How can you make that happen?

- How did you feel being the leader when walking the horse? How about when you weren't the leader?

- What was it like waiting your turn to walk your horse?

- If you could choose to do one over the other and for a longer period of time, would you have chosen to walk your horse or take your horse into the magic room?

- What did or didn't you like about this activity?

Application

This activity has a variety of applications and can be used over a period of time depending on group size, children's needs, unexpected individual and group dynamics, and session time allotment. This technique was created for children and adolescents residing in a residential treatment facility, but it offers other meaningful applications, including family counseling. Interesting discussions can arise from exploring a family's definition of "magic," whether the family allows for creativity, if there is cooperation and mutual respect, and how decisions are made. This activity can also be conducted in silence. Inquiries on how the activity was different with or without words can lead to great insight about communication, self-expression, and personal needs. Adding the partnering of the nonverbal horse can bring about a powerful experience.

References

Kersten, G., & Thomas, L. (2005). *Equine assisted psychotherapy and learning un-training manual.* Santaquin, UT: Equine Assisted Psychotherapy and Learning Association (EAGALA).

Trask, L. (2010). *Helping with horses: Equine assisted psychotherapy (EAP).* Southern Seasons. Retrieved from: www.freshsteps.net/index.html

☐ Safe Touch Using Horses to Teach Sexually Abused Clients to Value Their Bodies and Themselves

Tracie Faa-Thompson

Introduction

While working as a therapist for young people in the juvenile social services system, I first used this technique to assist a teenage girl who had a history of interfamilial chronic sexual abuse to learn about safe touch and self-protection against further abuse. Children who have been the victim of chronic interfamilial child sexual abuse are often not very skilled at future protection of themselves and will fall into additional abusive relationships as they go through their childhood. They are especially vulnerable when they reach puberty and become more aware of the increasing importance of their peer relationships.

Martin and Beesley (1977) found among other behaviors that sexually abused children and young people often presented with pseudo-mature behavior, meaning a false appearance of independence and indiscriminate affection to any person who shows an interest in them. This is why the teenage years are times of special vulnerability. Teenage boys begin to take a sexual interest in girls and are initially encouraging and then are very quickly rejecting of girls who allow themselves to be sexually touched.

Rationale

Howe (2005) relates that sexual abuse impairs children's ability to regulate and make sense of their emotions and levels of arousal. Trickett (1997) found that frequently seriously and chronically abused children and young people often present with inappropriate and unusual sexualized behavior toward peers. Their sexually labile behavior resulted in children and young people of both genders experiencing regular social difficulties and peer rejection. Children who have been sexually abused need assistance with body boundaries to identify safe and unsafe touch. In addition, they need to actually *experience* safe touch and to be in control of touch and touching.

Horses are large and sensitive creatures who are also very touch sensitive and will let their feelings be felt immediately if they are touched or approached in ways they do not like. A number of controlled studies have demonstrated the efficacy of animal assisted therapy (AAT) with a wide range of issues including children at risk of or victims of sexual harm (Bowers & MacDonald, 2001; Trotter, Chandler, Goodwin-Bond, & Casey, 2008). Chandler (2005), in an equine assisted counseling (EAC) program with at-risk teens found that highly troubled teens of both genders displayed new positive behaviors. She observed:

> At risk teens reduce and eliminate manipulative behaviours, over-come fears, display courage, develop and practice stress-management and anxiety-reduction skills, become less self-focused, increase communication skills, support and help one another and look out for and encourage one another. (p. 112)

For children who are victims of sexual abuse, all these changes are essential self-protective factors, especially in the need to have supportive peer relationships based on mutual respect and trust rather than allowing themselves to be sexually manipulated.

Cattanach (1992) states that play therapy gives sexually abused children the space to, as best as possible, come to terms with the stress and multiple losses they feel. She advises that it is important to assist children to repossess their bodies and find an identity other than one bound up in their past abuse. Zimmerman and Russell-Martin (2008) noted the features of EAC that are similar to those of play therapy. Like play therapy, EAC is conducted in a setting that is inviting to children. Both methods help children communicate with others, express feelings, modify behaviors, develop problem-solving skills, and learn new ways to relate to others. Play therapy, like EAC, builds on the natural ways that children learn about themselves and their relationships to the world around them. Both approaches can assist children in developing respect for self and others, body awareness, self-esteem, and better awareness and assurance of their own abilities.

Teenagers who have been sexually abused may struggle with the idea of traditional play therapy and may feel it is too "childish" for them. Relative to this are their often-desperate attempts to "connect" with their peers and present themselves as "normal." By using horses to replicate safe touch, trusting relationships, safety, and caring the teenagers can experience the differences between safe and unsafe touch through the medium of the horse. Gilligan (2001) states that this sense of "lovability" conveyed to the person by the animal may help with building on the teens' self-esteem.

Description

This is approximately a 10-session model, where the first 4 sessions are spent working on the ground and becoming familiar with the horse before progressing to riding; clients then work first with the saddle and then bareback so they feel the horse skin to skin. Clients can either choose to ride the horse bareback first on their own or with the therapist; either way is effective for building up to both safe equine and human touch at the clients' pace. A detailed case study is provided next to further illustrate all 10 sessions of this technique.

Materials

For best results I suggest you use a safe large horse that has the capacity to carry both the therapist and the rider—a tickly horse. A tickly horse is a horse that objects to being brushed too hard or too softly; some horses are more touch sensitive than others. You will also need grooming equipment and a trusted helper for the riding stages of therapy.

Treatment Goals

- Learn safe and appropriate touch

- Gain an increased sense of self

- Find the opportunity to experience close contact with others without having a sexual element

- Experience feeling safe and trusting others, both human and animal.

- Increase the sense of acceptance by others

- Experience being in control

- Have the courage to begin new relationships

Case Study

Micha* was a 14-year-old teenage girl who was believed to have suffered severe and chronic sexual abuse by many family members of both

---

* Names have been changed to protect identities.

genders. She had been in a therapeutic unit for 8 years and, at the time of therapy, was in foster care, waiting for placement in a residential school. Micha was referred for life story work, but it soon became clear that her risky behavior with her male peers was seriously affecting her peer relationships and was leading to further rejection and risk of further sexual abuse, which took priority over life story work.

Life story work is undertaken with children and adolescents in the looked after system who are struggling to understand their history and how they came to be in foster or adopted homes. Often children fantasize about their early life history, and half-remembered stories become reality. Sensitive life story work alongside a therapist assists children to understand fully their own personal story and to clarify any unanswered questions they may have.

I took Micha along to my local Riding for the Disabled Centre and introduced her to a horse named Tickly that objected by swishing his tail and lifting his leg up if brushed too strongly on his genitalia and other tickly spots. I demonstrated with Micha how to brush a horse, pointing out the parts of the horse. Micha was too wary at first to touch the horse. I talked about new situations and meeting new "people" being scary as it was difficult to know how to approach them and wondered aloud if it might feel the same for horses. Micha spent the first session meeting the horses and finding out their stories. She discovered that some, like her, had not experienced very pleasant beginnings. On the drive back, Micha was able to reflect on the horses and wanted to brush her "special" horse next time.

On the second session after watching the therapist brush the horse, Micha felt able to brush him herself. Micha brushed a little too hard, and the horse swished his tail and tossed his head. Micha stood back, and we discussed what the horse must feel like to be touched by someone he doesn't know and in "private" places. Micha was able to acknowledge that he didn't like it and showed it. Over the next two sessions Micha worked with the horse and worked out what kind of touch was acceptable and not acceptable to him and why. Once Micha knew how to groom the horse, he accepted her touch but was quick to let her know when she made a mistake and brushed too hard. On the drives back in the car, Micha would reflect on the progress that she had made and was able to talk about trust and relationships and not letting others touch her in her private area when she did not know them, just like her horse was able to set healthy boundaries.

By session 4, Micha felt confident enough to mount the horse with a saddle on, as she was not yet confident enough to ride bareback. She rode the horse while being led around the arena by the therapist and spent time stroking his mane and tail and getting the feel of him. Micha was able to talk about how it felt to put her trust in both the horse and the therapist as the leader. She talked about how she trusted the therapist would not allow her to be harmed, so she didn't have to be vigilant all the time. After that session Micha slept most of the journey home and stated that she felt very relaxed. As Micha was mostly in a state of hyper vigilance this was a huge move forward for her.

The next session Micha again rode the horse on a lead with its tack on. In session 5, Micha was invited to ride the horse bareback. Micha was not able to do this on her own but wanted to do it with me as she was too scared to ride the horse bareback; luckily, both Micha and I are light, and the horse was more than able to carry our combined weight. I got on first, Micha was helped up behind me, and together we rode the horse around the school. Micha was invited to put her arms forward around me and grasp the horse's mane, which she did. Micha loved this experience, and we did this for an additional three sessions. By the therapist riding the horse and Micha being very close behind, she experienced very close touch with another adult, which was safe and nonabusive and for which she did not have to give anything in return.

After the third bareback session Micha disclosed further sexual abuse by an uncle, which she had blocked out for over 7 years. Micha was always confused as to who abused her. Micha was interviewed and was able to make an excellent statement to the police. The last two sessions Micha was able to ride bareback on her special horse while being led by the therapist, and she said good-bye to her horse. The next week she moved to her new school and was able to develop more positive peer relationships. Her uncle had died since her reception into care. Micha did not know this, but when she found out she felt that this was his just deserts for his abuse of her. Micha is now 20 and is doing well. She holds down a job and has formed healthy relationships with others.

Application

Although primarily developed for clients who are victims of child sexual abuse, safe touch can be used with children and adults with attachment difficulties who are struggling with physical boundaries and recognizing their own and others' personal space. This process is ideal for clients with loss and bereavement issues and helps them learn to begin to trust in relationships and closeness. Safe touch is also an effective modality for victims of domestic violence, where building trust in relationships and getting comfortable with close safe touch is a fundamental need. Due to the nature of clients' issues, this method is best used as an individual model.

References

Bowers, M. J., & Macdonald, P. M. (2001). The effectiveness of equine-facilitated psychotherapy with at-risk adolescents. *Journal of Psychology and the Behavioral Sciences, 15*, 62–76.

Cattanach, A. (1992). *Play therapy with abused children.* London: Jessica Kingsley Publishers.

Chandler, C.K. (2005). *Animal assisted therapy in counseling.* New York: Routledge.

Gilligan, R. (2001). *Promoting resilience: A resource guide on working with children in the care system.* London: BAAF.

Howe, D. (2005). *Child abuse and neglect: Attachment, development, and intervention.* Hampshire: Palgrave Macmillan.

Martin, H., & Beesley, P. (1977). Behavioural observations of abused children. *Developmental Medicine and Child Neurology, 19*, 373–387.

Trickett, P. (1997). Sexual and physical abuse and the development of social competence. In S. Luthar, J. Burack, D. Ciccetti, & J. Weisz (Eds.), *Developmental pathology: Perspectives on adjustment, risk, and disorder* (pp. 67–92). New York: Cambridge University Press.

Trotter, K. S., Chandler, C. K., Goodwin-Bond, D., & Casey, J. (2008). A comparative study of the efficacy of group equine assisted counseling with at-risk children and adolescents. *Journal of Creativity in Mental Health, 3*(3), 254–284.

Zimmerman, D., & Russell-Martin, L. (2008). Connecting with kids: The EAGALA model with young children. *EAGALA in Practice, Autumn*, 18–21.

☐ Equine Facilitated Psychotherapy for the Treatment of Trauma

Molly DePrekel

Introduction

Equine facilitated psychotherapy (EFP) can be an effective approach for clients with a history of trauma. This is particularly true for clients with attachment issues, because equines can provide relational attunement as described by Perry (2006). It is the belief of the clinician that clients with a history of posttraumatic stress disorder (PTSD) can find value and healing when working with a qualified mental health professional who partners with equines in mental health therapy.

In my experience, building a framework in equine psychotherapy sessions that involves competency-based interventions, mindfulness, cognitive reframes, somatic approaches, play, and attachment work can provide a healing milieu for clients experiencing trauma. Van de Kolk in his work and research often refers clients struggling with trauma to mindfulness-based stress reduction, yoga, eye movement desensitization and reprocessing (EMDR), and other movement-based therapeutic interventions (van der Kolk, 2005). Dr. Allen Shore (2001), a leading researcher in attachment and trauma, states, "I have suggested that an interdisciplinary approach that focuses upon attachment experiences and their effects on regulatory structures and functions can offer us more comprehensive models of normal development" (p. 201).

Rationale

As a licensed clinical psychologist working with clients who are survivors of trauma, I believe that therapeutic interactions with animals hold value in their healing process.

According to Perry (2006), "Beginning the recovery process for relational neglect can start with animals" (p. 38). As a part of the recovery process, equine assisted psychotherapy (EAP) sessions can provide clients with a safe environment to begin to deal with the traumatic events, or series of events, that have shaken their ability to function or feel emotions as a result of creating negative belief systems about their self, others, and the world.

According to Perry (2010), when working with children and adolescents it all goes back to regulation and how children who have experienced trauma have had the development and biology of their brain altered. If you want the children to get better, you need to be able to help them regulate and calm down so that they can internalize new information and so the brain can develop the portions of its functioning that did not develop because of the trauma or neglect. The brain develops from the bottom up. Verbal interactions are less effective when a client is unable to access the higher levels of the brain, such as the prefrontal cortex. Different interventions are necessary for dysregulation located in a low level of the brain versus a higher level of the brain.

I believe that as researchers and clinicians better understand the brain and the effects of trauma and attunement–misattunement as well as attachment, we can develop quality interventions and define why working with equines may be one prescription for regulating the brain and limbic system. Perry (2010) further states that there are several areas of regulation: self-regulation, somatosensory regulation, and relational regulation. He believes that relational regulation is needed for good milieu work. Pharmacological regulation is necessary for containment but not change, and medication cannot provide any relational piece. It is Perry's belief that proximal rewards and consequences are needed for healing. He believes the best proximal reward is relational. There are numerous ways to best help with these regulation areas. He states that other forms of therapy help tremendously, such as yoga, drumming, and martial arts. Animal assisted therapy (AAT) is effective because it has a relational element along with a sensory element to help with learning regulation (Perry, 2010).

Movement activities with equines can help with self-regulation and skills to maintain an internal locus of control. For example, moving forward with a goal in mind and knowing where you are going while leading a 1,000-pound horse requires some internal locus of control, and increasing that somatic sense for clients can be empowering. Building on that skill and leading without a lead line can teach the concept, "If I know where I am going I can lead in my own life." According to van der Kolk (2005), a leading researcher in trauma recovery, movement therapies can provide healing and self-soothing for trauma clients. He further states that mindfulness and centering techniques assist clients in trauma recovery. Equine assisted therapy can play a key role in movement and mindfulness with clients.

Description

During AAT sessions, clients are provided with opportunities to observe the effects of their arousal state on another. Clients practice regulating their own affect to regulate the equine's arousal state and therefore the horse's behavior. This dynamic form of relational affect regulation teaches clients, in an interactive context, that affect can be modulated. Animal assisted therapy can reduce disruptive behaviors because it creates a culture and a community in which self-regulation and cooperative skills can be practiced again and again. Equine assisted activities and interactions should be designed to support clients in reaching increased levels of intimacy. The activities also should allow clients to practice managing a wide range of emotions with appropriate affect, and should allow influence from others, both human and equine.

It is critical for clinicians working with clients and equines to have an understanding of the neurobiology of the brain and the subtleties of the sensorimotor systems in the body. Work with equines that calms and soothes the brain and body is necessary to achieve healing and help clients to stay in their window of tolerance (Ogden, Minton, & Pain, 2007). Also gaining mastery and skills is critical for clients experiencing PTSD.

Working with a large animal that demonstrates fight, flight, freeze, and fidget, which many of our clients experience in hyperarousal and hypoarousal states, can provide metaphor, sensorimotor experiences, and narrative opportunities for healing. Helping clients expand their window of tolerance and stay grounded and present in the presence of a horse while always allowing challenge by choice gives clients mindful experiences that can lead to opportunities to build new neuropathways. Clients with PTSD often lose their access to the prefrontal cortex, which allows for response versus limbic systems reactions. The wise mind of "What do I feel, what do I think, and then what do I want to do" is often lost when clients are triggered or are hyper- or hypoaroused. In working with an equine, clients develop an ability to remain connected to the animal during moments of uncomfortable arousal. For example, while leading a horse through a frightening obstacle, clients must remain calm and act to soothe the horse to accomplish the task. (The terms *horse* and *equine* are used interchangeably throughout as equines can include donkeys and minis.)

Case Examples

In one case a client had a hard time with dissociation and staying present. In sessions she was taught breathing techniques and Tellington TTouch (Tellington-Jones, 2010), ear slides that she did on the horse to help her gain skills to stay present and mindful. She could also have feedback from another living being about her impact and see her ability to help another being calm and breathe deeply.

In another case, a student in a social and emotional learning school-based program who had very quick movements and presented as very anxious reported the horses moving fast and sometimes leaning away from him when he groomed or attempted to help bring them in from the pasture. His work involved walking down the barn aisle as he normally presents in the world and then at a slower pace with calmer micromovements and voice tones. He then was asked to notice the horses in each of these instances, and he walked up to the clinician and said, "Okay, I get it," adding that he understood how his teachers must feel with him. In explaining, he talked about when the horses backed away in their stalls and had wide eyes as he came through. He saw and felt his impact and wanted a relationship with them, so he tried another way. The horses' faces softened, and they stuck their heads out to be petted. The intervention then became to work with this young man to take his newfound learning back into his everyday life. In this program his teachers came to the group and were involved with the program. If they were not there, we had releases of information so we could talk with teachers. It was important to share information so this student could be reminded about the horses and practice with human interactions. He even had a picture of what the horses looked like when he was calm so he could have this picture on his desk and learn on many levels.

Modeling safe, respectful, mindful interactions with equines can help clients feel safe, connected, and able to build relationships with the clinician and another living being. Clients report to me that they feel like they are waking up in the presence of the horses, and one client even reported they knew they could trust me by how they observed my positive, polite, and calm interactions with the horses. Assisting clients to get in touch with their body brains and not just rattle cognitive thoughts is one way equines can be additive in therapy. Often when clients are grooming or doing TTouch (Tellington-Jones, 2010), they will report, "I feel better; I like this." It is then that the clinician expands this opportunity by saying, "Tell me about this: Where in your body do you feel better? What do you notice?" Clinicians often have to do some psychoeducation about sensation and the body and what stored memory the body can hold, as sensory experiencing may be a new concept. Also, the information may be a helpful explanation and understanding of what clients are experiencing and going through in their own trauma. Teaching breathing, mindfulness, and sensory experiencing to clients can help them gain self-soothing techniques to use away from therapy to deal with symptoms of PTSD. Equines are masters of being in the moment and can be cotherapists in this work of calming, gaining symptom reduction, coping with triggers, letting go, and recovering.

Building equine interactions and activities that increase attachment, attunement, competency, mastery, challenge, and cognitive reframes promotes healing. Also, teaching self-soothing skills, management of symptoms, social and emotional learning, and involving movement creates a healing environment for clients to recover. In the powerful work of equine therapeutic interactions, creative goal-directed sessions that allow clients to gain skills and self-regulation and allow for relational regulation are key. Clients can learn to be self-motivated and change their behavior in a positive fashion. Work with equines can help clients to communicate with others in an appropriate manner instead of using punitive methods, and they can gain relationships versus using a "power over" approach to get what they want. Often they can share feelings with the equines and just experience mutual gaze by looking into a horse's eye and breathing while practicing calming. Clients can show compassion and nurturance for other living things through energy work of TTouches (e.g., hair slides and ear slides, which are done by sliding one's fingers either up the ears or down the mane/tail with very light pressure—if the equine is accepting of the touch) and get feedback when a horse lowers its head or if the horse backs away. This powerful treatment work creates mastery for clients as they gain new skills and knowledge. Clients in trauma recovery often report not feeling like they have anything to offer or they can't state a lot of positives about themselves; for these clients, giving back to another living being may challenge their cognitive belief that they are unworthy or bad.

In psychotherapy groups with young women who are sexual trauma survivors, equine partners help bring clients out of their shells. The horses motivate the women to talk while at the same time soothing them. In my experience with leading groups in various treatment settings, adolescents, in particular, often find it awkward to connect with group facilitators. However, in the process of developing a relationship with an equine partner, an adolescent is often better able to move beyond initial discomfort and build trusting relationships. Clients can grow in confidence and gain a more positive sense of power in a world where they have historically felt powerless. Often these clients in particular can benefit from gaining self-regulation skills, learning boundaries and assertiveness, developing problem-solving skills, and demonstrating cooperation. All of these can be done with the assistance of an equine partner. In group work with trauma survivors, cooperative riding can be beneficial as peers learn to trust each other, ask for help, seek support, and show empathy and give each other support. The movement of the horse can be incorporated also as clients can learn to breathe and take some risks as they move forward on the horse and in their life.

It may be crucial that clients have opportunities to be on horseback as part of their movement therapy and rebuilding of new neuropathways that create options other than just reacting. In some mounted work, clients move through cones on the ground in the ring to create bilateral stimulation of the right and left hemispheres of the brain. This is a technique used in trauma models of therapy. This is also used in eye movement desensitization and reprocessing (EMDR). This helps clients maintain a less distressed stance and increase emotional regulation as they tell their story of trauma. It is contraindicated and can potentially reimprint trauma to a client if therapists ask a client to talk about the details of the trauma or feed them trauma questions when they are in a distressed emotional state. This process can reactivate the trauma or hardwire it deeper (McClelland, 2006).

The mechanisms of moving the body and the balance required in riding creates increased blood flow in the body, assisting the cingulate, which helps regulate a distress response (McClelland, 2006). Clients who have cut off parts of their body may begin to reconnect while on the back of a horse; the clinician can work with them to regain sensation while using calming techniques so they can have a sense of control. When clients have a powerful reaction while riding, the clinician can stop the movement and have them process what is occurring while sitting on the horse or getting off and reconnecting with their feet on the ground.

When trauma occurs early in development, equine facilitated psychotherapy may offer healing. As equines became domesticated, they became especially attuned to changes in affective states of humans. Equines respond to very subtle cues and affect, similar to parent–child affect communication and mutual regulation. Horses could offer a corrective emotional experience, reflective dialogue, and interactive repair when clients have experienced misattunement and attachment issues with a parent or caregiver.

These windows of opportunity can then be processed cognitively, somatically, and experientially with the clinician in the presence of the horse or in an office setting. The process of interaction and possibly training or caring for an equine becomes a developmental journey in which inevitable moments of misunderstanding and disruption can be identified and repaired. This interactive repair teaches clients to transition between emotional states and self-regulation. It also can enable clients to experience positive affect following negative experience. For example, if an interaction or task is not working, the clinician can help clients find another way to accomplish the goal or transform the interaction. If an activity needs to stop because of safety or frustration or because it is not working, then petting, play, and other activities can follow the experience. This repair can reinforce that the equine is still a "good horse" and that the clients are still a "good person," thus increasing frustration tolerance and allowing affect regulation and reconnection to occur (DePrekel & Fredrickson, 2004).

Often it is interpreted that animals provide unconditional love and positive regard. An animal's response to people is contingent on the verbal and mainly nonverbal cues received from the individual. Actions such as eye contact, facial expression, tone of voice, body gestures, and timing and intensity of the person's emotional state affect the animal's response. To work effectively with equines, clients must be aware of their nonverbal impact on the animal. Thus, the animal's behavior and interaction that happens is contingent upon individuals' nonverbal communication skills. In treatment programs we often refer to these interactions as *contingent collaborative communication*. For example, clients' tone of voice, body posture, and eye contact impact their success in catching a horse in a pasture. Some nonverbal types of communication that can be seen as aggressive, such as stiff body posture, staring, and loud tones, will chase the horse away. Meanwhile, softened tones, indirect eye contact, and fluid body movements will cause the horse to approach. Thus, human–animal interactions provide clients with a less threatening process for developing a congruent sense of self (Fredrickson, 2004).

Well-planned experiences with equines provide opportunities for clients to recognize the signals sent by the equine. Clients are assisted by clinicians in making sense of the signals, such as a horse's head shaking and pawing. The clinician can ask for clients' interpretation or story and can also help them to explore reasons for the equine's behavior. These interactions develop the capacity to create an understanding of the mind of others and of the self. Clients recognize the equine as another unique individual who may behave differently than they do. They can learn to respond to the animal as a separate entity on which they have an impact and vice versa. This learning and concept can then be taken into everyday life as clients can begin to see their impact on those around them and how they let others impact them.

In school-based social and emotional learning therapeutic work, some students who barely participate in school and groups eagerly cooperate, maintain positive behavior, and show empathy while in equine assisted social and emotional learning groups. I learn much more about these students in our equine groups than I have ever been able to in a traditional office therapy group. I believe the focus shifts for these teens from being psychoanalyzed to gaining mastery skills, cooperation, and practicing self-control. The horses and interactions become a focal point that unites the groups and allows for cooperative ventures. These equine interactions challenge group members, as well as school staff, to stay calm, exercise restraint, and play together. All involved in the groups teach and learn from each other.

Another example of participants' willingness to try new things and learn alternative healing is Tellington TTouch (Tellington-Jones, 2010). We often go to the participants' program site to conduct work on the first day of the equine group. One of the first days of a school-based program we went to one of the school sites, and the group was together only for the second time. They displayed very unfocused, argumentative, and disjointed behaviors. My group cofacilitator was watching the chaos and just picked up the therapy dog that was assisting in group. She put her on a table and started to teach TTouch. I watched in amazement as the group became quiet and focused, and many of the students began trying the touches on themselves. One participant who had her head down the entire first hour of group was doing python lifts on the dog's leg and ear slides as directed. The energy in the whole room became different as students became quiet and attentive. They watched my colleague demonstrate the touches on the dog, Mariah, and then try the touches on themselves. I was amazed and realized these students were hungry for new ways to relax and relate to one another and eager to try another way of being. We incorporate TTouch, as well as yoga stretches and body-centered work, in all our work with clients. The adolescents in these groups respond great and practice the TTouches on the equines each week of the program. (Note: TTouch should be taught as energy work on animals and oneself rather than on other people.)

The following is a quote from one of the school social workers working with teens with persistent mental illnesses. It relates to relaxation and guided imagery exercises we incorporate into our work with students and clients:

> Yesterday on the way home from Equine the guys were talking about medications and their side effects. One said he had problems getting to sleep at night. The other student told him he should use the imagery relaxation exercise that Molly taught them in group—about the horse and going to a safe place. He said he would try it. The next day he came to my office and said it worked. I thought this is exactly what we wanted—it is carrying over from the barn to real life. YEAH. (K. Neznik, personal communication, 2005)

One useful concept and framework that is inherent in equine facilitated therapy and interactions is play. The Association for Play Therapy (2010) defines play therapy as "the systematic use of a theoretical model to establish an interpersonal process wherein trained play therapists use the therapeutic powers of play to help clients prevent or resolve psychosocial difficulties and achieve optimal growth and development." Furthermore, play therapy is "the means by which licensed mental health professionals use developmentally appropriate play therapy theories and techniques to better communicate with and help clients, particularly children!"

Some examples of play in equine therapy work could include running in the pasture pretending to be horses (horses should not be in the pasture at the time), picking flowers, and whistling using a blade of grass. Having done this exercise with a group of older teen girls, I was amazed by their enthusiasm for play and the giggles and laughter from this otherwise serious and dramatic group of young women. At the suggestion of an intern, the described play was done with a therapy group focusing on trauma recovery. This clinician assumed they would not participate and would think it was a lame activity. The power of play won out, and laughter was abundant. Play could involve games with the horses. Other play could involve the seasons of the year. In hot summer, fun and play could include finger painting on the equines or putting a sheet on a tolerant equine, making a mural, and then washing the horse. In the fall, jumping in the leaves and collecting apples for the horses are fun activities; in the winter, try cooperatively making a snow labyrinth for the equines to walk through, and in the spring plant horse treats. Often the system of play can be accessible only when clients are able to calm and self-soothe and allow themselves to let go and access the creative brain. Imagine and incorporate treatment plans and goals that include play, laughter, and expressive arts.

Expressive arts often allow outlets and healing for clients recovering from trauma. Making horse masks or posters with feelings using horse pictures allows for self-narrative without having clients have to cognitively "tell" their story again. Many times the projects created can serve as transitional objects and tangibles for clients. These transitional objects can represent the recovery being sought at the barn while clients are going about their daily lives. One client reported that the wood barn sign she painted with a soothing word on it, along with a picture of her therapy horse, hangs above her bed to help with nightmares.

Application

In clinical work, the EFP clinician is always cognizant of how the human–animal connection acts as a catalyst for communication, insight, and change. Through their body language, equines give immediate feedback to clients on how they are functioning and handling their feelings. This feedback helps clients learn how to pay better attention to the connection between their body and mind so they can inhabit their body in a new way. Processing this feedback also offers clients insights, which assist them in a more productive and healthier expression of their emotions.

In one group session, for instance, a group member grew quite frustrated when she could not get her equine to follow her without a lead. She became visibly agitated, so we asked her to take a minute and relax before she tried again. As soon as she let out a breath of air and relaxed her body, the equine came up to her and nuzzled her. This gave her immediate feedback on how she processes tension in her body when she gets stressed. Because the equine responded positively to her physical calming "out-breath" response, the client was able to reorganize what she did. This gave her and the group a different approach to talk about how she deals with daily frustration and ways that might work better for her. This experience was applied to family work, and this client was able to relate differently to her mom and ask for her needs to be met rather than display further angry outbursts and leave the family sessions (DePrekel & Neznik, 2008).

Summary

In treatment for trauma, brain-based therapeutic interventions may help alter neuropathways and provide opportunities for clients to try out new behaviors and ways of being in the world. Equine assisted interventions can be a treatment option because it is an unconventional experience and is relationally based. In the brain, what is fed grows, so providing opportunities for nurturance and helping clients gain sensory input from their environment, the equine, and their own body may help get brain and body memory to create lasting change. When clients are able to work toward riding and developing balance while directing the horse through micromovements in their body, this can be a powerful dynamic for healing.

In one study involving preteen girls in a YMCA horse program, the comments from a focus group of participants showed that the girls felt a sense of protection and power while riding. Comments included, "You feel like you're protected because they're so big" and "Awesome, 'cause when you're on a horse, no one can ever get you" (Krawetz, 1992, p. 28). Studies are needed that can begin to show how the brain and body is impacted by equine and animal interactions. There have been some studies conducted with school-based youth struggling with emotional and behavioral issues over the last 15 years that show some promise of the efficacy of this work. The aforementioned study showing statistical significance in global self-worth was a YMCA equestrian program that worked with preteen and teen girls. The research question was, "Will learning to ride and care for horses improve the self-image and school behavior of 5th and 6th grade girls with emotional and behavioral problems?" The domain subscale of global self-worth and social acceptance showed a statistical significant increase. The three measurements included were the Harter Self-Perception Profile for adolescents, a modification of the Harter Teacher's Rating Scale of Student's Actual Behavior, and an informal focus group interview with participants. Three overall themes emerged during the interviews: relationships with the horses, feelings of power and protection, and responsibility (Krawetz, 1992).

Another study comparing equine assisted counseling (EAC) to school-based counseling using the BASC self-report found that EAC students achieved statistic significance on five scales of increasing positive behavior compared with only four subscales within the school counseling program (Trotter, Chandler, Goodwin-Bond, & Casey, 2008).

Working with clients to positively impact their equine partner is critical in this work. TTouch energy work and movement such as the TTouch labyrinth walk, positive reinforcement using clicker training, and mindful grooming are all interventions clients have reported to me that reinforce their ability to self-soothe and cope with stress associated with their mental health issues. Interventions that require assertiveness skills, boundary setting, cooperation, and risk taking by the clients provide opportunities for them to try out new behaviors and see options rather than just reacting.

It has been my experience that using animal assisted therapy and activities to work with clients is an effective alternative to traditional therapy in an office setting. The opportunity for learning and self-discovery is often accomplished through watching horse-to-horse behavior and then making metaphorical comparisons to human-to-human relationships. In group work, the experiences with the horses provide a shared experience with others that allows for communication regarding emotional states and responses. The process of working with an equine becomes a developmental journey in which clients can practice reflective interactions. Opportunities exist for clients to see the horse as another unique individual that may behave differently than they do. This can be the beginning of empathy, and the work becomes having clients respond to the animal instead of reacting. Work with equines also offers opportunities for emotional communication. In working with an equine, clinicians must assist clients to develop an ability to remain connected to the animal during moments of uncomfortable arousal. This is particularly important in working through symptoms of PTSD. For example, when leading horses through frightening obstacles, group members must work cooperatively or offer support and remain with the horses. Clients must act to soothe each other to accomplish the task.

Animal assisted therapy may be the treatment of choice for some people because it provides opportunities for experiences that mimic parenting skills. Animals, particularly companion animals, horses, sheep, and other livestock, respond to human arousal or emotional states in much the same way that children respond to parental emotional states (Levinson, 1972; Melson, 2000).

Further solid research is needed to understand how and if work with equines has a lasting impact on clients with trauma and emotional issues. The research questions I propose are

- Can it be proven that this work alters cellular memory or transforms brain waves and activity?

- What do clients who seek equine therapy report about their PTSD symptoms before, during, and after sessions?

- How do we as clinicians promote the calming, peace, and serenity clients report they feel in the presence of the equine when they are in other areas of their lives?

It will continue to be a journey to bring about healing for clients who suffer and recover from traumatic life-altering events, and assisting them in how they relate to these traumas continues to be an honor. It is truly a blessing to partner with animals as cotherapists in this healing and spiritual process.

Resources

- Clicker Training, http://www.clickertraining.com

- M. DePrekel, Cairns Psychological Services, molly@mwtraumacenter.com

- EPONA, http://www.taoofequus.com

- Featherbrookfarms.org

- M. MacNamara, MSW, Animal Systems, animalsystems@gmail.com

- Midwest Center for Trauma and Emotional Healing, http://mwtraumacenter.com

- M. K. Neznik, MSW, kneznik411@hotmail.com

- B. Rector, Adventures in Awareness, http://www.adventuresinawareness.net

- M. A. Ruiz, *The Four Agreements: A Practical Guide to Personal Freedom*, Hay House, 1997.

- Sensorimotor Psychotherapy Institute, http://www.sensorimotorpsychotherapy.org

- F. Shapero, EMDR, http://www.emdria.org/

- A. Shore, Affect Regulation, http://www.allanschore.com/

- L. Tellington-Jones, TTouch, http://www.ttouch.com

References

Association for Play Therapy. (2010). *Play therapy defined*. Retrieved from: http://www.a4pt.org/ps.index.cfm

DePrekel, M. (2005). Working with adolescents in a school-based experiential therapy group. In *Strides equine facilitated mental health*. North American Riding for the Handicapped Association.

DePrekel, M., & Fredrickson, M. (2004). *Animal-assisted therapy for at-risk youth and families*. In *Penn Proceedings—Can animals help humans heal?* Animal Assisted Interventions for Adolescents in Mental Health.

DePrekel, M., & Neznik, M. K. (2008). *Manual: Animal assisted therapeutic group interventions for survivors of trauma*. Self-published.

Fredrickson, M. (2004). Animal-assisted therapy for at-risk youth and families. In *Penn Proceedings—Can animals help humans heal?* Animal Assisted Interventions for Adolescents in Mental Health.

Krawetz, N. (1992). *The effect of riding horses On self esteem in 5th and 6th grade girls*. Unpublished master's dissertation, University of Minnesota.

Levinson, B. M., & Mallon, G. (1997). *Pet-oriented child psychotherapy* (2nd ed.). Springfield, IL: Charles C. Thomas.

Melson, G. (2001). *Companion animals and the development of children: Implications of the biophilia hypothesis.* In A. Fine (Ed.), *Handbook on animal-assisted therapy* (pp. 376–382). San Diego, CA: Academic Press.

Ogden, P., Minton, K., & Pain, C. (2007). *Trauma and the body.* New York: W.W. Norton.

Perry, B. D. (2006). Applying principles of neurodevelopment to clinical work with maltreated and traumatized children. In N. Boyd Webb (Ed.), *Working with traumatized youth in child welfare.* New York: Guilford Press.

Perry, B. D. (2010). *Child Trauma Academy: The impact of trauma and neglect on the developing child: Focus on youth in the juvenile justice system.* Presented at the Juvenile Justice Coalition in partnership with the Minnesota Department of Education.

Shore, A. N. (2001). The effects of early relational trauma on right brain development, affect regulation, & infant mental health. *Infant Mental Health Journal, 22,* 201–269.

Tellington-Jones, L. (2010). Tellington TTouch for your horse. Retrieved from: http://www.ttouch.com

Trotter, K. S., Chandler, C. K., Goodwin-Bond, D., & Casey, J. (2008). A comparative study of the efficacy of group equine assisted counseling with at-risk children and adolescents. *Journal of Creativity in Mental Health, 3*(3), 254–284.

van der Kolk, B. (2005). Trauma workshop, Minneapolis, MN, in cooperation with the Minnesota Society of Clinical Hypnosis. Retrieved from: http://www.traumacenter.org/

CHAPTER

Techniques That Explore Anxiety and Depression

☐ Healing Through Horses: Equine Assisted Counseling—No Place to Hide

Judith S. Schneider

Introduction

Susan* has survived more than any human being should ever experience: teenage pregnancy as a result of a rape, giving up a child for adoption, suicide of one of her children and her abusive husband, severe domestic violence, mental illness in her family of origin, terminal illness of a partner, substance abuse, and abandonment.

When Susan arrived for her first session, she was being treated for major depression with psychotic features and posttraumatic stress disorder (PTSD). She arrived with emptiness in her eyes, observable anxiety, and a stiff and stilted gait as a result of her psychotropic medications. Susan did not go out much. In fact, the only place she would go was to

---

* Names have been changed to protect identities.

her therapy appointments. Susan revealed that any activity outside of her home triggered her PTSD, fear of being harmed, and guilt for enjoying herself. These limiting emotions played like an old tape from years of abuse by her husband and her high level of anxiety and depression.

Rationale

If you think about anxiety, what comes to your mind? You may be thinking about signs of overt distress, such as sweating, rapid and shallow breathing, limb twitching and shaking, or the hidden physiological changes we cannot see with our naked eye. What happens to you, as the clinician and human being, when you become anxious? Now multiply that by 100 times more. Most of us cannot truly fathom the degree of distress our clients carry with them on a daily basis. Since Susan has been diagnosed with PTSD, this anxiety disorder will be the focal point of discussion. The *Diagnostic and Statistical Manual of Mental Disorders*, 4th edition, text revision (*DSM-IV-TR*; APA, 2000) states:

> The essential feature of Posttraumatic Stress disorder is the development of characteristic symptoms following exposure to an extreme traumatic stressor involving direct personal experience of an event that involves actual or threatened death or serious injury, or other threat to one's physical integrity; or witnessing an event that involves death, injury, or a threat to the physical integrity of another person; or learning about unexpected or violent death, serious harm, or threat of death or injury experienced by a family member or other close associate (Criterion A1). The person's response to the event must involve intense fear, helplessness, or horror (Criterion A2). The characteristic symptoms resulting from the exposure to the extreme trauma include persistent reexperiencing of the traumatic event (Criterion B), persistent avoidance of stimuli associated with the trauma and numbing of general responsiveness (Criterion C), and persistent symptoms of increased arousal (Criterion D). The full symptom picture must be present for more than 1 month (Criterion E), and the disturbance must cause clinically significant distress or impairment in social, occupational, or other important areas of functioning (Criterion F).

Susan met the full criteria for PTSD. She startled easily, was at times emotionally numb, lost interest in what was once pleasurable, had trouble feeling affectionate, was constantly triggered by external stimuli that reminded her of the traumatic event, was disassociated, and had flashbacks of certain events she experienced. It was not unusual for Susan to be triggered during her equine assisted counseling (EAC) sessions. The sound of a hunter's gun going off, a large truck driving down the road, the smell of the hay barn, or a storm moving in would often trigger Susan. For those who suffer with PTSD, grounding is an especially important coping skill to develop before the issues that created the PTSD can be addressed. EAC was effective in helping Susan learn grounding skills.

The horse is a prey animal. When fear is detected, the horse will usually flee rather than fight. Prior to this decision, the horse assesses the degree of harm and responds accordingly. When Susan arrived, she was not able to differentiate between what was to be feared or faced. She became overwhelmed with emotions and would often disassociate. Through the horse's behavior and her observations of the horse, Susan was able to understand that all events are not life-threatening. A particular event may provoke a sense of intense fear, however, it could be dealt with if she was able to assess the level of harm or threat. When she was triggered, we would have Susan firmly place her feet into the sand of the arena. We would encourage her to feel the earth, stand in the fear, and rely on the horse as her barometer. If the horse did not react (flee) to her trigger she began to understand that she could protect herself from harm. She initially saw the horse as her protector. Later, she realized that if the horse did not fear her trigger then she could wait for the fear to pass and protect herself from intrusive thoughts and feelings. Interestingly enough, Susan chose one of the most sensitive horses when we were helping her learn grounding skills. Herman (1997) suggests that recovery can take place only within the context of relationships; it cannot occur in isolation.

The rationale behind EAC is very similar to the old adage that horsemen use in their daily work: "If you move their feet, the mind will follow." This simple yet profound phrase has been cited by the masters— Ray Hunt and Tom and Bill Dorrance. We, as clinicians, are ready to offer up some *relaxation techniques* to our anxious clients. We observe them in our office. We then invite them to find their own way to relieve their symptoms. Many times, we will hear, "If only I had a friend to talk to, I would not feel so anxious. If only I...," and the list goes on. McCormick and McCormick (1977) write, "When we develop a special relationship with a nonhuman creature, we experience something mysterious, something not easily understood—the human–animal bond" (pp. xx–xxl). There may be an immediate sense of belonging and attachment. With a simple touch, our clients have a cognitive shift from anxiety to the comfort of being with another sentient being (we can change *living thing* to *sentient being*) that accepts them completely in the present moment. The horse senses what kind of connection is needed and, in their intuitive way, give it unconditionally. In this, we are allowed a safe haven to shed our facades.

Description

It is best practice to have an equine specialist (ES) present and involved in every therapy session. The role of the ES is to ensure the safety of the client and horses. The extra set of eyes and ears is essential due to the subtle nuances that manifest between the client and the horses.*

If EAC is the primary treatment modality, I begin it in the same manner as I would with a non-EAC client. A comprehensive clinical interview occurs, and then a treatment plan is formulated by both the clinician and the client. All treatment, regardless of modality, is client driven. My approach to each EAC session begins upon clients' arrival. I observe their gait, eye contact, the way they greet me, their physical form, level of energy or fatigue, and engagement. I observe how clients interact with the horses, how the horses respond to their presence, and how they may respond or react to the horses' behavior. Throughout the EAC session as well as the duration of treatment, I am always assessing clients.

Prior to clients' arrival, I do think about a possible intervention (activity) that may help facilitate their ability to move closer to their stated goal. However, I am also mindful of not getting "stuck" in my own preconceived ideas. Based on my clinical experience and as a seasoned horse person, I will allow my intuition to guide the session. We may start out with one activity, and, depending on how the client and horse are interacting, I may change my intention of the session, in the moment, to meet clients where they are. In other words, I follow their affect as I would follow the feel of the horse if I were to be working on a certain task solely with the horse. A detailed case study is provided to further illustrate how sessions were structured for this technique.

Not every EAC session incorporates an ES into the therapy dynamic. At all times, the counselor is very aware of the comfort and safety of both the client and the horse. Several models of EAC strongly suggest that an ES be present and active in every session. Depending on the tone of the session, I may request that specialists both observe from a distance and be directly involved in the session. When there appears to be a shift in

---

* Editor's note: This book does not endorse any specific model. References to any treatment or therapy model or to any program, service, or treatment are solely the views and opinions of authors.

the client and horse, I will ask equine specialists to offer their equine observations. I am a strong believer that two sets of eyes are more effective than one. I will always have an ES present when I am working with a child who is very active, presents with aggression, and has a history of being violent. In addition, the ES is also present when I am working with a couple, group, or family. However, based on the clinical presentation and request of the client, I have conducted individual sessions without the presence of an equine specialist.

Case Study

The intention of this first session was to assess Susan's level of anxiety and for her to gain an understanding of what it is like for her to be in her body while still being removed from her emotions. As we offered Susan a tour of the program area, she kept her eyes to the ground. When she was introduced to the horses from the outside of the arena, she looked up from the ground with the curiosity of a young child and asked, "Can I touch him?" Prior to this moment, I was not sure if I had been successful in setting a tone of safety and reassurance and in establishing some level of rapport.

The horses were instrumental in elevating Susan's engagement and sense of inclusion. Upon making eye contact with the horses, Susan's body language and verbal expression immediately changed. Her tone of voice became stronger, and she was able to express what she wanted to do. She was both validated and encouraged to do what she wanted to do at a pace that was comfortable for her. Through this, her sense of control was increased. She made the decision to move closer and to stay longer even though she was uncertain of what might happen.

We then entered the arena. When we conduct a session, we usually have all three of our horses loose in the arena or pasture area. We encourage clients to spend a few minutes observing the horses, ask which animal (I usually don't ask which animal; my phrasing is *who* or *which horse*) they feel drawn to, and then invite them to select *their horse* they want to be with for their session. The intent behind this approach is twofold. First, it allows clients to make decisions for themselves. Second, it gives them permission to *stand in their truth*; that is, choosing a horse empowers them to do what they feel is the right thing at the given moment. This simple offering tends to be very powerful when someone has felt powerless, victimized, and negated as a human being and has not been allowed to assert themselves in their relationships with other people.

Susan chose Jack, yet she hesitated and was not sure when she should walk to him, how she should approach him, and if he would like her. When I see and hear this from clients, I keep it in mind and use it as an assessment tool to gauge clients' sense of themselves, locus of control, fears, self-doubt, self-esteem, self-worth, and assertiveness versus compliance, along with many other facets of the traditional biopsychosocial assessment model.

I have successfully used this process with all of our clients. I simply ask them to observe the horses and pick one that they would like to be with for the day. Sometimes, the horse they want to be with has another plan. The horse may not come to the client; the horse may decide it wants to be with its herd and walks off. This allows the opportunity to observe and respond to clients' expectations, preconceived ideas, intentions, and reactions when *their* plan or ideas do not manifest in a manner they envisioned.

The information gathered from an activity can be useful when developing a treatment plan. Observations made by the clinician during an activity are fuel to help clients reach their goals. With the use of metaphors, we offer our clients ways to recognize and break down barriers that exist for them and gain a better understanding of both their thought and behavior patterns. We ascertain if they are hesitant or fearful they may fail; or if they wonder about being liked and accepted by the horse. I am in a position to examine and assess how this is played out in their human relationships and how it perpetuates a negative outcome.

I had no idea why she chose Jack. I suppose I could have speculated, made an assessment of her decision-making process, and then come to a hypothesis for her decision. Instead, I asked her to explain her choice of that specific horse. Susan's response was quite clear and simple. He was the "closest to us," and she "was tired of walking around." As clinicians, we follow the affect of our clients to better assist and support their process. Susan was encouraged to "follow the feel"—to experience Jack herself (a metaphor for her own process). At this point, Susan began to talk to Jack as she approached him. Her instincts took over. Susan began to trust herself again. Jack walked up to her, stopped, and waited. Susan's touch was gentle. She did not display any overt change of emotion. Her gait remained stiff. Her eyes and facial expressions did not change. Susan extended her hand to him, allowed him to get to know her. And when Jack touched her hand, she embraced his neck with a warm heartfelt hug.

Jack is our largest and eldest horse. In the past he has had seizures but had been seizure-free for many months. Just after her first touch, her anxiety triggered the horse to have a petit mal seizure. Susan did not notice this, nor did I point it out, fearing this may have an unknown meaning to her that I may not have understood at the onset of therapy.

Following this, Susan was asked if she wanted to do anything else with Jack. Her body language and behaviors indicated she was not ready to leave. She did not move away from Jack. She continued to rub his neck and talk to him. By this time, Susan's level of anxiety had lessened. Susan looked beyond her immediate area. At this point, she was invited to take Jack for a short walk from the arena to the round pen. With a brief overview of how to lead the horse, Susan and Jack walked in tandem to the other enclosure. An emotional connection between the client and the horse was establishing itself. Within a few minutes, she and Jack entered the round pen with ease. For those not familiar with this, it is an enclosed circular area, usually 60 feet in diameter. There are no corners, no places to hide.

Due to her anxiety, she was given all the time in the world to acclimate to her new environment. I noticed Susan looking around, taking mental notes of the surrounding pasture, checking to see where I stood. We waited in silence, perhaps for about 5 minutes. Susan finally said, "What are we waiting for?" At this moment, it appeared her hypervigilance and anxiety had faded. As she continued to establish a rapport with the horse, she began to relax. Her breathing was more even, and she was able to smile. Perhaps for the first time in her life she was able to see and be in the presence of another living being she could trust. We got her up on a mounting block made out of an old cottonwood tree trunk and invited her to lie over Jack's back. Initially, Susan was not sure about this and looked a bit puzzled. She was encouraged to, again, "follow the feel" and figure out how to hang over Jack in a comfortable manner. She tried several different positions until she found one that was comfortable for her. She then was able to hang her arms over him, head and legs dangling. She was now totally dependent on Jack and us to keep her safe. Susan thought this was funny. She began to giggle a bit and hung out for awhile. When she was ready to take a few steps, she let us know.

As we began to walk around the round pen, Susan was not aware she was holding her breath. This was detected by the horse's stiff gait and his hesitation when he did move forward. I pointed this out to her and encouraged her to feel Jack's movement and to breathe with him. She slowly began to relax. Her limbs were less tense. She rested the side of her face on the horse's side and placed her palms on Jack's stomach. When we finally stopped, Susan remarked she was not aware she "always" held her breath.

This was the beginning of Susan's ability to reconnect with her body. This aspect for Susan was paramount in her recovery. She stated she always felt "that I am not in my body—I cannot feel anything." This was a recurring theme for Susan. Frequently, she would disassociate and hallucinate during a session. Although I was very close to her during each session, I could not detect this. The horses did. Their gaits changed. It appeared to me that they had a stilted quality to their walk not unlike Susan when she was very anxious.

At the end of the first session Susan was able to describe a sense of lightness as she walked around the round pen. She noticed different scents in the air and realized she felt happy. She was able to feel parts of her body that previously had been inaccessible to her and was more aware of her emotions. This was just the beginning of her many breakthroughs.

Application

Equine assisted counseling, an experiential approach or model of therapy, has been successful with children, youths, teens, and adults who have experienced trauma, loss and abandonment, abuse or neglect from a caregiver, peer bullying, domestic violence, conflict within both the nuclear and extended family units, a life-threatening illness, and just about any other combination of experiences that has created emotional discord. In addition, it has been effective in treating individuals who struggle with substance abuse, chronic mental illness, anxiety, mood, eating, impulse control, and childhood disorders such as conduct disorder, oppositional defiant disorder, and attention-deficit/hyperactivity disorder (ADHD), as well as others not mentioned here (a complete list can be found in the *DSM-IV-TR*; APA, 2000).

References

American Psychiatric Association. (APA). (2000). *Diagnostic and statistical manual of mental disorders*, 4th ed., text revision. Washington, DC: Author.

Herman, J. (1997). *Trauma and recovery.* New York: Basic Books.

McCormick, A., & McCormick, M. (1977). *Horse sense and the human heart.* Deerfield Beach, FL: Health Communication, Inc.

☐ Therapeutic Trail Riding for Children and Adults With ADHD and Anxiety Disorders

Judy Weston-Thompson

Introduction

For several years, the many benefits of equine assisted counseling (EAC) with both children and adults have been demonstrated (Chandler, 2005; EFMHA, 2010; Fine, 2006; Trotter, Chandler, Goodwin-Bond, & Casey, 2008). In my practice as a Certified Equine Interactive Professional-Mental Health (CEIP-MH) and a Licensed Marriage and Family Therapist (LMFT) of 23 years, I have built on the more traditional equine interventions (NARHA; therapeutic horseback riding, recreational trail riding, and horsemanship classes) and have expanded my EAC program to use a unique, highly beneficial exercise: trail riding.

Years ago, when I interned as a wrangler at Eaton's Ranch in Wyoming, one of my favorite duties was taking people of all ages out on various challenging trails and witnessing firsthand their increase in confidence, focus, and self-esteem in a *nontherapeutic* environment. I clearly saw how trail riding helped people push through the immediate experience of fear toward increased competence. At this point I began strategizing, testing out assumptions, and organizing a trail riding program to incorporate into my therapeutic practice.

Both the anticipated incidents and the surprises on the trail are, in my opinion, metaphors for life and opportunities to negotiate life's challenges. It is all about developing a balance between letting yourself be carried (trusting) and finding your inner place of attention and authority. We work on paying attention and being highly present in a state of relaxation. We work on acknowledging the tasks and following through in appropriate sequence. Trail riding is therapeutically rich with opportunities to address in the moment the many issues arising from attention-deficit/hyperactivity disorder (ADHD) and anxiety disorders.

Rationale

I began this process with a thorough review of the *Diagnostic and Statistical Manual of Mental Disorders* (*DSM*) diagnostic criteria for generalized anxiety disorder (and related anxiety disorders) and ADHD and compared these criteria with the presenting issues in many of my EAC clients, especially children. Some of the symptoms that most frequently appear in my practice include restlessness, difficulty concentrating, symptoms of inattention, difficulty with task completion, distraction by extraneous stimuli, lack of focus, poor impulse control, and need for immediate gratification. I then considered what I knew to be true about the results of my work with horses and anxious, unfocused humans. Out of this review I designed a program for treatment of anxiety and ADHD with an emphasis on therapeutic trail riding.

The psychological, emotional, and somatic benefits of my therapeutic trail-riding program are numerous. Guiding one's horse requires one to be present in nature's bounty. The magical motion of the physical experience (clip-clop) along with the thorough engagement of the senses causes relaxation, awareness, and presence (Hargreaves, Westerman, Westerman, & Verge, 2007). Body follows thought and feelings. The mind becomes still, and thus the body quiets. The delicate relationship between the rider's physical being and the horse's momentum creates balance and focus on the physical sensations (Hallberg, 2008). In my experience, this all translates to rapid growth in awareness and improvements in concentration in both home and school environments.

My first profound confirmation of the healing nature of trail riding occurred when 9-year-old Grant* overcame excessive anxiety and shyness, feeling sufficiently confident to take the lead part in a school play. I knew without a doubt that my horse facilitator, Caesar, was meant for this work and felt validated in my belief in the extraordinary healing benefits of EAC.

Description

Creating a Safe Therapeutic Environment

Both individual work and group work begin with a thorough demonstration and discussion of horse and therapeutic trail-riding safety. It is essential that the horse have the appropriate temperament as well as a history of reliability and experience with novices on the trail. The appropriate human–horse match is an important part of creating a safe therapeutic environment; for example, an anxious individual would require a gentle, reliable horse, and an ADHD client would match well with a more spirited horse (Moreau & McDaniel, 2004). Other matching criteria include consideration of relative horse–human size and concern for a person's psychological makeup. The horse must, above all else, be dependable and experienced on the trail (CHA, 2001).

---

* Names have been changed to protect identities.

Therapeutic trail riding always begins on a trail that is familiar to the facilitator and the horses yet is appropriately challenging to the client. Each trail experience is unique, just as each traditional therapy session is unique, because I don't know what will be triggered in my client during the ride. As we proceed on the loop trail, both my horse and my client's horse are focused, and therapy is happening in a variety of ways (as described in the section "Application on the Trail").

Therapeutic trail-riding group sessions are similar to the individual sessions in that they consist of horse selection, grooming, tacking, mounting, and riding. Since there is much more you must attend to in a group setting, it is recommended that you have another professional with you. I use a therapeutic intern who assists in all aspects of the group process.

The 2-hour children's group (of up to six participants) is usually more intense than an individual session because it involves social interactions and the particular social challenges of ADHD and various anxiety disorders, such as not listening to others, self-centeredness, and difficulty setting and maintaining appropriate boundaries. Therapeutic trail riding triggers not only individual issues but also relational issues by exposing a participant's weaknesses, fears, or vulnerabilities in a group situation. For three or more children, I find it mandatory to use a trained intern. If I have three or more adults with severe anxiety, I will also use an additional facilitator.

Trail Ride Components

Whether individual or group, the therapeutic trail-riding program may be divided into four different components, each one building on the benefits of the previous.

Grooming

After horse selection, grooming is the first component of the program. Grooming teaches and fosters preparation and organization, sequential learning, impulse control, and delayed gratification. The repetitive and grounding nature of the grooming exercise helps regulate affect by physically slowing down and calming an anxious or hyperactive human (EFMHA, 2001; Hallberg, 2008).

For an ADHD child in particular, grooming captures the attention, creates focus, and requires, under my guidance, task completion before moving on to the next step. Grooming is always considered a prerequisite to trail riding. Nurturing an animal through touch and the magic inherent in the horse–human interaction also creates focus on the tactile experience of repetition and completion of task. Grooming actually sets the tone of the ride because the horse–human connection is already building a sense of empowerment in the client.

Tacking

Though more technical than grooming, tacking also supports a sense of empowerment in both child and adult clients. Following a sequential order—blanket, saddle, and bridle—is required when tacking. The task must be done correctly and thoroughly for safety reasons.

For instance, 10-year-old Carl just wanted to rush through the tacking due to the impulsive nature of ADHD. Now he's learning that everything we do to prepare for the trail ride has a reason and an order to it. My intervention with Carl has been to ask, "Why does the blanket go on before the saddle?" (for the horse's comfort) or "Why do we always tighten the cinch around his middle?" (for both horse and human safety). Thus, Carl is learning the purpose and consequences of following directions.

Mounting and Dismounting

After tacking comes mounting and dismounting of the horse. This is another sequential exercise that requires skill, patience, listening, and paying attention. Impulse control is needed to learn to mount correctly.

Because group riding involves social interactions and boundary issues, I begin each group trail ride with a group check-in, which fosters bonding and connection. My intern helps provide more individual attention, and everyone is encouraged to help each other along the way. Understanding horse herd behavior and safe trail behavior (e.g., keeping the correct distance between the horses) also helps with boundary issues. Trail safety is taught in the first session and reinforced throughout.

Application on the Trail

The ride itself offers unlimited opportunities for therapeutic insight and growth. For example, it is important to pay attention to the leader. (Generally, I lead with my assistant at the rear of the group. Because leading is helpful in self-esteem building, occasionally one of the more seasoned riders may have an opportunity to lead). It is essential for clients to remain focused on their own horse as well as to keep the appropriate boundary between self and others while also remaining present with the task of staying on the trail. Attention to their body positioning also requires focus. I set the order of the horses in a manner that is most likely to foster an experience of individual competence and control.

For example, the horses are arranged according to how they get along. The anxious horses do better in the middle, whereas the braver ones are out in front. The riders are responsible for the cooperation of their horses and must always be aware of the boundary between horses. I find it useful to pay attention to the trail "chatter" because riders often project what they may be feeling onto their horses. An anxious child, for instance, might say in reference to his horse, "He looks like he's scared!" And my response would be, "What do you think he's scared of? How do we help him become less anxious?" An ADHD child might remark, "My horse isn't paying attention." My response would underscore that horses focus when the rider focuses on them. So I might ask, "What are some of the ways we get horses to focus?"

Because horses have to be on the lookout for predators, sometimes even the most trustworthy horse may be spooked by a surprise in its line of sight. I will announce when my horse has a startle response by saying something like, "Look how Caesar's looking at the log; what do you think he's thinking?" This type of intervention encourages anxious children to relax (self-soothe) and to soothe their horse. Then I encourage them to push past their fears if the situation doesn't warrant a fear response. I use the situation to teach about the nature of appropriate and unnecessary fear.

When Carl's horse trotted up a small incline to catch up with me, Carl asked me why the horse responded that way. I replied, "What do you think?" This naturally became a teachable moment in which Carl learned about anticipation. Carl was learning both to anticipate a horse's change in momentum as well as the importance of trusting his horse.

Often we will discover a tree branch intruding on the trail. First, I anticipate its coming. Then, I demonstrate how I use my leg to steer the horse around it. This teaches appropriate anticipation of obstacles and use of proven methods to avoid them, creating a balance between alertness and relaxation and teaching that the locus of control is within oneself and is not external to self.

Horses have impulses just like humans. A horse may stop along the trail and begin eating grass. I tell the rider that there is a time and a place for everything but that this is not the time for grazing. Thus, this is another teachable moment in delayed gratification, self-control, and self-monitoring.

Application

In my therapeutic trail-riding program, I work with individual children and adults as well as with groups. In addition to being a useful therapeutic tool in the treatment of ADHD and anxiety disorders, therapeutic trail riding may be helpful with the following types of clients:

- Socially anxious clients: Therapeutic trail riding offers an opportunity for children and adults with social anxiety to practice new and effective ways of communication with others.

- Narcissistic clients: This technique allows clients who lack normal empathy and are over concerned about their own needs to better appreciate another's perspective.

- Depressed clients: Horses provide depressed people with a feeling of connectedness.

- Traumatized clients: Horses, with their powerful ability to empathize, can help heal the damage caused by trauma.

Besides the ones listed here, there are countless ways horses may be involved with therapeutic healing.

References

American Psychiatric Association. (1994). *Diagnostic and statistical manual of mental disorders, fourth edition* (DSM-IV). Washington, DC: American Psychiatric Association.

Certified Horsemanship Association (CHA). (2001). *CHA combined horsemanship and trail manual.* Lexington, KY: Author.

Certified Horsemanship Association (CHA). (2010). *CHA trail guide manual.* Lexington, KY: Author.

Chandler, C. K. (2005). *Animal assisted therapy in counseling.* Boca Raton, FL: Taylor & Francis.

Equine Facilitated Mental Health Association (EFMHA). (2010). *EFMHA.* Retrieved from: http://www.narha.org/resources-education/publications/efmha-news-archives

Fine, A. (2006). *Handbook on animal-assisted therapy, third edition: Theoretical foundations and guidelines for practice.* Philadelphia, PA: Elsevier Science.

Hallberg, L. (2008). *Walking the way of the horse: Exploring the power of the horse–human relationship.* New York: iUniverse, Incorporated.

Hargreaves, H., Westerman, P., Westerman, D., & Verge, M. (2007). The benefits of animal assisted therapy with children that are survivors of abuse. *CSA Sociological Abstracts Database.*

Irwin, C., & Weber, B. (2001). *Horses don't lie: What horses teach us about our natural capacity for awareness, confidence, courage, and trust.* New York: Marlow & Company.

Kohanov, L. (2001). *The tao of equus: A woman's journey of healing and transformation through the way of the horse.* Navato, CA: New World Library.

Moreau, L., & McDaniel, B. (2004). Equine facilitated mental health: A field guide for practice.

Rector, B. (2005). *Advances in awareness—Learning with help of the horse.* Bloomington, IN: AuthorHouse.

Trotter, K. S., Chandler, C. K., Goodwin-Bond, D., & Casey, J. (2008). A comparative study of the efficacy of group equine assisted counseling with at-risk children and adolescents. *Journal of Creativity in Mental Health, 3*(3), 254–284.

☐ Exposed Anxiety With Equine Assisted Counseling

Steven B. Eller

Introduction

Appropriate response to emotions is a crucial skill needed to maintain healthy relationships, problem-solving ability, and normal functioning. Anxiety has the ability to decrease and inhibit these necessary daily controls of an individual. Exposure to anxiety-provoked sources can assist the individual in building a knowledge base of experience to function and control their behaviors and decisions, empowering them with a sense of well-being and balance when dealing with the global stresses of daily life. Equine assisted counseling (EAC) is a resource available to help expose, walk through, and process emotions of an anxious client. The metaphors and symbols of interaction offer the opportunity to assist an individual in overcoming incapacitating anxiety.

The uncertainty of anxiety can be a debilitating experience. The unknown is always present and may evoke heightened symptoms of evoking unhealthy emotions and low self-esteem. There is a biological purpose for anxiety that resides in our innate core of functioning. For there to be a positive outcome from this emotion, it must be engaged and explored rather than avoided and feared.

EAC is a therapeutic model for helping people face their fears and overcome the anxiety that seems to immobilize healthy decision-making processes. It provides an opportunity to introduce the client to pressure points in a controlled, safe environment. These interactions may then give a more positive model for processing the experienced and frequently blocked emotional states.

Rationale

The nature of the horse is a prey animal, with an instinct of self-preservation. A normal horse response would be to run when faced with threat and danger. A horse will turn and look back at this pressure point only when it feels safe. This safety guides its interactions with new stimuli and will create a pattern of understanding and responsiveness to danger (Parelli, 1993). Horses provide a real-time interaction for an individual to learn how to match internal thoughts with external behaviors. They do not allow discrepancies between thoughts and behaviors without responding in some way.

Horses will mirror and reflect the authentic energy given off rather than the image clients desire to convey. The only way horses will cooperate and forgive some of our discrepancies toward them is when we explore our part in the problematic interaction. As a result, the horse gives permission to remove the false external images we portray to protect us from danger and threat. Such an encounter can then allow us to move toward true responses to our emotions. This offers a path toward self-realization and improves self-regulation of emotional reactions to pressure (McCormick & McCormick, 1997).

The solution-focused goal of EAC offers the therapeutic relationship, an attentiveness of the presenting symptoms, and the desire for control. "Client(s) come to therapy not because they needed a solution, but because they realized what the solution was, and were terrified" (Walter & Peller, 1992, p. 100). Anxiety can arise when the client feels a lack of control over this solution. The therapist would then facilitate an awareness that what seems to be out of control is really in their control and thus repeatable. This guides the task to help the client choose and identify those meanings, changes, and ways of creating, becoming, and maintaining what they desire to experience more of in their life.

Healthy fear guides action, but those who face anxious fear on a continual basis often become frozen by the mere possibility of an undesirable outcome. Unhealthy anxiety is then produced within an individual as the person attempts to deal with the perceived threat and danger. The brain and body work together to survive during these moments. Hormones are produced and help guide the physical being toward self-preservation (Cozolino, 2006). Physical exhaustion and emotional breakdown result when these fears become repetitive over an extended period of time.

One study has noted a connection with anxiety and the intolerance of uncertainty (Chen & Hong, 2010). This uncertainty about the future and present situations impairs behavior and internalizes as unfair and disconcerting within the individual (Sexton & Dugas, 2009). It is believed that the intolerance of uncertainty can enhance anxiety by increasing the perceived threat, thereby prolonging the exposure to uncertainty for an unknown period. Individuals then tend to have a weakened problem-solving ability, thus intensifying the response to existing symptoms of normal stress (Chen & Hong) and creating an unbearable experience of feeling out of control.

Experiential therapy provides an interactive model for the participant to learn through doing rather than lecture and education. There is also the presence and power of emotional processing of the experiences that take place within the arena with the horse. Global distress can be a difficult battle with someone who is continually reacting to perceived threats. This promotes daily, continuous anxious moments of uncertainty toward healthy decisions and relationships. When an individual continues to attempt to repress these aroused feelings, it can lead to negative self-image and a core representation based on a maladaptive emotional schema (Greenberg & Paivio, 1997).

It is important for the therapist to interface with emotional processing and the global distress of clients. The therapist is then able to move toward a rational and empirical model of relief by giving images and control through the newly experienced interaction. This invites clients to assess their beliefs, to discuss points of anger, fear, and shame, and to move toward the goal of acceptance and self-agency (Pascual-Leone & Greenberg, 2007). Clients are then presented with a new method of resolving a perceived reality of frozen choices and providing new meaning from the possible-present of fear and what ifs to the actual-present of feeling loved and worthy. The goal, then, of clients and the interactions with the horses is promoting self-soothing and regulation when fear and anxiety appear.

The outcome for working with clients presenting with anxiety may look very different for each one. Building and growing confidence seems to be a by-product of this emotional state as well as exploring, evoking, and restructuring emotional and physical responses (Pascual-Leone & Greenberg, 2007). Clients leave the arena with new tools and symbols for interacting in their world and relationships. Brainstorming and safety become an option rather than a perceived method of failure in tough or dangerous situations.

Description

Offering an opportunity to clients to relive and be exposed to their anxiety can bring about increased fears and emotional uncertainty. This invitation of interaction politely asks the client to search for and create a new meaning for situations that previously caused emotional distress (Walter & Peller, 1992). A solution-focused therapist would agree that everyone has the ability to change. It is just finding an arena for persons to create and experience this ability, which gives them the knowledge and wisdom to apply positive new processes to their daily life skills and interactions.

The Anxiety Brainstorm

The purpose of the anxiety brainstorm, a cognitive-behavioral therapy-based activity, is to help participants feel safe in the arena. They are instructed, prior to stepping in the arena, to come up with three different options they may want to use should they feel afraid, uncomfortable, or fearful after stepping into the arena with the horses. The therapist should ensure that clients know that the options presented are not concrete and unchangeable and that at any moment it is acceptable for clients to make a new decision. This time of brainstorming is used to process with clients their current emotional and physical state as well as how they would define and identify the moment of encroaching fear and discomfort.

Rating Scale

To help recognize and identify these moments, clients are asked to rate their level of anxiety on a scale of 1 to 10, where 10 is marked as the highest possible level of anxiety. This allows the clients and therapist to talk through the influence of anxiety at different points during the sessions and provides a quick and easy response to stimulus and emotions. It is also helpful for the therapist to provide new information about the influence of anxiety on decision-making processes as well as what biological assessments can be made to gauge the level of anxiety. Blood pressure, tense muscles, shaking hands or body, rambling speech, and unfocused attention may be a few biological attributes discussed to help comprehend, express, and even stabilize clients' fears and discomfort.

For example, clients may rate their anxiety as a 5 while standing outside the gate. They mention there are some nervous but controlled thoughts about what to expect inside the arena with the horses, there are some fears and worries about what might happen, and there may be some stories that arise in their mind as they recall worst-case scenarios for this interaction. As the therapist walks through the scale, it would be helpful for clients to know what a 6 might look like in the arena as well as how a 4 may look and feel. This equips them with the possibility that the interactions within the arena will not be purely negative and destructive. Allowing space and time for clients to predict both possibilities creates new alternatives and unique situations that may not have been an option in the past. The therapist also portrays a new example to the externalized part of their internal dialogue during these anxious moments by introducing self-confidence.

Safe Zones

During this activity, two externalized metaphors are created with clients. The first is an intervention of anxiety by creating a zone of safety and trust for them. In the arena, the therapist introduces the safe box. This space drawn in the dirt is a place where clients may retreat when feeling the anxiety level increase or becoming uncomfortable with the activity and surroundings. The safe box would nonverbally express to the treatment team that there is a needed break and would invite them to intervene if possible in separating clients from the horse and activity. This intervention is aimed to teach the client the possibility of choices when anxiety is encroaching on their physical and emotional security. It also directs clients in unique ways to communicate with others about what is needed during these anxious moments. There is a false assumption within human relationships that if you do not say or do anything to express current interactions then you are OK. An important reminder to clients is the value of expressing these needs when the brain and emotions are operating from true reality, prior to being flooded by the influence of uncertainty.

The second externalized metaphor is the awareness of physical and emotional separation from the root of anxiety. This may coincide with one of the brainstorming options presented by clients but may also be introduced as an alternative to navigate them toward a unique but mimicked reaction to anxiety. Outside the arena, the therapist talks about the alleyway. This is a place where clients can go to get away from the source of anxiety. There are guidelines setup for this escape to assist clients with managing the pressure of anxiety and stress. One guideline to clients is they can go to the alleyway at any time during the activity but must express to the treatment team the need to remove themselves from the arena. Second, there is a time frame put on clients to not abandon the experience and activity completely. The intent is for clients to go to a safe place (similar to the safe box) and consider the implications, intentions, and current interactions they are experiencing with anxiety. The therapist can discuss the biological responses at this point and how good decisions are not made during moments of crisis and fear. The alleyway is an example to clients of taking a break from perceived attack or fear, to go to a place where they are able to move freely while using the time to calm their mind, body, and spirit. Lastly, clients are given the choice that they may reenter the arena prior to time being up.

Giving clients choices and input into how long they need to be away presents the concept of learning coping skills and stress management techniques. When clients reenter the arena, they are asked to commu-nicate with the treatment team the level of anxiety experienced on the rating scale and how they were able to talk through the pressure of dis-comfort and fear caused by anxiety.

Treatment Team

The therapists' role in these three interventions with clients and their anxiety is presenting alternatives. Using the rating scale throughout the sessions teaches clients to monitor and adjust current interactions to maintain a reasonable level of functioning. Clients learn to recog-nize and talk about their level of anxiety in the space and time granted through the alleyway and the safe box. The goal is not to completely annihilate anxiety but to learn how to manage and understand its role and influence on decision-making ability.

As already noted, anxiety presents itself in a variety of ways. It can be seen through the physical, emotional, and internal encounter of the client. For clients who are either afraid of the horse or its unpredictable nature, it is good for the therapist to walk through the nature of the animal with the client. The therapist can explain that horses are a prey animal, and their nature is not to attack but to feel safe and trusting of the new presence in the arena (Parelli, 1993). When horses are uncertain about people, animals, or any new object they will slowly approach it from all directions before accepting it for what it is. Just because something or someone is presented to the horse does not mean it will be immediately welcomed. Even when it is presented by a trusted source, the horse will maintain comfort and safety above grand risk taking.

Clients are asked to relate the nature of the horse in this manner, allowing them the opportunity to learn how humans can mimic this innate response to new relationships, interactions, and anxiety. People will usually jump right into something new without assessing their physi-cal and emotional safety, finding themselves trapped and even in danger. Granting clients permission to take time to adjust to the new object and activity, much like a horse would, grants permission to find new ways of relating the new encounter to the influence of anxiety.

The discussion with clients can take place within the arena in a nonconfrontational activity. As clients and treatment team stand inside the arena, there can be a moment of observation of the horses and their interactions. During this time, the therapist can continue to gauge the response of the client to their anxiety level and monitor the distance between the horse and client. As observation continues, the treatment team can talk about the relationship of the role of horses in their herd and humans in their community. Horses may bring about fear because of the lack of understanding and even unwillingness to approach them from a new perspective. Anxiety is then defined and described with clients as an imagination of fearful situations and how there is no foundation to predict outcome with a created false reality. For clients who are afraid of being eaten by a horse, they are able to counter the imaginative fear with real interactions with a horse that did not eat them.

Clients also benefit from learning why horses are used in this type of therapeutic setting. Horses have an honest interpretation of human emotions and physical demeanor. They are able to pick up on the discrepancies of verbal and nonverbal communications. Therefore, they act and react to either the honesty portrayed or the confused and chaotic interpretation of those discrepancies. This image of that interaction is beneficial in assisting the client to promote self-growth, awareness, and understanding relationships. The horse then becomes a teacher and mentor to clients rather than a basis for fear and anxiety. A new meaning is created for something they were once afraid of, complemented with new language and an engagement model for fear and anxiety in their life.

Case Study

The client's presenting problem was with relationships. Anxiety appeared to be present during our traditional in-office therapy sessions but did not appear to be an emotional or behavioral compromise toward decisions. EAC was offered as a suggestion to this client to help with relationship stress, and it became evident during the first session that the client was extremely anxious about the session. She described her anxiety as hitting her as she drove down the dirt road toward the arena. There was a definite intolerance of uncertainty present in her demeanor and level of engagement, yet she knew that she should come to learn something about herself and to grow through this experience.

We would rate her level of anxiety as we stood outside the gate to the arena. She started out with a 7, which means she could be seen shaking and nervously talking through her week and activities. As we entered the arena, the therapist continued to monitor and walk through her anxiety scale acting as a secure point within the arena. At one instance, one of the horses was showing off and engaging the other horses in a perceived frightening manner to the client. She positioned herself so that the treatment team was between her and the horses, so as not to be anywhere near the source of pressure. She commented that she was now at an 8 but felt fine separated from the horse. This horse became her nemesis as we talked about relationships and unhealthy points of stress in her past. But as our sessions progressed, it become evident that we needed to work toward providing resolution to her anxiety and giving the ability to self-sooth and self-regulate during those moments of 7 to 10 on her scale.

During a subsequent session, we used the brainstorming activity to help her create her own rules about safety and comfort. She decided her three options are moving away, getting behind the treatment team, or leaving the arena. We talked about how all three of these choices looked the same, but with different levels of separation. She agreed and stuck with these three choices. We did discuss that later down the road there may be a need to reevaluate the options to ensure validity.

During our sessions, we also created a square in the dirt that represented a safe box. At first, the mental health professional was the one directing her to the box for a break and to process some of the activities that were taking place. However, at one point, her level of anxiety rose to a 9 or 10, and she removed herself from the arena. We walked her out of the arena, recognizing the level of anxiety and fear that had been presented. We asked her to take a walk down the alleyway to cool down and gather her thoughts. She was told to return when she felt like her anxiety had dropped to a controllable level, around a 7 by her own standards. After a few moments she returned to the gate, and we reentered the arena.

The exposure to anxiety for this particular client proved beneficial. There were sessions later where she was seen pushing and pulling on the horses to get them to move and respond to her commands as well as helping others in group settings with the knowledge and skills she had gained in her own interactions. The safe box, the alleyway, and the three choices of brainstorming were useful interventions and metaphors for this client to use outside of the arena. She expressed how she visualized her walk down the alleyway to regain composure and allow her the time to process the emotions she was experiencing. In the past, these emotions would have crippled her ability to make good decisions, therefore keeping her engaged in heightened anxiety and prolonged emotional fears. She has portrayed the power of working with the horses and facing her anxiety in the following statement:

> I think asking for help is important, humbling, and good to know, but I don't think that was the most crucial lesson I learned from Sierra (the horse). I think I learned how to let go. That is hard. That strips a person. Letting go of what they know, how they cope, people's expectations, etc. I let go for me. I let go to say I can't do this and lead my life anymore. I cannot fake it, or even try to fake it.

EAC proved to be an effective and helpful method for her by providing new experiences where she was able to identify her level of anxiety. This experience also provided new language and symbols of understanding fear and anxiety as a useful response to daily interactions. These responses have provided her the choice to grow through global stress, to have power over her own choices, and to recognize the unwanted negative impact of emotions in certain relationships.

Application

This technique can be used with clients of all ages wrestling with anxiety of all different flavors. Exposing clients to their anxiety in this safe arena can help them explore ways to implement safety and boundaries in their current life challenges. It provides insight into how their expectations to normally freak out are challenged with opportunities and options during anxiety-provoking situations. The technique offers clients an ability to identify and understand their emotional experiences rather than fearing the worst possible scenarios. Clients may also learn the cause of most episodes of increasing anxiety levels are due to being unaware and unfamiliar with new interactions. They can also begin to understand how previous moments of anxiety do not always predict future symptoms and struggles.

The anxiety brainstorm teaches clients to think through the situation they are encountering prior to being overwhelmed by fear. Using the rating scale of anxiety, clients are also learning how to identify, understand, cope, and navigate through situations. The safe box and alleyway are key symbols of externalization to clients, assisting them with new language to process rising levels of anxiety, the expectation in situations encountered, and finding points of trust to share these struggles. These points of trust may be found through friends, family members, spouses, ministers, counselors, and even in dialogue with one's self. The technique is useful in beginning to build a foundation of reliability as clients begin to understand and use anxiety to their benefit.

It is important to note the interventions and activities described are not the only way to help walk through anxiety with clients. The power with equine assisted counseling is creating and adapting activities to match the needs of clients while ethically providing maximum benefit through those interactions.

Conclusion

Anxiety presents itself in normal interactions as a motivating force to make decisions. When anxiety gives way to fear and sustained emotional alertness, individuals may seek out equine assisted counseling as an option to regain control and build a knowledge base of experience. Emotional arousal and processing facilitates the healing process. By providing a safe arena for clients to experience these emotions, they will build confidence and identity and the ability to perform well in the presence of global stress and uncertainty.

References

Chen, C. Y., & Hong, R. Y. (2010). Intolerance of uncertainty moderates the relation between negative life events and anxiety. *Personality and Individual Differences, 49,* 49–53.

Cozolino, L. (2006). *The neuroscience of human relationships.* New York: W.W. Norton.

Greenberg, L. S., & Paivio, S. C. (1997). *Working with emotions in psychotherapy.* New York: Guilford Press.

McCormick, A., & McCormick, M. D. (1997). *Horse sense and the human heart.* Deerfield Beach, FL: HCI.

Parelli, P. (1993). *Natural horse-man-ship.* Colorado Springs, CO: Western Horseman, Inc.

Pascual-Leone, A., & Greenberg, L. S. (2007). Emotional processing in experiential therapy: Why "the only way out is through." *Journal of Counseling and Clinical Psychology, 75,* 875–887.

Sexton, K. A., & Dugas, M. J. (2009). Defining distinct negative beliefs about uncertainty: Validating the factor structure of the intolerance of uncertainty scale. *Psychology Assessment, 21,* 176–186.

Walter, J. L., & Peller, J. E. (1992). *Becoming solution-focused in brief therapy.* New York: Routledge.

☐ The Tellington Method™: A Technique for Equine Assisted Counseling

Tanya Welsch

Introduction

The Tellington Method™, also commonly known as TTouch, was developed by Linda Tellington-Jones and is a way of interacting with other sentient beings to support body awareness and improve functioning. Over the past 4 decades, this technique has evolved from Linda's background as a pioneer in the field of equine massage in the 1960s; cofounder and director of the 9-month residential Pacific Coast School of Horsemanship in the 1960s and 1970s; and was influenced by her training in the Feldenkrais Method. The Tellington Method includes work with species ranging from snakes, whales, and chimpanzees to dogs, cats, and humans; however, the foundation animal for Tellington-Jones's work is the horse. With horses, TTouch has three components: circular touches, lifts, and slides; groundwork exercises, also known as the "playground for higher learning"; and mounted exercises. The intention for all TTouch sessions is to help awaken the body and the mind and to support "behavior, health and performance while developing the human–animal bond" (Tellington-Jones, 2006).

Incorporating TTouch activities into equine assisted counseling (EAC) programs provides clients with an opportunity to develop an increase in sensorimotor integration, awareness of the external and internal environment, and cooperative social and peer development. According to Welsch and DePrekel (2008),

> Reading an animal's body language is a core component to a successful TTouch session. Through some of the basic TTouch circles and lifts, participants sharpen awareness of what the animal partner is conveying through subtle tail carriage, ear and head posture, and skin ripples. As a person is able to hone the ability to read body messages, this knowledge may then transfer to human-to-human communication and the person can develop a greater understanding of social cues. (p. 125)

Rationale

Equine assisted counseling is one modality that can address the historical importance animals have had in people's lives, that can provide practical applications of research results showing how animals help facilitate daily wellness, and that can model new directions and discoveries from the fields of neuroscience and mental health.

Historically, mental health therapy often seems to forget not all clinical practice happened in an office or on a couch. One of the earliest accounts comes out of Geel, Belgium, in the ninth century where patients deemed *mentally ill* were taught how to care for a variety of farm animals in an effort to establish some sense of regularity, skill mastery, and relationship (Stein & Cutler, 2002). Paradoxically, Sigmund Freud also brought his dog, Jo-Fi, to his therapy sessions because he believed his dog to be an accurate judge of his patients' character (Bougerol, 2007). More recent studies have shown animals decrease feelings of social isolation, increase community support and integration, and increase social capital (Allen & Blascovich, 1996; Garrity & Stallones, 1998; Putnam, 2000). Animals also facilitate human social approach (Melson, 2002), social contact (McNicholas & Collis, 2000), and conversations between strangers or casual acquaintances (Rogers, Hart, & Boltz, 1993).

Within the field of mental health, advancements in understanding brain functioning and neuroplasticity, especially in relation to healing trauma, support holistic counseling practices that stimulate both sides of the brain, that engage the body (somatic) while the mind attends to new thoughts and feelings, and that provide clients with techniques for self-awareness and self-regulation (Garland & Howard, 2009). "Psychology and psychiatry, as disciplines, have paid scant attention to the deficient orientation and action patterns that are triggered by sensory input, and, instead, tend to narrowly focus on either neurochemistry or emotional states" (van der Kolk, 2006, p. 5).

By incorporating TTouch activities into EAC sessions, a bridge between *doing* and *being* is easily achieved and also helps support a respectful, mutually beneficial relationship between horse and client. A common assumption many clients make when engaged in EAC sessions is doing—What are we going to do to the horse? When can I ride?—and the concept of *being with* the horse is much more unusual. TTouch provides a consistent framework of saying hello to each horse coming to join a session and is a measured way to check out any areas of sensitivity with each horse from a multisystemic perspective while also assessing each client: Are they able to track left and right? What tempo is used? Have they retained learning from the last session? Are they easily distracted? What initial conversations appear while spending these introductory moments with the horses?

Furthermore, TTouch helps build a sense of community and respect and helps release tension and slow down the excitement and anticipation individuals or groups feel upon arrival. Over time, the consistency and care shown to each horse supports the development of a trusting relationship between client and horse because the horse comes to rely on the client for such kind behavior, the client builds confidence in reading each horse's cues, the client adds new skills to behaving in the world, and the client is allowed the initiative to choose which TTouches each horse likes or which TTouches should be conducted during the session.

Description

TTouch is an application fun to teach and fun to learn, and there are no "rules." The basic TTouch is a circular touch, where the skin under the pads of the fingers is gently moved in a one-and-a-quarter circle, usually clockwise. Visualizing a clock face also helps to demonstrate the path of this circle and helps to activate the whole brain. The numbers on the clock stimulate the left hemisphere (i.e., logic) and creating a mental image stimulates the right hemisphere (i.e., intuition and creativity).

For the circular touches, begin at 6 o'clock, follow all the way around past 6 o'clock, and continue up to 9 o'clock to end—this is the basic one-and-a-quarter circle. The circular TTouches are micromovements, meaning only the skin directly under the fingertips or hand is activated. The circles are not wide, sweeping gestures with the fingers and hand to cover a large patch of the body. There is intricacy and focus when doing the TTouches, and this allows, if applicable, further practice in meditation, breathing, and mindfulness.

The tempo and pressure of each touch also varies based on the needs of and feedback from each horse. Generally, each circle is completed in 1 to 2 seconds with mindful pauses after several circles to allow the body to digest the information. A parallel benefit can also be observed in human clients who are agitated, distracted, or stressed, as slower circles have produced similar calming and attunement, whereas, logically, speeding up the circles may help provide pep to a session. Pressure ranges from 1 to 10, and generally most people will use a 2 to 5 pressure. A 3-pressure can be discovered by making a smooth, even circle over the cheekbone on a human's face. It is important to note TTouch is not massage or acupressure, because contact is relatively light and meant to move only the skin and hair. Once a circle-and-a-quarter is completed, clients pick up or slide to a new area and repeat the process. Some participants like to follow horizontal or vertical lines with a TTouch series.

Abalone TTouch and Clouded Leopard TTouch are good "generalist" circular touches. Abalone TTouch uses the entire hand to conduct the circles, and fingers are brought together with a slight cup in the palm in the same manner used to shake hands. Only the skin underneath the entire hand and cupped palm is moved in the one-and-a-quarter motion, and when completed, clients lightly slide to the next spot. Clouded Leopard TTouch uses the pads under the first joint or knuckle of all four fingers to move the skin while the thumb stays anchored in place to provide stability. The heel of the hand is lifted off the horse's body and the fingers are slightly apart and curled. A TTouch that is fun to teach is the Llama TTouch. It is especially helpful with shy or hesitant horses. Use the same basic hand position described in the Abalone TTouch, and flip the hand over, using only the backside of the hand to touch and move the horse's skin in the one-and-a-quarter circle pattern.

Lifts and slides comprise the description of other TTouches, and some also combine with circular touches for systemic effects. Favorite TTouch lifts and slides are Ear Slides, Hair Slides, Zigzag, and Lick of the Cow's Tongue. For the ear TTouch, teach clients to lightly cup their hand around the base of the horse's ear. While supporting the ear, gently move it in a circle and then slide up to the top of the ear. Repeat with the other ear. Some horses are unsure about this activity or do not like the inside of their ears touched, so clients can begin by touching just the base of the ear and sliding the back of the hand over the ear like in the Llama TTouch. Hair Slides have a calming effect and can be reminiscent of finger combing or mimicking behavior some humans do when twirling their long hair. Select a section of mane or tail hair and gently slide the hair through the thumb and forefinger until reaching the end; then repeat the motion with a new section of hair. For Zigzag, separate the fingers, bend them slightly, and diagonally stroke back and forth, usually over the horse's side and back, in a zigzag pattern. Horses commonly enjoy this TTouch because of a similarity to mutual grooming. Finally, Lick of the Cow's Tongue is a smooth stroke with the entire flat of the hand. Start at the girth area at the midline on the belly of the horse, draw your hand toward you, and once you are halfway up and around the barrel rotate your wrist so your fingers are pointing toward the topline, continuing until you have reached the horse's back. Repeat these movements over the horse's entire barrel until you reach the flank area.

There are approximately 20 different TTouches to date, and each is identified with an animal name. Each TTouch provides support to the body in different ways, and the TTouch books, DVDs, and clinics are strongly suggested to assist in refining the method. Furthermore, TTouch is appropriate for all ages and abilities and can be modified in whatever way is needed, perhaps using an elbow or even the top of one's forehead. Sensibility and caution is also encouraged, just as with any human–equine activity. Best practices suggest introducing your equine cotherapists to the various TTouches, assessing their reactions, and once your client or group has received an overview of equine and barn safety you are able to support all the participants by helping select the most appropriate options.

TTouch Ground Exercises

In addition to the TTouches previously mentioned, a variety of ground exercises help to further complement an EAC session, and, similar to the touches, there are no rules aside from common sense and safety. Leading and the Playground for Higher Learning—a groundwork course containing various elements such as poles, barrels, boards, and tarps configured to simulate real-life experiences a horse may face—make up the majority of the groundwork exercises and provide rich comparisons to mental health goals and objectives. One TTouch leading position is called the Homing Pigeon.

Homing Pigeon

Its uniqueness comes from two clients working cooperatively to safely guide their equine partner. Spatially, each client stands about 4 feet to the side and forward of the horse's head instead of the common position of leading at the horse's shoulder. The horse is connected to each client with zephyrs, special leads made up of a nylon section attached to a shorter, thinner white rope that can be woven through the horse's halter in various configurations depending on the level of support and direction needed.

One client is designated the pilot, and the other person becomes the copilot. The zephyrs are attached to the side rings of the halter and, ideally, the pilot's zephyr is fastened in an advanced fashion, either up the side of the halter or over the noseband. Together, they create a plan for leading their horse to a designated area, which can range from something very simple, such as walk five steps and stop and then walk three steps and stop, to very detailed, with turns, ground poles, and jumps.

For additional guidance, the human team uses wands, a deliberate reframe and rename of the traditional whip. The wands serve as an extension of the arm and a way of providing visible direction and boundaries for the horse. Clients hold their zephyr with both hands, and the outside hand maintains the lead's end, any slack, and the wand. When standing in idle position, both wands may be crossed in front of the horse's chest to signify *stand*. At times, one person may also use the wand to stroke the horse all over its body as a way of maintaining focus and minimizing restlessness or pawing on the ground.

To begin walking, the pilot cues the horse with a slight lift of the zephyr, both wands are opened slightly and point forward, and a verbal cue is given slowly, such as "and waaaaaaalk." Ideally, the space between each client and the horse is of equal distance to help maintain balance and not crowd the horse's head. To stop, "and whoaaaaaaaa" is spoken slowly, the wands are brought together, and a half-halt cue is given with the zephyr. The clients do not stop walking until the horse halts; otherwise, they will end up behind the horse's head and produce an imbalance. Homing Pigeon can also be used as a way to lead while navigating specific ground objects like the labyrinth and the star.

Labyrinth and the Star

Using eight basic ground poles or any other object that helps provide an outline, the Labyrinth can be thought of as two F's facing each other, with one flipped upside down. The Star is constructed with four poles that radiate out from a common point, and the poles can be elevated at their mutual connection, or all the poles can remain flat on the ground. These objects increase the level of skill required from the horse and clients, further engaging the body and providing a new challenge as clients advance in their work. For diagrams of the Labyrinth and the Star, see http://www.ttouch.com/horsePlayground.shtml.

As with any experiential counseling technique, it is advised for counselors to practice these exercises with their horses prior to initiating with a client. It is also recommended that counselors first do this activity as the client so they get a deeper understanding of how experiential-based counseling activities have an impact in actual sessions. Furthermore, clients will also benefit by first leading another client in the Homing Pigeon, as well as walking through the Labyrinth and the Star before partnering with a horse. These practice sessions provide an embodied experience and empathy for the horse, support skill mastery so the client is not frustrated, and provide a "sense of inner assurance and competence" (Fidler, 1981).

Application

Incorporating TTouch methods in EAC helps bring focus to a session and gives it purpose while also supporting the *doing* and *being* each client needs to balance for success. "Doing provides the means to develop and integrate sensory, motor, cognitive and psychological systems. It allows an individual to experience reality, to achieve, to fail, to explore and to grow. Mind, body and social self are developed through what we do" (Creek & Lougher, 2008, p. 362). Once the basics are learned, clients can be encouraged to experiment with different TTouches and ground exercises to match a need they might identify in their horse. For example, during Homing Pigeon a horse might repeatedly trip or walk sluggishly. The client or group could review the TTouch books and discuss how to give the horse more support. Because there are many concrete options, the brainstorming is not overwhelming and the creativity makes it fun. Also, because the focus is on what is best for the horse, there is less pressure for perfection or attachment to the outcome.

In addition to the doing, clients also experience being with the Tellington TTouch Method. Relaxation and breathing techniques can be taught by suggesting that clients breathe in when stroking up on a horse's belly and breathe out as they push away, such as with Lick of the Cow's Tongue. Because horses often provide immediate feedback with the different touches, skills can be gained in monitoring cause and effect, reading social and environmental cues, and deciding what actions, if any, to take in response. This exploration of how to best honor the horse combines a way to practice competency with external and internal assets such as support, empowerment, boundaries, and positive identity (Search Institute, 2007).

A core principal of TTouch is the balance of doing and being, using the full brain and activating both hemispheres while also supporting calming and relaxation (Hartmann, 2006). "It is my belief that the whole brain activation that occurs when a person practices enough of the basic TTouches leads to a more productive and satisfying life. Being able to use one's analytical as well as intuitive faculties enhances life and opens one to compassion and a connection to one's fellow beings" (Tellington-Jones, personal communication, August 2, 2010).

An example of whole-brain activity is with the ground work exercises, especially the Labyrinth, which provides clients and horses a type of bilateral stimulation. Clients can walk the Labyrinth prior to working with the horses, especially if there are high feelings of anxiety or sadness. They can also visualize fun, successful past sessions when walking the labyrinth with the horses. In this manner, the body is in motion in a neutral state while the brain can go back to a different memory and emotion, something enjoyable, and make a different neural connection than the unpleasant, immobilizing one that anxiety or depression can create. Furthermore, labyrinths in general provide therapeutic symbols for living one's life and making choices (Artress, 2006). A labyrinth has only one entrance and one exit, and if the path is followed the end will appear. If confusion arises when walking the path, a break can help one regroup before continuing on the journey.

Overall, because TTouch is an integrated body–mind intervention, it helps clients modulate their emotions, provides a healthy sensory or touch experience and is physically engaging, is intrinsically enjoyable and rewarding, provides context for altruism, and is a transitional activity clients can continue to practice when away from the horses. TTouch teaches acceptance and patience, especially when working with horses; it facilitates communication without words and supports the perfection in each living being.

References

Allen, K., & Blascovich, J. (1996). The value of service dogs for people with severe ambulatory disabilities. A randomized controlled trial. *Journal of the American Medical Association, 275*, 1001–1006.

Artress, L. (2006). *Walking a sacred path: Rediscovering the labyrinth as a spiritual practice.* New York: Riverhead Trade.

Bougerol, E. (November 1, 2007). *Ten dogs that changed the world.* Retrieved from: http://www.cnn.com/2007/LIVING/wayoflife/11/01/ten.dogs/

Creek, J., & Lougher, L. (2008). *Occupational therapy and mental health.* Philadelphia, PA: Elsevier.

Fidler, G. S. (1981). From crafts to competence. *American Journal of Occupational Therapy, 35*, 567–573.

Garland, E. L., & Howard, M. (2009). Neuroplasticity, psychosocial genomics, and the biopsychosocial paradigm in the 21st century. *Health & Social Work, 34*(3), 191–199.

Garrity, T. F., & Stallones, L. (1998). Effects of pet contact on human well-being: Review of recent research. In C. C. Wilson & D. C. Turner (Eds.), *Companion animals in human health.* Thousand Oaks, CA: Sage Publications.

Hartmann, T. (2006). *Walking your blues away: How to heal the mind and create emotional well-being.* South Paris, ME: Park Street Press.

McNicholas, J., & Collis, G. (2000). Dogs as catalysts for social interactions: Robustness of the effect. *British Journal of Psychology, 91* (Part 1), 61–70.

Melson, G. (2002). *Why the wild things are.* Cambridge, MA: Harvard University Press.

Putnam, R. (2000). *Bowling alone: The collapse and revival of American community.* New York: Simon & Schuster.

Rogers, J., Hart, L. A., & Boltz, R. P. (1993). The role of pet dogs in casual conversations of elderly adults. *Journal of Social Psychology, 133*, 265–277.

Search Institute. (2007). *40 developmental assets for adolescents.* Retrieved from: http://www.search-institute.org/content/40-developmental-assets-adolescents-ages-12-18

Stein, F., & Cutler, S. (2002). *Psychosocial occupational therapy: A holistic approach.* Albany, NY: Delmar.

Tellington-Jones, L. (2006). *The ultimate horse behavior and training book.* North Pomfret, VT: Trafalgar Square Publishing.

Tellington Ttouch: A playground for higher learning. Web site provides diagrams of how to create LABYRINTH and STAR plus components of the Playground for Higher Learning. Retrieved from: http://www.ttouch.com/horsePlayground. shtml

van der Kolk, B. A. (2006). Clinical implications of neuroscience research in PTSD. *Annals of the New York Academy of Sciences*, 1–17.

Welsch, T., & DePrekel, M. (2008). TTouch in support of psychological, emotional, or behavioral concerns in youth. In L. Tellington-Jones & C. Wendler (Eds.), *TTouch for healthcare*. Santa Fe, NM: Tellington TTouch Training.

☐ Conflict Resolution: The Crosswalk

Janet Nicholas

Introduction

Most families enter the therapy process due to some type of challenge or struggle. Professional help is often sought to assist family members in some type of direction or resolution of their issues. While some may have experienced challenges for years, others may have been proficient at dealing with their problems. Yet a family can realize a change or loss propelling it into a crisis and unknown territory, such as a death, illness, career change, or a move to a new location. Another type of change can be children approaching or in adolescence. Parents formerly able to reason with their children may observe transitions in their preteen's cognitions and actions.

Communication problems and conflict can evolve as children approach and enter adolescence. Additionally, families can represent a microcosm of society. They have their own rules (spoken and unspoken), nuances and postures, voice inflections, rituals, and emotional dances (Napier & Whitaker, 1978). When a family enters therapy, some of these details may remain unseen by the family therapist. While these myriad issues may be familiar for the family, it takes time to see how they function, communicate, and deal with conflict.

Rationale

As children approach adolescence, developmentally their styles of coping, cognitive processing, and self-identity and how they view their parents begin to shift. While this process is normal, it can create daunting new relationship dynamics for parents and other siblings in the family. As children begin this transition, they often challenge familiar family dynamics. Erikson's (1963) psychosocial stages of development describe ages 12–18 as adolescence and a time between childhood and adulthood. His theory posits that this age group experiences a time of transition that is known for testing of limits, separation and questioning from parents, and establishing a new identity. The term he uses to illustrate adolescence is *identity versus role confusion*.

Assisting preteens, teens, and their family members through this transition can lead to long-term positive outcomes. Helping parents to adjust to new communication strategies can enable the family to navigate the conflict while giving the developing teen healthy boundaries and teaching problem solving skills. These preadults need coping and decision-making strategies that will assist them during this new developmental stage. As more complex situations present for teens, more sophisticated skills are helpful to make healthier decisions when not in the presence of adults. Brain anatomy explains why this can be challenging, since the frontal lobe is one of the last places to mature. The frontal lobe is the seat of reasoning, making judgments, and thinking through situations prior to executing a decision or choice (Barlow, 1995).

Equine assisted counseling (EAC) creates a unique opportunity to engage in an experiential counseling environment. Since horses can mirror back attitudes, behaviors, or actions, they can allow for deeper insights in an individual or family therapy session. Due to their prey nature, horses are experts at observing body language, innuendo, and emotions. These attributes assist the horse in survival and safety. Upon observing oneself in an equine session, participants can increase in awareness as the horse reflects back information or behaviors we convey. These can be behaviors or patterns we are oblivious to, yet they affect our relationships and our communication (Kane, 2007).

Horses can be similar to people and teens, in that they are herd animals, they want to be with each other, and they can have moods. As teens gravitate to a "new herd" mostly outside of their family system, challenges are experienced for parents in negotiating new and appropriate boundaries. EAC offers an additional resource as it incorporates kinesthetic dynamics of sight, sound, touch, and olfactory. Due to these attributes, horses allow for metaphorical reflections about life and relationships in a pasture or arena setting rather than within the typical four walls of an office (Mandrell, 2006).

Most often, issues arise and are left unresolved due to poor conflict resolution skills. Several diversions often prevent resolution or lead to communication breakdowns. One area is the inability to identify the issue, diverting to numerous issues, or manipulation to avoid the key issue. Another challenge in resolving conflicts is differences in styles of communication. These differences may thwart the communication process and lead to misunderstandings or hurt feelings (Looney, 2010).

Description

As therapists, we all encounter daily the challenge of assisting clients in finding healthier ways to resolve conflict. Since most adults and teens

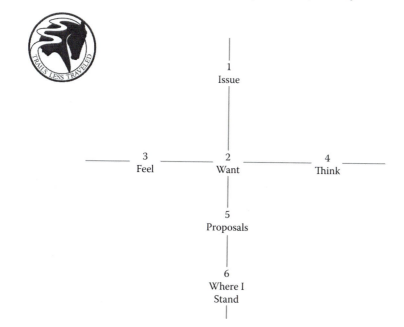

FIGURE 4.1 A crosswalk map.

have experienced the frustration of conflict and becoming stuck or angry as the result of unresolved conflict, participants understand the metaphor of needing a road map. Therefore, a family or individual participating in an EAC can create a road map in the representation of a "crosswalk." Looney (2010) suggests six steps in creating a crosswalk map:

1. Identify the *issue*.

2. State what they wish or *what I want*.

3. Share *feelings* or emotions stirred by the issue.

4. Clarify *thoughts* on the issue.

5. Make one or more *proposals*

6. State *where I stand*.

A paper copy of the six steps is placed in a crosswalk configuration on the ground. The therapist demonstrates by choosing a simple issue and walking the crosswalk for the clients. After the demonstration, the family is given a 10-minute time frame to determine a simple issue, to choose items for their crosswalk, and then to set up their crosswalk creation in the arena.

The key aspects of the crosswalk are straightforward and self-explanatory with the exception of the *where I stand*. This final piece of the road map represents a statement of commitment to the relationship or an affirmation to the others engaging the issue. This is a powerful pause in this conflict resolution exercise. Most often people do not stop and reflect on a positive or affirming trait of the conflict-inducing person or relationship. Doing so helps to keep the conflict respectful even though it may be a difficult issue. It is recommended that participants start with easier issues and learn how to have a healthy, respectful conflict before trying their more challenging issues.

Items Needed for This Exercise

- One to six participants

- One to two horses (one horse is haltered for the crosswalk)

- Halter

- Clipboard with paper to write down proposals

- Paper, tape, or paint for the "issue statement" and for labeling the crosswalk

- Six items for the six steps of the crosswalk (e.g., barrels, cones, jumps, pool noodles)

Important aspects of the crosswalk are that only the person actively walking the crosswalk can speak and that the haltered horse represents the issue. A second horse left free to roam in the arena can offer interesting metaphors. As the person walks the crosswalk, the haltered horse walks alongside the client. The client can have the issue written on a piece of paper and tape or even "paint" the issue onto the horse. This keeps the issue succinct and prevents diverting to another issue.

Allow no more than 10 minutes for the clients to determine the issue and to create their crosswalk map. Having items to use for the crosswalk available in one spot will keep clients more focused and keep the process moving. The facilitator also hands out paper, tape, and markers so the clients can identify items representing the issue, wants, feelings, thinking, proposals, and where I stand. After setting up their crosswalk, one participant begins the walk while the remaining clients watch and listen. They start at the item labeled *issue* and then proceed with the horse labeled with the issue; next they state what they want, then how they feel, and then what they think. Next is what they propose (one or two proposals) and last, where they stand on the issue.

This is a timed activity; 30 minutes are allowed after the crosswalk is created. It frequently can take up to 10 to 20 minutes to prepare, discuss, demonstrate, and physically create the crosswalk. After walking the crosswalk with the horse, the next participant must *reflect* what the initial family member said and check in with that person to make sure they have an accurate understanding; if so, they are ready to take a turn on the crosswalk. After the second person walks the crosswalk, the next person reflects back their responses and then also walks the crosswalk. It becomes apparent that to recall proposals, one participant needs to follow the person walking the crosswalk and write down the shared proposals. Participants can take turns being the scribe. Writing down every word can be laborious; it can be more practical just to write the proposals. Most of the time people can recall the wants, feelings, and thinking, but after one or two people have walked it they begin to forget the proposals. After all participants complete the crosswalk, the process can be repeated until either the 30-minute time limit has been met or when resolution is achieved. Often participants reach resolution by taking one turn each, due to practicing on an easy issue that ensures success. However simple the issue, some families may experience challenges during this exercise. It is possible that some clients may have difficulty even identifying the issue. This can be therapeutic for clients to see where they become sidetracked or confused.

If the second horse begins to interfere with the crosswalk process, what does this uninvited intrusion represent to the individual or family? Also, if this exercise is with an individual, the therapist can assist by role playing to create conflict resolution efficacy. The 30-minute limit prevents the conflict from continuing too long and allowing tempers to flare or polarization to occur. The family or group can take a 5-minute pause after everyone has completed the crosswalk and consider the proposals brought forth. They may realize that resolution has been achieved. If resolution has not been achieved, the break can serve as a time for each to review the proposal list apart from the group and consider any areas of compromise or new proposals. Time permitting, another round of walking the crosswalk can continue if there are new or improved proposals. (Having done this exercise many times, a 5-minute pause is not recommended until all have finished one round of the exercise. Clients get sidetracked and bogged down and often stop listening, and the exercise deteriorates.)

In some cases total resolution is not possible, but the value of the crosswalk is that each person may speak freely and be heard. Parents and children may not be able to agree with their teen's proposals; however, that teen gets to speak her or his issue, feelings, wants, and thoughts and to offer proposals in a safe therapeutic environment. Likewise, teens hear their parents' feelings, wants, thoughts, proposals, and affirmations. Often families will come up with new proposals as they navigate the crosswalk.

When a family or group becomes stuck, they can learn an important key dynamic in resolving conflict. Stopping this exercise after 30 minutes is powerful. First, it teaches participants to be concise and keep moving. Second, more complex issues cannot be resolved after just one walk through or one session. If resolution has not been achieved, the therapist can teach the family to take the proposal list and make a copy for each participant. This allows for time to review the proposal list individually, thwarting the possibility of ongoing arguing, demands, or manipulating one's view of the issue. Often, when the proposal list is studied individually, variations or compromises can form. Depending on the issue, the family may be able to take a quick break and begin to resume the crosswalk or may even see where they can agree. However, continuing to argue the same key points repetitively is unproductive and leads to communication breakdown. It can also illustrate how the lack of communication has been playing out in the family.

If the issue can wait, then consider the following example. It is March 1, and the issue is, "Can the teen go to summer camp for the first time?" The deadline for registration is May 31, and the family has 6–8 weeks to make a decision; therefore, this conflict does not necessarily need to be completely solved today. The proposals can, in this case, be incremental—the teen will check out the cost and transportation involved by March 15. The teen proposes she or he will find out the meeting time for parents and the church team leader. The parents' proposal list may include that Mom and Dad will check the budget and determine if the family vacation reservation can be changed and report back by March 20.

When the issue is time related, it is paramount to set a specific time to meet again and see if the proposals are still relevant or if new proposals become necessary as additional information unfolds. This teaches the family other important resolution tools of time, negotiation, and follow-through. This also allows the family to work on the assignment and present their new proposal list at the next equine therapy session. Additionally, this keeps the family accountable and the therapist role models the importance of follow-through.

Case Study

I had been working with a family for several sessions, and it was clear that resolving conflict was a significant issue. One day, the mother and daughter arrived at the session alone. We decide to use the crosswalk. After demonstrating the crosswalk for them, they chose different items to create a life-size crosswalk in the arena (the crosswalk is created by choosing six objects and then taping the appropriate crosswalk words on the items: issue, wants, feelings, thinking, proposals, and where I stand).

For example, we identified the issue and mounted a sheet of paper on a barrel with the words "Wanting to get ice cream." We also used an additional piece of paper and taped the issue to the horse. This reminded both mother and daughter to stay on the same issue. The girl had been very upset with her mother just prior to the session. She wanted ice cream, but there was not enough time to stop on their way from school to the session. Though the mother explained they could not stop without being late, her daughter could not understand why her mother would deny her what she wanted. The preteen was accustomed to working her parents to get what she wanted. Often, she would simply persist in her demands until she wore them down. This was a common dynamic she witnessed from her family.

The girl proceeded first. She identified the issue and taped it to the horse and began proceeding to each item in the crosswalk labeled wants, feelings, thoughts, proposals, and *where I stand*. The horse was very cooperative, stopping at each station in the crosswalk as the girl talked about her *issue*. Then the mother began reflecting back what she heard her daughter say. The mother had significant difficulty recalling the details of her daughter's communication. Even more surprising, the girl couldn't offer much assistance, as she couldn't remember what she herself had said. Both mother and daughter seemed stunned that they could not recall any of what had just been shared.

Then the mother took her turn walking the crosswalk. The last stage of the crosswalk was a piece of paper stating *where I stand* taped to a mounting block. Upon arriving there, the previously calm and cooperative horse began pawing the mounting block repeatedly. Mother and daughter were both surprised at this behavior and asked, "What is he doing? Why is he doing this?" As the therapist, I simply replied, "I don't know; what is he doing?" Then the horse kicked the mounting block numerous times and reached down and ripped the paper off the mounting block, stomping it until it was barely discernable in the deep sand of the arena. The *where I stand*, written in red marker, now appeared as *E-S-ND* with ripped edges in several places on the paper.

We watched in silence for quite some time as the horse finally calmed down and stood quietly. I asked the mother and daughter, "What does this mean to you?" After another lengthy silence, the mother spoke up: "I know exactly what this means. This is exactly what we do in our family. We don't listen to each other; we just wait for the other person to be quiet so we can go on the attack. We don't stand for each other." Mother and daughter were quiet and reflective.

After this profound realization, we proceeded to work toward proposals acceptable to both mother and daughter. Then the daughter proceeded to take a leftover piece of paper and began drawing out the crosswalk diagram. She carefully rewrote the words, issue, wants, feelings, thinking, proposals, and *where I stand* statement on her paper and left that day with her copy of the crosswalk.

The impact of what unfolded in the *arena of life* would not have been as apparent without the intervention of the horse that afternoon. The horse reflected back a key struggle in their family system, and that struggle became completely clear that day. I walked away that afternoon shaking my head in awe as I loaded up the horses to head home.

Application

Used in a psychotherapy session, the crosswalk is a powerful conflict resolution tool. Coupled with the experiential nature of EAC this tool is even more significant. The equine modality in counseling can create experiences that illuminate life struggles. An uncooperative, moody, or fearful horse in such an exercise can mirror back aspects of a family dynamic not immediately visible to the therapist or even the family.

Another positive aspect of teaching such a conflict resolution map is the dynamic of only one person speaking during the "walk." Listening is one of the most difficult but important tools of communication and conflict resolution. The ability to listen thoroughly and then accurately reflect back offers the listener and receiver an additional opportunity to review the information shared. Especially during the frequently difficult time of transition to adolescence, parents tend to become more reactive in their communication. As their teens begin to push the boundaries of the family, parents can become more anxious and rigid. This can lead to less listening and more overreacting on both the part of the parent and teen.

As teens begin to navigate new relationships and more activities away from their parents, they need to know how to address conflicts in such situations. Since they are entering new arenas of life, they need to know how to deal with peers, school, parents, and new situations that increase in complexity. The crosswalk conflict resolution tool along with equine cofacilitators can assist parents in learning new skills of listening, time boundaries, follow-through, and negotiation. These skills role modeled by parents can then be instilled in their teenagers, assisting in those crucial developmental transitions from childhood to adulthood.

References

Barlow, D. H. (1995). *Abnormal psychology: An integrative approach.* Pacific Grove, CA: Brooks/Cole Publishing.

Erikson, E. H. (1963). *Childhood and society* (2nd ed.). New York: Norton.

Kane, B. (2007). *The manual of medicine and horsemanship.* Bloomington, IN: Author House.

Looney, P. A. (2010). *Crosswalk: Getting to the other side of conflict.* Manuscript submitted for publication.

Mandrell, P. (2006). *Introduction to equine assisted psychotherapy: A comprehensive overview.* Lubbock, TX: Author.

Napier, A. Y., & Whitaker, C. A. (1978). *The family crucible.* New York: Harper & Row.

Techniques That Speak to Atypical Behaviors

☐ Heart-to-Heart Rainbow: An Imagery Experience to Facilitate Relationship Development

Pamela Jeffers, Erin Lucas, and Kristina Houser

Introduction

The heart-to-heart rainbow is an experience created to develop relationship skills and repair the misinterpretation of nonverbal cues that may have evolved through trauma. The equine specialist (ES) and mental health professional (MHP) work together to bridge three relationships for the child: inner relationship and self-awareness, relationship with horse, and relationship with others.

The heart-to-heart rainbow is a threefold experience. First, it requires developing self-awareness and connection with the inner being. This awareness is then used as a bridge to forming a relationship with the horse. Finally, the relationship with the horse is used as a bridge to restructuring the relationship with the parent through the heart-to-heart connection. Once the family has achieved the full experience of the heart-to-heart rainbow, they are asked to use this experience to practice being connected in a comfortable way as a family.

Rationale

In his groundbreaking work on attachment theory, Bowlby, observing orphaned children with staff as caretakers (Bowlby, 1969, 1973, 1980, 1988), reported that infants and young children became listless, uninterested in their environment, and unable to take in emotional and nutritional support because of separation from their primary caretakers. Ainsworth (Ainsworth, Blehar, Waters, & Wall, 1978), observing young children, described three categories of attachment: secure, insecure, and anxiously attached. With the *strange situation* (1978), Ainsworth et al. evaluated the level of attachment in children. A *securely attached* child was one who would be able to respond appropriately and flexibly with affect, cognitions, exploration, problem solving, and social interaction. An *insecurely attached* child could be expected to go back and forth between socially appropriate interactions in certain situations and inappropriate responses in others. An *anxiously attached* child would be expected to display irritability, apathy, and failure to respond cooperatively with a caring adult.

According to Hughes (2000), children without a rich 18-month period of interaction with birth parents immediately after and subsequent to birth will not seek comfort, safety, or pleasure with adoptive parents. The child can be expected to manipulate caretakers with short-term charm or aggression. Control struggles will be common, since the child's brain has developed an automatic flight-or-fight response to previous inadequate caretaker interventions and may not anticipate that needs will be met. The child will want to be in charge, uncertain that adoptive parents will actually be able to provide for emotional, physical, or spiritual needs. In addition, the child's understanding and communication of these needs will be undeveloped, because the earliest experiences of response to the child's needs will have been inconsistent or entirely lacking. To retrain the brain to respond differently after neglect or trauma have elicited the child's self-protective, entrenched, and unproductive pattern of behavior, van der Kolk (2005) has suggested the individual may need to be given another opportunity to develop the ability to have a mutually reciprocal and nurturing relationship.

It is proposed that an equine assisted counseling (EAC) program consisting of a step-by-step building block process can provide an empowering adjunct treatment to the attachment-based therapy model. This proposed program follows the format of the work of van der Kolk (2005). According to van der Kolk, "Only after children develop the capacity to focus on pleasurable activities without becoming disorganized do they have a chance to develop the capacity to play with other children, engage in simple group activities and deal with more complex issues" (p. 407). Typically, talk therapy helps the family identify the origin of the problems the family is experiencing and teaches skills for new patterns of interaction. As a result, it is presumed that the equine experience will provide the hands-on experience to increase the traumatized child's awareness of skills and then the opportunity to practice these skills to apply them in their home. "At the center of the therapeutic work with terrified children is helping them realize that they are repeating their early experiences and helping them find new ways of coping by developing new connections between their experiences, emotions, and physical reactions" (van der Kolk, 2005, p. 408). Thus, families can start building a bridge to new relationship patterns and interactions by participating in EAC experiences.

Equine assisted counseling, encouraging the development of a relationship between an individual and a horse, is proposed as a medium in which this new opportunity to establish healthy relationship skills might occur. Horses have the ability to reflect and telegraph the emotions of an individual in proximity due to perception of themselves as prey (Irwin, 1998). Through the horse's typically congruent behavioral responses to human behaviors, the horse's body adjustments would inform the child about the positive or negative progress of interactions. The essence of the modality presented here is to enable the child, heretofore resistant to loving caretakers' parenting, to acquire relationship skills with a horse in a safe and developmentally appropriate sequence, accompanied by adoptive parents. It would be anticipated that the child's ability to relax, to respect, and to emotionally connect with the horse would be observable in the horse's behaviors of comfort and relaxation (head lowered, relaxed ears, front feet squared, body still, eyes soft; Irwin, 1998); ability to follow communication from the child; and reciprocal exchanges of affection. In an arena out of the realm of acquired human relationship experience, which may have included trauma, the child might be more willing to explore relationship building. The child's previously absent skill set of appropriate responses to adoptive parents' nurturance would be developed by relationship to the horse in a sequence that includes (1) the presence of parents, (2) the support and assistance of parents, and (3) in tandem with the parent. Through this process, it is hoped that relationship skills with horses would generalize to receptivity and relationship skill building with adoptive parents.

Description

Inner Relationship and Self-Awareness

To develop self-awareness and connection with the inner being, the child is guided through several activities, with the parent providing supportive observation. Each session starts with everyone seated in a circle. In this setting, the parents, children, ES, and MHP participate in centered breathing (Jeffers, 2010; Kane, 2007). In this exercise, participants are asked to put feet flat on the ground, sit with their back straight, close eyes, and place hands in a relaxed, open position on their legs. The ES or MHP then directs the group to draw awareness to body parts from the head to foot and to take long, deep breaths throughout the exercise. The task-oriented nature of this activity makes it an easier way to begin the therapy. It is explained that horses respond to various breathing patterns and that the herd members display calm, nonverbal cues when the humans around them take long, deep breaths. Thus, it is a key element to beginning the time with the horses as we respectfully enter their world. During the centered breathing, the participants are asked to take long, deep breaths. They are instructed specifically when to breathe in and when to breathe out and where they should feel the breath in their body.

The centered breathing activity leads into the body awareness activity. Participants are asked to focus their attention on specific body parts, from head to foot, as directed by the ES leading the seated circle. They are encouraged to take note of the sounds they hear, the smells they experience, the sensations they feel on their skin, and the level of relaxation or tension they notice in their muscles throughout their body. Remembering that trauma affects one's ability to interpret sensory information, it is important for the ES and MHP to be in conversation about the children's trauma history and its effect on this exercise. Sounds, smells, and other sensory input may remind children of other times in their lives that they have experienced similar sensory input and could arouse memories that interfere with their ability to attend and relax. The MHP will need to be ready to identify and label what might be happening for children and to provide emotional support and empathy. The ES will need to be ready, as well, to describe the way horses respond to threats that could inform human reactions. More time may be necessary to facilitate sufficient relaxation. Once participants appear relaxed and centered, they are asked to begin visualization.

During this exercise, the participants are to visualize a space of peace, relaxation, and unconditional love. This can be done through use of a script (Murdock, 1987) or informally by reminding them of their centered breathing. This experience of peace is then used to begin the rainbow for the heart-to-heart rainbow experience. This centered feeling is then referred to throughout the time spent with the horse to reenter the horse's world as we encounter distractions or become anxious or nervous when faced with unfamiliar tasks. Because horses reflect and respond to human behavior, participants are encouraged to use the nonverbal cues of the horse to build awareness of internal energy states and their effect on others.

For example, when participants are anxious, they are encouraged to notice how horses' nonverbal cues mirror their energy and then are asked to use centered breathing and observe the effects on the horses' behavior. During these activities, it is helpful to encourage the participants to verbalize what it felt like to affect another's energy state with their internal energy to help them integrate the experience. In addition, it is important to call attention to the nonverbal cues that the horse exhibits mirroring the child's internal feelings and external behavior to raise awareness of the client's internal state.

Relationship With the Horse

Bridging the heart-to-heart rainbow from the child's inner being to the horse is the next step in the experience. This is facilitated weekly during the grooming, visualization, and leading activities. When focusing on bridging the connection from the child to the horse, parents are asked to provide supportive observation of the children's experience. During the grooming activity, the ES is to loosely hold the lead rope, being careful to perceive if children are centered and grounded to assure that the horse is reacting to participants and not the ES. Children are asked to approach the horse at the animal's shoulder to begin the activity. The ES allows the horse to move freely as the ES remains stationary holding the rope. If the horse moves away from the child, the child is asked to take a long, deep breath and reapproach the horse, slowly advancing and then retreating until the horse displays comfort with the child's inner energy. Throughout these activities, the advance and retreat approach is used as needed (Parelli & Kadash, 1993). The advance and retreat technique involves approaching the horse to engage in the activity and then walking away to take a centered breath as needed in response to nonverbal cues of the horse. The grooming activity is done with the ES in proximity to the horse and holding onto the rope because of the child's possible difficulty interpreting nonverbal cues and perhaps interpreting the horse's initial retreat as a personal rejection.

When children are connecting with the horse through grooming, they are encouraged to notice the horse's response to their presence and begin to interpret what this means. The ES offers interpretation of nonverbal cues as the child, parent, or MHP notices the cues. Comments and questions by the MHP to the ES often help the child identify and internalize the nonverbal cues. During the grooming, it is important to help the child transition from a task-focused experience to a relationship-focused experience. Reminding the child of the visualization that occurred in the seated circle and asking the child to use centered breathing as a way to return to that state of being can help to accomplish this transition.

Once a relaxed relationship is achieved, children are led through the next step in the heart-to-heart rainbow experience. They are asked to visualize this magical rainbow from their heart to the horse's heart as they groom the horse. With each stroke of the brush or placement of their hand on the horse's neck, they are encouraged to imagine the heart-to-heart rainbow getting brighter or stronger. Observations of the horse's nonverbal cues are verbalized and discussed at the end of the activity. By observing typical nonverbal cues of the horse such as soft eyes, low neck, front foot alignment, and resting fee (Irwin, 1998), both parent and child can become aware of how their inner state of being affects others around them.

After experiencing the heart-to-heart rainbow in a stationary position, children are guided by their parents and the ES in leading the horse. To communicate their desire to move forward, children are asked to use the heart-to-heart connection. Children are to visualize what they would like the horse to do (Hunt, 2004), to clearly communicate this request, and to act toward it. When the ES notices a break in the heart-to-heart connection, they request a pause in the activity to help children regain the connection and then proceed.

As children are able to maintain the connection to the horse through the leading exercise, they are then challenged to let go of the lead rope. This challenge is posed in a relationship context. Children are encouraged to use their awareness of the heart-to-heart connection to let go of the lead rope when they and the horse are ready and to continue walking. The children can pick up the lead rope as necessary to reestablish the connection with the horse.

Relationship With Others

After a basic awareness of the heart-to-heart rainbow is achieved with the horse, the children are to expand this rainbow to their parents. This is accomplished through grooming, visualization, and leading activities, again using the advance and retreat approach as needed (Parelli & Kadash, 1993). These activities differ only in that parents are asked to join their children, providing synchrony in the grooming and guidance in the leading. In addition to the previous activities, the heart-to-heart circle and heart tone exercises are used.

The Heart-to-Heart Circle Exercise

This exercise consists of creating the heart-to-heart rainbow between the child and the horse and then bridging the horse's heart to the parent's heart and then back to the child's heart. This completes the other half of the rainbow and makes it a circle. The parent and child are asked to take one long, deep breath. When they exhale, they are to imagine a rainbow joining from their heart to the horse's heart, and then as they inhale the horse's heart joins to their heart in a circular motion. Parents are asked to imagine this circular flow of energy from them to the child to the horse and then back to them.

The Heart Tone Exercise

This exercise involves all participants present. The ES or MHP vocalizes a tone that resonates in the throat and upper chest; this tone is then matched by the person next to the leader. Once it is matched, the next person vocalizes the tone until all participants are in tune, creating the same tone together. The group is asked to sustain the tone for a couple of minutes with participants pausing for a breath as needed at different intervals throughout the experience.

The bridge of the heart-to-heart rainbow experience between one child and the parent is the next stage in the process. In families with more than one child, this heart-to-heart circle can then be expanded to include all of the children in the family. This relationship is bridged through use of grooming, visualization, leading, and heart tone.

To bring the parent into the horse–child relationship, parents first enter the grooming activity. During this activity, they are to match their child's strokes and practice use of centered breathing to regulate their own affect and in turn to regulate the affect of their child. Once a relaxed inner state of being is achieved for parent, child, and horse, the child and parent begin the visualization activity standing next to the horse. They are to use the heart-to-heart circle imagery, visualizing a magical rainbow from the child's heart to the horse's heart to the parent's heart and then back to the child's heart. After the heart-to-heart circle is experienced standing with the horse, the parent, child, and horse are ready to move forward together.

During leading exercises, the parent starts out walking next to the child. After the relationship connection is achieved and the heart-to-heart circle is experienced among the parent, child, and horse, the parent moves to one end of the arena with the MHP, and the ES and child move to the other. The child leads the horse in a circle from the parent and MHP to the ES, maintaining the heart-to-heart circle connection with the child, horse, and parent throughout the exercise. The role of the MHP is to support the parent in maintaining the heart-to-heart connection while the ES coaches the child through the leading activity.

The Heart Tone

This activity is used as a way to create another experience of connection and mutual peace, relaxation, and unconditional love. It is practiced in the seated circle after the centered breathing and body awareness exercise. Initially, the ES or MHP begins the tone. As the family becomes more comfortable with the exercise, one parent is to take over the role of leader. The tone is then passed to the person sitting next to the leader and continues all the way around the circle. Participants are asked to notice when others pause to breathe so that they can stagger their breaths. They are also asked to listen to each other so that each can modify their tone, volume, and intensity, as needed, to coordinate with each other.

When working with a family that includes multiple children, the heart tone can serve as a way to bridge the connections formed between each child and the parent to include a heart-to-heart circle experience for the entire family. The family participates in the seated circle together. After the centered breathing and body awareness exercise, the family participates in the heart tone exercise. Once the heart tone has been achieved, the family is ready for the heart-to-heart family walk.

The Heart-to-Heart Family Walk

The goal in this exercise is for the family to experience a feeling of peace, relaxation, and unconditional love together as a unit. All of the participants form a line: horse, child, and parent. The ES and MHP are positioned on either end of the line. (To integrate another parent, the activity can be repeated with the parents trading places.) The child and parent connect holding a piece of crepe paper in between them. The crepe paper connects the family as a unit yet allows enough give and flexibility to accommodate individual fluctuations in movement. The participants are asked again to imagine the magical connection of a rainbow starting at one end of the line, flowing through the horse and family members, and continuing all the way to the other end of the line. The group then creates a heart tone, with the parent leading. Once the heart tone is created, the group is to move in unison across the arena while maintaining the heart tone. The group is to stop when the parent stops the heart tone. The rainbow connection is reinforced as needed for unification of the family unit.

Application

The heart-to-heart rainbow is an experience created to develop relationship skills and repair the misinterpretation of nonverbal cues that may have evolved through trauma. The ES and MHP work together to bridge three relationships for the child: inner relationship and self-awareness, relationship with horse, and relationship with others. This activity is appropriate for children of all ages, their parents, and families. It is not appropriate for abusive parents in the early phase of treatment or for psychotic parents or children.

References

Ainsworth, M. D., Blehar, M. C., Waters, E., & Wall, S. (1978). *Patters of attachment: A psychological study of the strange situation.* Hillsdale, NJ: Erlbaum.

Bowlby, J. (1969). *Attachment and loss: Vol. 1. Attachment.* New York: Basic Books.

Bowlby, J. (1973). *Attachment and loss: Vol. 2. Separation and anger.* New York: Basic Books.

Bowlby, J. (1980). *Attachment and loss: Vol. 3. Loss: Sadness and depression.* New York: Basic Books.

Bowlby, J. (1988). *A secure base.* New York: Basic Books.

Hughes, D. (2000). *Facilitating developmental attachment; The road to emotional recovery and behavioral change in foster and adopted children.* Lanham, MD: Jason Aronson.

Hunt, R. (2004). *Cowboy logic.* Idaho: Bruce Publishing.

Irwin, C. (1998). *Horses don't lie: The magic of horse whispering.* New York: Great Plains Publications.

Jeffers, P. (2010). What Cheyenne knew. *Angels on Earth, May/June.* New York: Guidepost Magazine.

Kane, B. (2007). *The manual of medicine and horsemanship—Transforming the doctor–patient relationship with equine-assisted learning.* Bloomington, IN: AuthorHouse.

Murdock, M. (1987). *Spinning inward using guided imagery with children for learning, creativity & relaxation.* Boston, MA: Shambhala Publications.

Parelli, P., & Kadash, K. (1993). *Natural horse-man-ship.* Colorado Springs, CO: Western Horseman Magazine.

Swift, S. (2002). *Centered riding 2.* North Pomfret, VT: Trafalgar Square Publishing.

van der Kolk, B. A. (2005). Developmental trauma disorder: Toward a rational diagnosis for children with complex trauma histories. *Psychiatric Annals, 35*(5), 401–408.

☐ You Gotta Crack a Few Eggs

Tracie Faa-Thompson

Introduction

Many people block out painful thoughts and feelings, especially around unwanted major life changes. This can lead to an apparent inability to recognize events that they may or may not have some control over. Shame or a victim mentality keeps them in the *stuck* position, where they either blame others for their own failings or are so ashamed they are unable to rationalize their experiences. Because of its focus on more than one major life event, the exercise "You Gotta Crack a Few Eggs" helps clients identify and track what changed their lives in unexpected ways and understand their own role in the process.

Rationale

In the field of addictions, clinicians struggle to gain a definition of the psychological nature of addiction. According to Shaffer (2010), one simple model for understanding addiction is to apply the three Cs:

1. Behavior that is motivated by emotions ranging along the craving to compulsion spectrum

2. Continued use in spite of adverse consequences

3. Loss of control

Equine assisted counseling (EAC) used as part of the 12-step addictions recovery program assists clients to examine these three aspects of addiction in a way that opens up choice. Clients believe they have no choice, so they give up or repeat the same behaviors that keep them addicted. Often this can mean the manipulation of others to get their needs met. Using EAC, clients begin to understand and accept that they cannot make anyone else do something and that they can change only themselves. They begin to learn that the choices they make are paramount, as is the fact that others may not behave the way they want them to. Relapse is caused not by environment, things, and people but by the addict's reaction to environment, things, and people (Shaffer, 2010). Horses are large and powerful (like an addiction is), which creates a natural opportunity for some to overcome fear and change and to develop confidence. The size and power of the horse are naturally intimidating (again, like addictions) to many people. Accomplishing a task involving the horse, in spite of those fears, creates confidence and provides for wonderful metaphors when dealing with other intimidating and challenging situations in life.

The egg represents the client, which is a useful metaphor since all human life begins as an egg. The horse is used as the carrier of the egg on its journey. As in all journeys, some are smoother than others, and the experiences with the egg allow for reflections on clients' experiences in their journey. In family work, the process and the differences in what might have been perceived as a shared journey are learning and reflective opportunities for families to view the same event from the other family members' perspectives. There may also be differences in what each family member perceives as *significant life events*. At the end of the sharing experience, families will have the opportunity to understand other family members' individual stances and to be mutually supportive.

Description

Clients are invited to catch a horse and bring it to one end of the arena (or whatever venue you are using). Clients are then given a hard-boiled egg and told that this egg represents *the beginning* for them. Leave it up to clients to choose the life milestone from which they wish to begin. It could be their birth, a graduation, a marriage or divorce, or any other significant point in their life that is meaningful to them. For example, we might see divorce as a significant life event, but clients must be free to choose their own significant life event for themselves and not be directed. Individuals will all have their own point where they wish to begin.

They are then invited to place the egg anywhere on the horse. The task is to get the horse and egg to the other end of the arena, which represents the present moment. If this is a group or family intervention, participants are told it is not a race and that there is no special recognition for getting to the other end of the arena first. Clients are not allowed to hold onto the egg in any way, although they are allowed to try to catch the egg when it is falling off the horse. Of course, the egg will fall many times on its journey to the here and now.

Each time the egg falls, clients are asked to write down another significant point in their life in the notebook provided. We choose to process these events at the end of the activity; however, you can process them each time the egg falls. By the time the journey has ended, the egg often looks very battered. In soft, deep arenas the egg can often get lost. Being battered or lost can be very symbolic reflections of clients' personal journeys. This powerful metaphor helps clients reflect on periods where they felt lost or out of control in their life. If they have trouble identifying numerous significant life events, the counselor can gently guide them on this path of discovery and reflection. At the end of the activity, clients are invited to look at their egg and describe it. Then they are invited to talk about the significant points in their life that they have jotted down in their notebook.

In a family model, each person takes a turn to describe each event. The counselor notes how each person offers a completely different perspective of the same event and how these very unique views impact the family dynamic. Each family member has his or her own horse and own egg, as significant events might be different for each member. (How exactly would you do this activity with a family or group?)

Processing Questions

- Where did your journey begin and how?

- What were the obstacles you encountered, and how did you effectively or ineffectively manage them?

- Did anyone catch his or her egg as it was falling?

- Did you lose your egg? What happened when it got lost?

- Ask each family member for his or her perspective, as each of them might remember or view the event in very different ways or there might be some shared understanding.

- Which events are remembered in the same way?

- How does the egg look different now than at the beginning of your journey?

- Did the horse you chose assist or hinder your progress? In what way?

- How does it feel to achieve the journey's end?

- Anything else?

Equipment Needed

Necessary equipment includes horses, a hard-boiled egg, a head collar, and lead ropes (extra ones can be left around); cones and some obstacles for winding around (optional but a useful metaphor as life is never a straight, smooth path); and a clipboard and pen for journaling (it helps if the pen is attached to the clipboard by string). Another adaptation is to have more horses than clients. The extra horses remain loose and can serve to impede the journey, invoking the metaphor that sometimes others get in the way of your goals and are sometimes out of the individual's control.

Application

This EAC technique was developed for use in the addictions field; however, it can be adapted for use with a variety of client groups. I have found it particularly useful in working with clients who are dealing with major life changes (in particular loss and bereavement) and with family work where there is family dysfunction

☐ Reference

Shaffer, H. J. (2010). *What is addiction?: A perspective*. Retrieved from http://www.priorygroup.com

☐ Treatment of Autism and Attachment With Interpersonal Equine Therapy

Sara D. Edwards

Introduction

While it is important to recognize symptom clusters in behavior, perception, sensation, and neurology to identify and classify differences in individuals identified as being on the autism spectrum, diagnosis alone takes us just so far in helping an autist adapt to a predominantly non-autistic society. There is an increasing awareness of autism from both professional perspectives (psychotherapeutic, medical, and neurological) and personal perspectives (autobiographical) that has moved us to a better understanding of autistic behavior and allowed us to more accurately describe the experiences of autists themselves. As a consequence, professionals are more able to reliably make valid diagnoses to classify individuals with this disorder. Using this information to create more effective treatment modalities is essential so that mental and medical health practitioners can be beneficial beyond the art of description. This essay presents the rationale, description, and application of using interpersonal equine therapy (IPET) as a form of equine mental health in the psychotherapeutic treatment of individuals with autistic and attachment disorders.

Rationale

As a psychotherapist I have witnessed autists struggle with traditional psychotherapies when the mode of intervention is an interpersonal didactic social experience because the sensory, perceptual, and intimacy factors essential to psychotherapeutic intervention and success are at the heart of the autistic struggle. Social exchange that emphasizes interpersonal intimacy to be psychotherapeutic heightens an autist's anxiety. The attachment and connection necessary for effective intervention can usually induce panic and cause an autist to interpersonally retreat into an intrapersonal safety zone, a withdrawal into their own world, which strikingly halts any further process of communicative exchange. How, then, does a therapist intervene in a psychotherapeutic and healing way when the very tools of intervention—sensory, perceptual, and experiential interpersonal behavior and exchange—heighten anxiety and are the immediate cause for disconnect and retreat for an individual on the autistic spectrum?

From patient clinical histories it becomes apparent that the predominant socially *dysfunctional behaviors* that make autistic symptoms first recognizable are witnessed at an early age (2–3 years). These behaviors, or the lack thereof, disrupt normal play and other interpersonal affiliative connecting behaviors—such as hugging and making eye contact—that not only define normal childhood development but are also the building blocks for healthy adult social adjustment. Clinical observation reveals that when these symptoms begin to surface, isolation becomes a defense against being unable to build socially connecting, interactive behaviors in a neurotypical manner. Isolation becomes a more valuable resource for the autist and is relied on frequently in development as a response when confronting difficulty in how to negotiate social interaction and expectation. With this in tow, impairments in reciprocal social interaction and in verbal and nonverbal communication increase, and, most importantly, a marked preference for repetitive, solitary, and stereotypical interests and activities grows for autists.

These aforementioned impairments are the three key features described by Szatmari (2004) that characterize all children with autism, no matter where they fall on the spectrum, from Asperger's to pervasive developmental disorder (NOS) and beyond to the most severe autistic disorders. These stereotypic autistic behaviors are very much like the self-comforting behavior observed in captive monkeys—rocking, self-grooming, restricted or repetitive focus and behavior—following exposure to stress (Harlow & Suomi, 1971). Stereotypy is indicative of and evidence for states of extreme stress. It follows that withdrawal and interpersonal isolation are defenses used by autists to better manage their anxiety. Personal reports from clients corroborate this line of reasoning.

John Robison (2008) explains in his autobiographical book, "Our responses may appear totally neutral, while inside we are crying. You cannot reliably evaluate our state of mind by our outward demeanor" (p. 288). How emotion is experienced by autists is described in different ways by Grandin (1996), Robison (2008), and Tammet (2006). However, consistent among these autistic autobiographers is that although the manner in which autists experience emotion is or was not like their neurotypical contemporaries, all were able to describe their unique ways of experiencing emotion and all were insistent on the isolation and stress they felt as a consequence of their and others' awareness of their being different. All were able to progressively overcome their childhood limitations and become successful adults through very different processes. Despite variable family situations and developmental experiences, Robison (2008) notes that the ability to negotiate emotional connection without fail increases with age. It appears then that social flexibility and competence grows and expands with interactive opportunities and working through trial and error efforts tested throughout life. While Grandin had more familial sources of consistent social intervention at an earlier age, Robison depended more on himself and learning opportunities from life experiences. Both identify the adults in their lives as not allowing them to retreat and enforcing compulsory social interaction as a key to their successful social evolution. Even though the development of autists' social skills may appear somewhat awkward, the ability exists in autistic individuals and is more effectively learned and accessible if social retreat, stereotypy, and perseveration are not supported or reinforced. Therefore, despite reports by Robison (2008) and Grandin (1996) that the social world does not have the same value and meaning for an autist as it does for a neurotypical person, there does still appear to be an intrinsic value for an autist to develop and learn social skills, which is evidenced by both Robison's and Grandin's professional and social successes.

One of the greatest difficulties for autists is how to make their own social expression adaptive to their environment, especially if their experience is different and their behavior not spontaneously socially embraced. The distinctions of *focus*, namely, *self*, and *other*, and the additional doctrines of interpersonal theory (Leary, 1957; Sullivan, 1953) are particularly difficult concepts for autists. These concepts are not learned without special effort. Social separation and isolation are defensive behaviors used by autists to comfort themselves and to reduce distress over a perceived awareness of his/her differentness. Autists appear to lack a social doctrine or intuitive understanding of themselves as individuals and, more particularly, themselves in relationship to others. These deficits in social adaptation include marked impairments in the use of nonverbal communication to regulate social interactions; difficulties in initiating, negotiating, and terminating social interactions; challenges in the recognition of complementarity and reciprocity; confusion in experiencing emotional social reciprocity (understanding the thoughts and feelings of others); and limitations in perceiving the impact of one's behavior on others. Dawson and Levy (1989) recognized that the autism population has a unique pattern of attention involving an ability to focus intensely on things that are of interest to themselves while they are unable to attend to things that are not of interest. As Szatmari (2004) surmises, "It may not be so much that children with autism are unable to speak as it is they do not have the motivation to use their communication skills for interaction" (p. 9).

It seems essential then that for any therapeutic intervention to be effective for an autist, it must primarily provide a safe and motivating situation for connection with others to occur as well as trial situations that enable the learning of interpersonal behavior doctrines and the constructs of social exchange.

Following this rationale, it makes sense that horses can provide a unique work-out situation for autistic individuals. Horses do not recognize prosody—things like flat, monotonic quality and unique cadence (Grandin & Johnson, 2004). Unlike humans, horses do not expect the labyrinth of social nuances that are meaningful to people. A lack of these nuances, or the disorganization of them, does not cause communication breakdowns between people and horses. A relationship with a horse can decrease anxiety about therapeutic work in a session as the connection with the horse increases. Autistic individuals can learn to interact with horses in an interventionist manner to induce change, facilitated by the therapist, both interpersonally and intrapersonally by incorporating observation and feedback imagery that can be translated into imagery that works not only with horses but also with people. Connection, focus, boundaries, reciprocity, and complementarity can all be identified and practiced with motivation inspired by the growing connection in the relationship between the autistic client and the horse. Grandin and Johnson (2004) reflect on how the relationship between human and horse is not just the human relating to and directing the horse; rather, "it's a relationship" where horses are "super-sensitive" and are responding to the person as much, if not more, than the person responds to the horse (p. 6).

In effect, doing interventionistic therapeutic work with horses and individuals on the autistic spectrum provides a medium through which autists can increase social connection with another to decrease anxiety within themselves. The interactions with the horse provide social exchange work-out situations for learning and practicing the doctrines of interpersonal theory. These are constructs from which autists can become more socially aware and skilled in developing social behaviors, both inter- and intrapersonally responding to themselves and another in the context of establishing a bonding relationship with the horse.

Description

The IPET Model

Based on interpersonal theory, Sullivan (1953), Leary (1957), and Smith-Benjamin (1974) provided circumplex models that can be used effectively to depict and understand interpersonal behavior. Mapping behaviors in the context of social interactions with self and others is a very useful tool when attempting to describe the behaviors involved in social exchange, be it with *self* (intrapersonal) or with *others* (interpersonal). Using these models, an individual's relationship with him or herself is called *introject* or intrapsychic, whereas any behaviors in the context of a relationship with an other are either intransitive (reactive) and called *self* behaviors or transitive (active) and called *other* behaviors. Refer to Smith-Benjamin (1974) for more details of the structured analysis of social behavior (SASB) to further understand these concepts. These models provide the basis for the IPET model that can be used to observe, describe, and analyze social behavior in the context of human–horse relationships (Edwards, 2011). Certain descriptions of interpersonal behavior, whether enacted by horse or human, can be analyzed using the same dimensional components of social behavior. One dimensional component is *influence*—differentiation and interdependence—whereas the other dimensional component is *affiliation*—love and hate (Figure 5.1).

Many may argue whether a horse feels love or hate, but there are clear behavioral indications of when a horse's behavior is affiliative or disaffiliative (Edwards, 2011). Analyzing these two-dimensional components, along with *focus*, allows for the identification and analysis of the interpersonal dynamics: complementarity, reciprocity, and internalization in the context of the horse–client relationship (Figure 5.2). These dynamics are the foundation of any interactive social relationship.

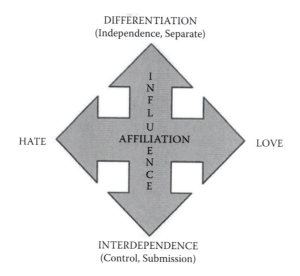

FIGURE 5.1 Components of interpersonal behavior. From Edwards, S., *A Clinical Model for Equine Psychotherapeutic Assessment, Intervention, and Treatment,* 2011.

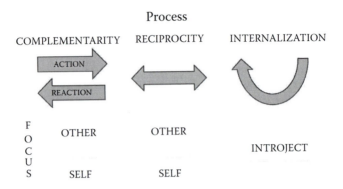

FIGURE 5.2 Interpersonal behavior dynamics. From Edwards, S., *A Clinical Model for Equine Psychotherapeutic Assessment, Intervention, and Treatment,* 2011.

Therapist Observation, Analysis, and Intervention of Horse–Human Social Interaction

Using the IPET model allows the therapist to identify, describe, analyze, and interpret the client's interpersonal dynamics with an other, with the horse as a representative of a significant other in the therapeutic session. The therapist can then identify significant psychological issues for the patient and apply a systematic interventionistic approach to the patient's evaluation and treatment from dynamics evidenced in the context of the client/horse relationship (Figure 5.3).

This type of behavioral analysis in the context of the relationship between horse and client not only reveals interpersonal and psychological dysfunction but also serves to outline potential means of intervention, based on whatever therapeutic outcome is desired. The IPET model not only organizes observation, identification, and analysis but also systematically outlines the path necessary to encourage the desired healthier behavioral change. The horse's dynamics—its actions and reactions—are essential in exposing and drawing out dysfunctional dynamics and equally essential in guiding and assisting in behavioral changes that create a healthier adjustment for the client. If the horse is allowed to express its own reactions to the patient without influence or censorship by the therapist, it becomes an extremely powerful source for providing accurate, effective social and psychological feedback. If the horse's behavior is controlled by the therapist, then valuable therapeutic material is lost. The horse can also provide feedback on the state of the client's nervous system, thereby helping them learn to self-regulate and manage their own anxiety, fear, tension, and focus.

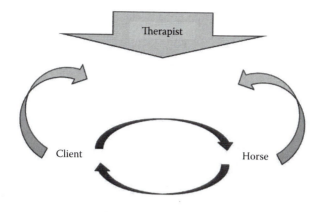

FIGURE 5.3 Therapist participant observation. From Edwards, S., *A Clinical Model for Equine Psychotherapeutic Assessment, Intervention, and Treatment*, 2011.

Therapeutic Intervention Using IPET for Sensory Processing

Attwood (2008) expressed concerns that there is presently little that clinicians and therapists have to offer autistic clients to help reduce auditory, tactile, and olfactory sensitivity. Sensory processing disorders in autism are common and are generally characterized by difficulties with processing the integration and management of internal and external sensory information, which then prevents adaptive functioning (Gabriels & Hill, 2007). Therapeutic work with the horse provides for the client an opportunity to discriminate between different stimuli and to learn how to center focus and practice self-regulation skills. Attention prioritization and disinhibition of extraneous stimuli are enhanced with the use of calming, relaxation, meditative, and self-hypnotic techniques practiced in relation to the horse. Some of the major critical processes that seem to be affected in autistic individuals can include vestibular (gravity and movement), proprioceptive (muscles and joints), and tactile (touch) senses along with vision and hearing. Many interventions can be used while on the horse's back to develop stronger and more accurate sensitivity and balance as well as build vestibular, tactile, and proprioceptive skills. It may be assumed not only that the neural centers coordinating these sensory and behavioral connections become better developed but also that the learning centers in the brain also become increasingly developed with continued practice and application. Not only can IPET be used to work with the social symptoms on the autistic spectrum, but the equine involvement helps also to address the cognitive and behavioral symptoms as well as the neurological symptoms.

Before proceeding to the description of various treatment paradigms, it is important to review what is integral to the social, psychological, and neurological adjustment of autistic individuals. Primary to all autistic function is the anxiety that evolves as a consequence of the autist's social experience of being *different*. Disruption of attachment is at the core of what generates this anxiety. Connection to oneself, others, and a horse reduces anxiety tremendously. Selective, prioritized focus also reduces anxiety, but with autistic individuals we want to transpose that inward regressive focus to a connecting focus with any aspect of the world outside of themselves. Psychological and emotional–social connection with the horse, when effectively achieved, decreases anxiety and increases a sense of confidence and competency, that is, one's own sense of being effective and powerful (Figure 5.4).

The development of the connection proceeds at the autist's pace. Great efforts, using many IPET-derived techniques, are made to facilitate social communication and behavioral interaction that create an intense and empowering connection between client and horse. Increments of success in their relationship serve to increase motivation and confidence in both the client and horse. These social achievements—cooperative join-up, intense bonding, and interpersonal skills—are then translated to the autist's relationships with people. Considering the hallmark symptoms of individuals with autism, a number of goals are essential to a healthier autistic adjustment and are the focus of therapy. These include the development of friendship and relationship skills, the management of emotions and impulses, the promotion of social understanding of self

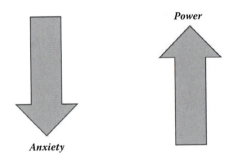

Power

Anxiety

FIGURE 5.4 Social interaction and communication with others. From Edwards, S., *A Clinical Model for Equine Psychotherapeutic Assessment, Intervention, and Treatment*, 2011.

in the context of others, becoming aware of how nonverbal behavior is perceived by others, the development of empathy and social skills that communicate interest in others, and, finally, the constructing of social and occupational applications for an autist's special intense interest in a particular subject. All IPET therapeutic interventions work toward reducing fear, anxiety, and frustration and increasing interpersonal mastery and effectiveness. Therapeutic work also focuses on individuals' ability to recognize their autistic differences and the implications of their differences. As part of the cognitive-behavioral work, social stratagems are learned through work-out situations with the horse so that relying on learned interpersonal skills and tools is chosen over withdrawal or retreat.

Treatment Paradigms for Autistic and Attachment Dysfunction

The autist's escape, whether it be relating exclusively with oneself or simply intrapersonally traveling away from the external world and interpersonal interaction, is an indulgence that causes considerable social awkwardness and *dysfunctional behavior* as perceived by others. This *autistic bubble* may serve many purposes for the autist but appears frequently in response to anxiety over perceived differentness and sensory overload and results in a lack of confidence and a sense of inadequacy in social situations.

Therapeutic Work With the Herd

Our initial work in IPET is to provide a peaceful place that autists are comfortable to retreat to, and one which is not full of anxiety or sensory overload. We let the client enter our horse herd by meeting one horse at a time, spending considerable time sitting in the pasture absorbing the social situation, and defining their experience in their own words. Clients are encouraged to recognize stimuli as perceived with the template of identifying, discriminating between, and prioritizing so that stimuli and sensation can be attended to independently without the effects of flooding. We have a herd of five horses that live in harmony and exist in a quiet, wooded hillside setting. In attempts to minimize horse neuroses we have created an established social network that replicates as close as possible a *normal* herd structure in the wild. This herd situation can be applied for learning with any individual or group system. Autistic clients experience a peaceful place beyond their internal world and a sense of kindred energy with the horses. If left to their own devices, horses naturally prefer a quiet, not overly stimulated world. Clients are encouraged to identify how they want to be part of the herd. With this sensory immersion there now exists a retreat that is peaceful and healing, and the client is in control of processing stimuli, one perception and sensation at a time. We build this as a cognitive and emotional perceptual template using sensory imagery so that the comfort and connection experienced with the horse herd can be a resource, employing visual and other sensory imagery, they can bring back to themselves cognitively at any time. This template also brings with it a retrieval of the confidence they have developed while processing and managing stimulus information with the horse herd. This recollection helps them refocus and more effectively manage stimuli processing in and out of therapy situations.

This process also provides an imagined retreat with the self-comforting attributes not unlike the *autistic bubble*; however, this retreat is not a bubble of isolation. The client is taught to be in control of his or her imagery, gaining the skills, peace, and the connection the client needs. He or she becomes a connected part of a nonthreatening social group and identifies each horse's role in the herd and what behaviors are expected from these roles. A widening comprehension of social cooperativeness and interpersonal behavior becomes nonthreatening and meaningful when the client increases his or her understanding of the horses' social and inter- and intrapersonal world. Gradual and guided recognition of how this relates to human social situations and the client's inter- and intrapersonal world is developed. The horse herd starts to become a social template to which the client can refer to better understand his or her own social world.

At this point the client is ready to work on social process and behavior. We use the horse herd as a model society that the client can learn from to understand the doctrines of social relatedness. These doctrines can then be translated to the client's own social world. We begin by introducing the concept of roles and defining the purpose of roles in a society (i.e., roles give information about what kinds of behavior individuals can expect from each other). We define the concept of *focus—other, self,* and *introject*—and identify the components of *influence* and *affiliation* while observing the interactions between the horses and their social group. Interpersonal dynamics (Figure 5.2) are identified and explored, not only among the horses but also between the client and the horses and again relating this to the client's world. The horse herd can be used as a model to explore social issues in other social groups (e.g., family, friends, work groups). The client explores how horses *join up* (Roberts, 1997) and speculates on each horse's *contract* with the others. Horses have *relationship contracts*, which are agreements among themselves that define the behavioral rules given their roles, and the *interpersonal behavioral tools of negotiation* (Edwards, 2011), which they use to manage each of their relationships.

The client is encouraged to reflect on each horse's experience in the herd as a whole as well as in each relationship, thereby increasing empathy and an understanding of an other's experience. At this time distinctions are clarified in terms of interpersonal versus intrapersonal communication, followed by speculation on the social and personal effectiveness of these communications. The client is asked to recognize how the horses share space, how they create and respect boundaries, and the underlying negotiations of their relationships that create and maintain their interactional niches of connection and independence in their shared space. The client is encouraged to evaluate what behaviors are successful and should be repeated versus what behaviors do not work well and should be extinguished, not only in the horses' world but also in reflection to situations of the client's social world.

Therapeutic Work With Individual Horse on Ground

After weeks of working with the herd, with psychotherapy sessions taking place sitting in the pasture among the herd of horses, the client is ready to progress to working on a relationship between him- or herself with and one of the horses. Careful selection of which horse the client will work with is determined based on their interpersonal style and needs as well as what the client has learned about each individual horse and the client's own particular therapeutic needs. Before any relationship work can begin, both the horse and client must be *in agreement* (Edwards, 2011) to work together. Horses involved in IPET are trained to communicate responses and choices in a respectful way, since their communicated experiences are essential to unveil the inner conflicts, strengths, and psychological workings of each client. Horse–client choice must be mutual. The horses at IPET are trained specifically to encourage expressed reaction to the client's behavior and affect. The process of *joining up* (Roberts, 1997) and *relationship choice* (Edwards, 2011) introduces many variables that need to be processed therapeutically. The client is now not only an observer of the horse's processes but is also an active participant of the relationship and its development.

After a horse is chosen, the client and therapist approach the horse. First there is the initial mutual greeting and investigation, and then the client makes a request (Edwards, 2011) for the horse to work with them. If the horse is in agreement (cooperative initiative join-up behavior; Edwards, 2011; Roberts, 1977), the horse is haltered and brought by lead rope out of the pasture to work with the client with assistance from the therapist. If the horse is not agreeable, then the client needs to look at his or her behavior and attempt further communication until the horse is comfortable leaving the pasture to work with them. This always illuminates important issues that the client needs to be aware of and to work on therapeutically. Following a session of *grooming, touching, sharing air, and sensing* each other, the next sessions deal with *lead rope negotiation* (Edwards, 2011). Lead rope negotiation is an IPET intervention that provides a visual and tactile representation of how interpersonal communications transpire and feel. This heightens the client's awareness of the potential impact of his or her behavior and the impact of others' behavior on him or her while her or she is a participant in interpersonal interactions. These concrete physical representations of interpersonal dynamics are very helpful to all clients and particularly to autists.

The essence of the following sessions is the building of the client–horse relationship: working on connection, *focus*, space and boundaries, roles, interpersonal negotiation, interpersonal consciousness (sensitivity and responsiveness), establishing a contract, and processing the client's intrapersonal relationship in juxtaposition with the development, and processing of his or her interpersonal relationship with the horse. All relationship development and negotiation is structured with the interpersonal components of *influence, affiliation,* and the recognition and understanding of these dynamics.

With constant recognition of dysfunctional interactions, analyses are made of ineffective behavior, and then corrective behavioral strategies are created and used. Effective behavior is always rewarded by a deeper connection with the horse in ensuing endeavors. Both client and horse feel more proficient with their collective efforts and more powerful in their independent contributions.

The stimulus processing and management skills are especially important to work with as the client and horse are developing their contractual relationship. The client can use various physical cues from the horse but must differentiate each stimulus and prioritize which ones to attend to by being responsive to the horse's reactions and behavioral cues. Specific physical features of the horse can also be used to trigger and practice responses in the client. The client also learns how disadvantageous it is to not respond and to ignore informational cues from the horse. This is paramount for interpersonal effectiveness with humans.

These practices are continued as the client and horse learn to walk together through different environments, do lunging work together, ride together through different surroundings, and navigate obstacles together in both walking and riding challenges. Many features come into play in the progression of this work. For example, walking challenges highlight spatial issues, boundaries, and assertive as opposed to dominating behavior. The lunging work builds on the prior but amplifies the demand on focus, relationship balance, cooperation, recommunication, and stimuli prioritization.

Therapeutic Work With Individual Horse Riding

Riding is all about developing a more intimate social and physical connection between client and horse. Social interpersonal awareness with behavioral adjustment and balance are paramount. As Hempfling (2001) expounds, it is about not only a person's responsibility to balance on the horse but also the horse's responsibility to balance the person as well. Interpersonal join-up, balance, cooperative effort, and accountability and responsibility are developed with riding. No saddles or bits are used so that responsive behavior can continuously be negotiated between horse and client. Clients do not ride a horse unless the horse agrees to it. The horse is an equal contributor to the relationship and is used not as an object to work on but rather as an individual to respond to and work with. All riding takes place with the therapist supervising and interpreting the interactions between horse and client. Once alignment, balance, reliable communication, and a trusting connection (Edwards, 2011) are achieved through these challenges, the horse and client are offered sessions of increasing complexity in which they need to work through problem-solving confrontations on rides or walks on nature trails. Autists work on *not* avoiding difficult situations and instead are taught how to construct *recipes* (Edwards, 2011) and stratagems for creating their own unique way to work through challenging situations.

Progression through these stages of therapy increases the client's sense of competency through continual recognition of success, while simultaneously the connection between client and horse becomes extremely strong and reliable. These experiences and this confidence may then be transferred to the client's relationships with people.

Interwoven into the aforementioned therapies are two additional therapeutic tracks. Therapeutic work on sensory processing integration, management, and coordination is done while the client rides the horse. Work-out sessions that build focus and refocusing skills are paired with imagery that can be used as an effective tool outside of therapy. It is postulated that these activities that coordinate different sensory modalities and demand cognitive and behavioral responses may serve to build stronger learning centers in the brain that can then be applied to new situations.

Another important track consists of clients learning their own meditative and self-hypnotic script, which they practice and use to help them manage anxiety, fear, and frustration and thereby learn to self-regulate their nervous systems. The infinite sensory imagery and the client's connection with the horse make these scripts powerfully effective.

Family therapy is also very important in that it potentiates the success of behavioral change and is an essential resource for clients to progress with their behavioral adjustments. Working in conjunction with school programs and teachers for school-age children is also imperative. Lastly, a very important part of our treatment program is group work, which all clients are recommended to progress to and is extremely important for social support and further independent therapeutic progress.

Application

The therapeutic work that can be done using IPET with individuals suffering from attachment issues and falling within the diagnostic symptom spectrum for autism is near limitless and can be used in conjunction with any underlying psychological theoretical approach. To demonstrate its effectiveness and application, a brief anecdote on client progress and a case study are presented. Names have been altered to protect confidentiality.

A family came to our office seeking help for their daughter, who was experiencing difficulty in her grieving process for a deceased family member. As their daughter progressed in therapy, they mentioned concern for their son Kurth,* who was being treated for Attention-Deficit/Hyperactivity Disorder (ADHD) with medication (Adderall and Focalin). Kurth presented symptoms of agitation, fear, and alienation and was distracted with extreme separation anxiety and panic. He lived in a bubble of anxiety that only his mother and, to a lesser extent, his family were allowed to penetrate. Kurth's clinical presentation was more indicative of and consistent with an autistic process rather than one of attention deficit. Medications were removed to gain a more accurate clinical picture. Kurth was diagnosed with Pervasive Developmental Disorder–Not Otherwise Specified (PDDNOS), and to rule out any medical and organic factors, he was referred to a nearby medical center specializing in childhood developmental disorders. Kurth's evaluation validated PDDNOS, and there was no evidence of an organic contribution. Accurate diagnosis was pivotal for Kurth's progress in therapy and life. Kurth's fear and anxiety were so extreme that he was unable to go anywhere other than school without his mother, and even that was difficult. He was isolated from his peers, irritable and manipulative with his family, and barely able to function at school. His mother was protective of Kurth, whereas his father

---

* Names have been changed to protect client confidentiality.

was overwhelmed by his behavior. The whole family was compromised by Kurth's condition, despite their dedication and commitment to him.

Kurth had an immediate reaction to the horse herd. He discovered an innate sense of peace and spent a considerable amount of time sitting and watching the horses interact. After doing therapeutic work with his individual horse, of whom he was initially terrified, Kurth enjoyed sitting and absorbing the peace he felt with the herd. It was a slow and progressive process for him to recognize anything outside himself and his constant state of anxiety. Kurth was compelled to work beyond his anxiety as his connection with his horse grew. Within 5 months of therapy, Kurth was off all medication and was using self-hypnotic meditative techniques practiced with the horse to effectively self-regulate his nervous system. Kurth to date is still not using any psychotropic medication, has broken out of his panic and anxiety, and since his first year in therapy has been able to start going places and experience more things. He has gone to camps, performed vocally, changed schools, traveled on extended school trips, and held a paying job.

Kurth has worked for 3 years with IPET and has built strong social skills and a keen sense of social awareness. He has achieved increased confidence and is now mainstreamed in his high school. He has traveled on class trips and attends most school events. Kurth's current challenge is to "notice when I'm losing people when I talk about things I am interested in and to be able to change my conversation so that I don't seem like I'm not normal." Kurth initially worked with one horse but has now worked with every horse in the herd, taking on difficult issues with each and always attempting more advanced challenges. He works not only on interpersonal behavior with the horse but also on strengthening his ability to focus, to be distracted, and then to refocus while riding the horse and negotiating many difficult challenges and obstacles. Kurth continues to work on his ability to maintain continued focus, to recognize when he loses it, and also to recognize learned social cues to reapply his attention.

To overcome his sensory problems, Kurth has worked on cognitive and physical connections in response to physical cues from the horse. This work has helped decrease visual motor delays, strengthen motor skills, and develop those cognitive learning centers that were formerly less developed. With continued challenges and confidence built from repeated successes, there remain very few situations Kurth is unable to attempt to work through. His family has diligently worked in IPET with Kurth, and due to their dedication in family systems work there have been major transitions in the family dynamics for Kurth's role to become more independent. Kurth currently works in individual and group psychotherapy. He is a role model and leader for his group, which is composed of other successful autists. In individual therapy Kurth continues to work on social connectedness as well as redefining his interpersonal presence and behavior so that he "seems normal" and does not stand out as uncomfortably different. Kurth is well liked by others and in mastering his negotiation skills is working toward deeper relationships. Kurth is learning to drive and continues to work on his competence in school and his job. He has a special education teacher who has worked collaboratively and most effectively with his therapeutic work with the horses and has significantly supported his academic success. Kurth now experiences very little anxiety and sees his fears as a challenge to work through with the support from his relationships with horses and people, using the strategic tools he has gained from his work in therapy. Being less socially isolated than ever before, Kurth states, "I really like where I am now and I never want to go back to that place where I was again."

It is unlikely Kurth would be as successful in his therapeutic work had his therapy not involved therapeutic work with horses. It was his desire to connect with the horses in a powerful way that motivated him to work so hard. Without his sensing the peace in their world, he may not have found the motivation to find his own peace and success, now and in the future. Without interacting with the horses and working through social negotiations with them, he may not have been as competent socially as he now is.

References

American Psychiatric Association. (APA). (1994). *Diagnostic and statistical manual of mental disorders*, 4th ed., text revision. Arlington, VA: Author.

Attwood, T. (2008). *The complete guide to Asperger's syndrome*. Philadelphia, PA: Jessica Kingsley Publishers.

Dawson, D., & Levy, A. (1989). Arousal, attention, and the socio-emotional impairments of individuals with autism. In G. Dawson (Ed.), *Autism: Nature, diagnosis, and treatment* (pp. 49–74). New York: Guilford Press.

Edwards, S., & Snowdon, C. (1980). Social behavior of captive, group-living orang-utans. *International Journal of Primatology, 1*(1), 39–62.

Edwards, S. (1982). Social potential expressed in captive group living orang-utans. In L.E.M. De Boer (Ed.), *The orang-utan: Its biology and conservation*. The Hague, The Netherlands: W. Junk.

Edwards, S. D. (2011). *Interpersonal equine therapy (IPET): A clinical model for equine psychotherapeutic assessment, intervention, and treatment*. Unpublished manuscript.

Gabriels, R.L., & Hill, D. A. (2007). *Growing up with autism: Working with school-age children and adolescents*. New York: Guilford Press.

Grandin, T. (1996). *Thinking in pictures: And other reports from my life with autism.* New York: Vintage.

Grandin, T., & Johnson, C. (2004). *Animals in translation: Using the mysteries of autism to decode animal behavior.* New York: Scribner.

Harlow, H. F., & Suomi, S. J. (1971). Social recovery by isolation-reared monkeys. Proceedings of the National Academy of Science of the United States of America.

Hempfling, K. F. (2001). *Dancing with horses.* North Pomfret, VT: Trafalgar Square Books.

Leary, T. (1957). *Interpersonal diagnosis of personality.* New York: Ronald Press.

Roberts, M. (1997). *The man who listens to horses.* New York: Random House.

Robison, J. E. (2008). *Look me in the eye: My life with Asperger's.* New York: Three Rivers Press.

Smith-Benjamin, L. S. (1974). Structural analysis of social behavior (SASB). *Psychological Review, 81,* 392–425.

Sullivan, H. (1953). *The interpersonal theory of psychiatry.* New York: Norton.

Szatmari, P. (2004). *A mind apart: Understanding children with autism and Asperger syndrome.* New York: Guilford Press.

Tammet, D. (2006). *Born on a blue day: Inside the extraordinary mind of an autistic savant.* New York: Free Press.

Techniques That Focus on Social Skills and Communication

☐ Out of the Starting Gate: A Practical First Approach to Equine Assisted Activities

Beverley Kane

Introduction

This chapter presents both a general and an activity-specific approach to conducting equine assisted group activities. For those of you new to this work, it offers some general remarks about the initial setting and kick-off stage of your program. It then introduces an outline for preparing, implementing, and processing an equine assisted activity. This template is a practical way of organizing our team's thoughts and coordinating our efforts. For those of you well seasoned in this work, the description format has proven especially useful for conducting programs with cofacilitators who have not previously worked together. It provides a focal point for getting everyone synchronized on expectations for how the activity will run. The activity outline also provides organizing principles for new activities as you conceive of and experiment with them. At the end of the essay, there is a sample activity that follows the outline. The activity is drawn from *The Manual of Medicine and Horsemanship—Transforming the Doctor–Patient Relationship With Equine-Assisted Learning*, Version 2.0, a Stanford Medical School-based equine assisted learning (EAL) curriculum for medical students and health-care professionals (Kane, 2011).

The Welcome Area

From the first moment the clients arrive at the barn, the tone is set for the group session. Tone makes as much of an impression as content. Good content cannot make up for poor tone. Many of your clients will never have been in a ranch environment. They might feel a sense of strangeness, even if on some level it feels better to be out in nature than in a classroom, clinic, or office. The sights and smells of horses (and horse droppings), although second nature and even pleasant to us horse people, might take some getting used to on the part of your clients.

What will your clients see and feel as they enter the space? Will they feel welcomed by beverages and snacks and flowers and a clean barn? Or will they be dismayed by manure, dusty chairs, and loose fence boards with nails sticking out? The convocation area should be welcoming and temperate—not too hot, not too cold. You may need to have on hand extra hats and sunscreen for the heat and sweatshirts, jackets, and blankets for cold and wind. A friendly, relaxed facilitator or course assistant should be there to greet clients as they arrive and to offer refreshments, hand out the syllabus, collect release forms, and answer questions.

Opening Ceremonies

Opening ceremonies suggests the Olympic Games and the idea of official beginnings. At several points throughout the session, we emphasize the ceremonial nature of human interactions. The formalities associated with communication rituals include proper introduction, proper conduct in the dynamics of the transaction, and proper closure. We are reminded of the subtle complexities of the Japanese tea ceremony, in which something otherwise commonplace and mundane—making tea—follows a proper protocol and assumes a sacred significance. Horses appreciate and are more relaxed with consistent rituals and routines for grooming, leading, and tacking up.

We arrange ourselves in a circle. Circles are containers for energy, a symbol of wholeness, and a uniform shape without the quadrangular heads and sides indicative of power positions in a boardroom. Circles for dancing, powwows, and religious initiations are universal across many cultures. There should be no empty chairs in the circle. If an expected participant is a no-show, remove that chair and bring the circle closer together. The story of Carla and Maci is in part a parable about the importance of the integrity of the circle.

The introductions segment that includes, optionally, clients' names, their reasons for joining the group, and their past associations with horses, is the icebreaker. A collection of strangers is sitting in each other's company. Those without previous horse experience and those who are psychologically introverted are apt to be the most apprehensive and reserved during opening ceremonies. Many times these reticent people are those for whom the lure of EAL barely overcomes the fear factor.

The principal facilitators introduce themselves, their introduction acting as an example of the type of information solicited and the length of time each person needs to take. Cofacilitators are introduced next. It is a good idea to specifically ask individuals what their previous experience is with horses. That way you can gauge how much time to spend on preliminaries with the horses and how comfortable each person is likely to be with the exercises.

Horse Activities Overview

The best sessions and workshops maximize time with the horses and minimize time spent on nonexperiential modalities such as reading, writing, and theoretical discussion. The latter activities dominate our lives. Equine experiential learning offers a balancing counterpoint to our generally overwrought intellectual patterns of functioning. In our workshops with medical students, note taking is discouraged. We emphasize an experiential approach that honors each experience phenomenologically, in real time, not as a recorded entity. We trust that each experience is sufficiently embedded in and retrievable from consciousness without a written record.

Especially for the benefit of clients without horse experience, activities with the horses progress in a stepwise manner from simple approach-and-touch to more complex hands-on tasks. Approaching a horse for the first time is an awesome experience for many people. Each horse activity must include ample time for discussion. This after-action review, to use a military term, is introduced by the facilitator's thoughtful choice of open-ended questions. It is essential to continue observing the behavior of the horses during the discussion period. Horses will often react to the tone and energetics of the discussion by behaviors such as drawing near, acting out, licking and chewing in a relaxed fashion, or selecting a particular individual to nudge or nuzzle. These behaviors are significant and should be treated as additional information for the activity.

In our experience, some of the most valuable learning comes from the horses' behavior during processing. One conjecture for why this is so is that the activities are contrived situations based on sometimes elaborate instructions and rules. When the structured portion of the activity has ended and we come out of our constraints to share and process, the horses are aware that we are more natural and real. We hear the word *authentic* used a lot. Horses respond to our *authentic* selves. So do not turn your backs on the horses during processing. Keep an eye out for what they are telling everyone as they return to their own authenticity when the charade is over.

Horse Activity Outline

Each activity has an infinite number of possible variations. Given the unpredictable and often surprising nature of working with horses, who haven't read the manual, many departures from Plan A and from "the best laid plans" are apparent only after they've begun to happen. Be prepared to come up with Plan B on the spot.

You will need to experiment with what fits with your style, your horses, your ranch facilities, and the type of clients in your group. You will need to err on the side of not overplanning, or at least of not being overly attached to your plans. You need to remain flexible and open to whatever spontaneous, unforeseen opportunities present themselves in the session. Sessions and workshops often have a life of their own—that is the beauty and the perennial freshness of this work.

Each activity description is divided into 10 parts as follows:

1. Activity type

2. Setup

3. Objective

4. Purpose

5. Metaphor

6. Procedure

7. Rules, violations, and consequences

8. Observations

9. Questions

10. Further discussion

Activity Type

Activities are *observational* or *hands-on, group* or *individual*. In observational activities, clients watch the facilitators or other clients interact with the horse. In hands-on activities, some or all of the group works with one or more horses. Some hands-on exercises are conducted with a client-to-horse ratio of 1:1. Some hands-on activities have as many as four clients working with one horse, and with some exceptions this ratio is generally as high as I will accept. Ideally, there is one facilitator per horse. This ratio goes from merely ideal to mandatory if no student in the group has experience with horses. There are benefits to all four kinds of activities, and you will want to balance them in your programs.

Ideally, the group maintains a unified focus even when only one client is assigned to work with the horse. However, what is most enriching for the individual tends to be least participatory, and therefore least interesting, for the rest of the group. The facilitator's challenge is to keep everyone engaged in each person's process. Not only is it polite to stay attentive, but also one of the few mishaps I have incurred in *Medicine and Horsemanship* happened when I neglected this principle, as described in this case example.

Case Example: Carla and Maci

It was toward the end of a long day in which I had tried to condense our 24-hour curriculum into an 8-hour pilot program at a new medical center. We were doing Uninformed Consent with a horse I'll call Maci, a young, slightly skittish quarter horse. Our group of eight medical students and house staff, two attending physicians, one veterinarian, and I were in a postprandial slump—that dull, sleepy state after lunch. The students were sitting on the railings of the round ring in pairs and threesomes.

Carla,* a first-year medical student, was having a difficult time trying to get Maci to venture across the spangly, flappy space blanket adorned with Mylar ribbons and a hot-pink wriggly feather boa. One person had the idea to cover the blanket with food to hide the reflections and tempt Maci. Two people left the round ring to get hay. In what seemed to be a hiatus in the activity, with two people out of the ring several side discussions broke out. I attempted to continue teaching yet had my back to Carla and Maci while speaking to the students on the fence. Suddenly, Carla yowled as Maci stomped on her foot.

Part of the cause of this mishap was the fact that the group no longer had a focus, and the horse and student pair was left outside the circle defined by me and the other students facing each other. (Remember, my back was to Carla.) Without the attentional support of the class, Carla was distracted from the task and lost her connection with Maci. If we had kept Carla and Maci in the circle with our focus on them, it is likely that Maci and Carla would have kept their attention on each other. Carla might have been more mindful of where she was in relation to Maci's feet.

Setup

The setup instructions indicate the size of space needed, the number of horses, and any special equipment or props required. It also describes the initial conditions of the activity, such as whether clients are in or out of the arena and whether the horses are tied. When time is at a premium or the layout involves a pattern of equipment whose set up by clients is not part of the activity, such as having clients build their own obstacle course, it's helpful to set up arenas before class.

Objective

The objective is the task that the clients are asked to accomplish. Examples are lead the horse around the arena, groom the horse, and pick up the horse's foot. In fact, accomplishing the objective is secondary to the self-awareness achieved in the process of getting to the goal. In EAL some clients require many sessions to accomplish a simple task such as haltering. The haltering itself is not the most important thing. The revelations about personal and interpersonal dynamics are more important.

---

* Names have been changed to protect identities.

Purpose

The purpose is the reason we pursue a particular objective. Some activities lend themselves to a particular objective more than others. We lead the horse so we become aware of our leadership styles. We ask a horse to do something scary so we develop compassion for our patients' fears. We longe or trot a horse to see how we convey intentionality and authority. We stage group activities to see how people behave on a team.

Metaphor

A metaphor is a description of one thing in terms of another unlike thing, often in a poetic or symbolic way. "All the world's a stage." "You are the sunshine of my life." "Med school is a hard row to hoe." Every *Medicine and Horsemanship* activity is designed to illustrate some aspect of patient care, particularly in regard to the doctor–patient relationship. In addition to the metaphors we provide, students are asked to recall metaphors and analogies from their own patient care experiences and even from their personal lives. Horses provide metaphors for patients because horses respond to us in ways that patients would like to but are too polite or well socialized to do. Corporate groups, couples, families, children—any client or participant—can draw their own metaphors from their personal and professional lives.

Procedure

Analogous to a lab experiment or research protocol, the procedural descriptions enable you to conduct the exercise even if you've never seen it. For many activities, you will want to add your own interpretation and variations.

Rules, Violations, and Consequence

Rules introduce both a real-life element and an element of play and humor to the activities. Life is a continual process of working around restrictions. Because the rules are somewhat arbitrary, the activities acquire the feel of a game. Lest anyone take himself too seriously, there is no harm in reminding the group they are there to have fun while they learn about themselves.

Most rules are stated as those things that clients are not allowed to do. By not phrasing rules as things they must do, clients should be freed from thinking there is only one way, or a few ways, to accomplish something. At some point it should occur to the clients that while there may be three or four things they cannot do, there is an infinite number of things they can do. For some exercises this means thinking literally outside the box. Do they go get some other tool or prop from outside the arena? Do they ask someone for information or help?

For some activities, the only rule is that the clients may not talk to each other. This requirement gives clients the opportunity to concentrate on the horse and on their emotions, intuitions, and physical sensations. Nonverbal interludes reinforce one of the main messages of the course and provide an instructive counterpoint to the intellectualizing and verbalizing that accompany most other aspects of life.

In the more contrived activities, breaking the rules may have consequences. Note that we do not use the word *punishment*. Clients can come up with their own consequences, or consequences can be assigned by the facilitators. Information about personal styles and personal integrity emerges from discussions about whether and how rules were violated. Often there is a difference of opinion about whether there has been a violation. Some clients easily admit to violations they may not have committed; some clients will deny or make excuses for violations that were witnessed by everyone else. It is not the facilitator's role to establish an "objective" truth in this situation but to facilitate the discussion and acknowledge the disparities in observations and interpretations.

Observations

Observations are, as much as possible, the objective descriptions of events and behaviors. Perfect objectivity is not possible to achieve. All observations are biased by subjective factors of mood, temperament, perception, and past experience, to name a few confounding factors.

In the observation step, we learn to say, "The horse pinned his ears when I came within five feet of him," instead of, "The horse was angry at me." The first statement is an observation. The latter statement is an interpretation. The distinction between an observation and interpretation is crucial for developing awareness of one's projections, biases, and misperceptions. Often it is the participant's inner critic that fails to distinguish what happened from what it might have meant. The most common response to horse behavior is to take it personally. "The horse doesn't like me" or "the horse is tired of me" is an understandable, but often mistaken, interpretation of nonspecific horse behavior, such as walking across the arena away from the client, that may have nothing to do with the human in proximity.

The chief role of the facilitators is to elicit observations about horse behavior. We frequently ask, "What is the horse doing now?" We provide our own observations if the clients are not forthcoming with what we think we observed. We must be open to the fact that even experienced facilitators have biased observations—what we think we saw may not have happened in quite the way we think we saw it.

In the postexercise processing, clients are asked to state their observations before facilitators do. As much as possible, observations should be elicited and not spoon fed. Many clients do not trust their own observations, especially of horse behaviors. When we ask questions like, "What did the horse do when Jason got in front of her?" we encourage students to speak up about subtle observations they may have dismissed. Interpretations become important at a later stage of discussion when we practice reading body language and trying to respond appropriately.

Questions

Much has been written on the psychology and techniques of asking questions (Leeds, 2000). The most important concept to remember is to ask questions from a place of curiosity and humility, not from a hunch about what might be going on with the client, much less a position of certitude about what the client needs (Rudolph, Simon, Dufresne, & Raemer, 2006). In the following activity, the Questions section suggests a few of the hundreds of possible questions to ask depending on each unique set of circumstances.

Questions can be saved for the discussion at the end of an exercise or may be asked at key points in the activity. There is always a tension between wanting to let the activity flow uninterrupted and wanting to make sure a remarkable horse behavior is not missed or forgotten. At Horsensei, we err on the side of calling attention to notable behaviors at the time they manifest.

Individuals in the group, whether hands-on with the horse or observing the hands-on person, should be asked about their experience of the exercise. In larger groups, this means keeping track of who has and has not spoken and inviting the latter to have their say. We alternate "going around the circle" type participation with random access opportunities to speak out. The former rota of questioning draws out both extreme introverts who may be reticent to speak and extreme extroverts whose attention has wandered outside the group. Be sure and ask the group if they have any questions of their own.

Discussion

Allow at least 20 minutes of discussion time at the end of every activity, 2 to 4 minutes per participant. Some activities may need a full hour to process. This time is for summary questioning about specific observations and reactions to the exercise as well as for spontaneous stream-of-consciousness conversations. Here again, introverts may need to be gently drawn out with a take-turns-around-the-circle question and answer format. At the end of each discussion period, we review and return to our metaphors, which in *Medicine and Horsemanship* are principles of patient care.

Sample Exercise from *Medicine and Horsemanship*

Uninformed Consent "White Coat Syndrome"— Dealing With a Patient's Fear

Type

Group observation, selected individuals hands-on. We have also conducted this activity with clients in teams of two to three.

Setup

One horse on a lead rope in an arena, round pen, or corral. A tarp or space blanket with a white coat and scary objects such as ribbons, streamers, or plastic bags.

Objective

To get the horse to quietly cross the tarp.

Purpose

To develop sensitivity to another person's fears.

Metaphor

Informed consent. Trying to educate, reassure, and convince a patient to undergo a frightening procedure, from a flu shot to open-heart surgery.

Procedure

A tarp or space blanket covered with other scary objects is laid out in the arena. One or more horses are asked, one at a time, to cross the tarp. Optionally, other scary objects might be laid out—a low jump festooned with fake plants, stuffed animals, streamers, or balloons. All clients are inside the arena, which should be large enough to accommodate the group. Time and group size permitting, each client will get a turn.

A variant, after everyone has taken a turn or if the group seems unusually restive, is to have one participant serve as chief resident, offering suggestions for the procedure. Another variant for larger groups entails having more than one horse in the arena. The next client in the arena might choose to work with another horse. A scared horse might follow, or imitate, a brave horse. This suggestion is not given; some students think of this tactic on their own.

Rules

Observers do not give advice until and unless asked by the client with the horse—however, facilitators do not mention this possibility.

Observations

- How does the client attempt to lead the horse over the tarp?

- Does the client look at the horse during attempts to lead the equine?

- How does the client acknowledge and work with the horse's fear?

- Does the client tug and tug against a horse that has its feet planted?

- Does the client give the horse respite from the scary thing?

- Does the client break the task down into smaller steps?

- Does the client pet the horse?

- Does the horse jump and pull?

- Do the whites of its eyes show?

- Does the horse sniff the tarp or show any other signs of curiosity?

Questions

- Ask about all the previous observations plus:

- What was your plan?

- What was the horse's response?

- Did the horse show any sign of getting closer to the goal?

Discussion

Patients are often afraid of even relatively noninvasive procedures, such as getting a flu shot. Many times their fears seem irrational to us. Some patients are phobic about needles, while others undergo open-heart surgery as if it were no more than a haircut. The white coat used for this exercise illustrates in a humorous way the condition called *white coat hypertension* or *white coat disease*. This blood pressure "disease" is caused by a white-coated professional, usually the doctor, who obtains higher blood pressure measurements than would be obtained by a nurse, medical assistant, or family member. Medical studies show that doctors in white coats can produce higher blood pressure readings than nonphysicians or non-white-coated nonphysicians (Helvaci & Seyhanli, 2006).

Two important principles of horsemanship apply to this exercise: (1) pressure and release; and (2) rewarding tiny steps toward the goal. Virtually all natural horsemanship practitioners, and many other trainers, vets, and farriers, use an approach-retreat or pressure-release strategy. This technique takes the horse to the point at which he or she becomes afraid, confused, or resistant and then allows him or her to retreat to the last place of comfort and understanding. Tiny steps made toward the goal are rewarded with release of pressure, relief from asking. Even if the horse merely looks at the tarp (or plastic bag or mailbox), he or she is rewarded.

This exercise reveals how comfortable clients are with being the type of leader who is more assertive and directive versus the more laissez-faire type who lets them make up their own mind. You may note that in every group there is at least one participant, and often many, who keep petting the horses to get the horse over the tarp. This generally has the effect of rewarding the horse for not going over the tarp and is usually counterproductive to achieving the goal. The best outcome from this tactic is the discussion that ensues over wanting to be liked versus respected, people pleasing, and whether making nice to a horse actually instills confidence and trust in our leadership.

The activity also reveals much about our patience with reluctant or noncompliant patients. How far are we each willing to go, in number of visits or level of assertiveness, before we give up on the patient? What does giving up look like? Do we cease to recommend follow-up visits? Do we refer the patient to a specialist or another practitioner? Do we stress out and burn out trying to get all patients to do what we believe is in their best interest?

Resources

Many repertories of horse activities can be found in the *Manual of Medicine and Horsemanship*, the Equine Assisted Growth and Learning Association (EAGALA) training manual, the EAGALA quarterly magazine *EAGALA in Practice*, and many EAC centers such as Horse Sense of the Carolinas (2007). You will soon devise your own unique activities and hopefully give back to the field of EAC by sharing your creative ideas with colleagues at conferences, in professional papers, and in online discussion groups such as maintained by the Equine Facilitated Mental Health Association (EFMHA), a part of Professional Association of Therapeutic Horsemanship International (PATHI).

References

Equine Assisted Growth and Learning Association (EAGALA). (2006). *Fundamentals of EAGALA model practice*: *UNtraining Manual* (5th ed). Santaquin, UT: Author.

Equine Facilitated Mental Health Association (EFMHA). (2010). *EFMHA Open listserve*. Retrieved from: http://health.groups.yahoo.com/group/EFMHA-Open/?yguid=252596338

Helvaci, M. R., & Seyhanli, M. (2006). What a high prevalence of white coat hypertension in society! *Intern Medicine, 45*(10), 671–4.

Horse Sense of the Carolinas. (2007). *Curricula & program manuals: Help you can use, programs your community needs*. Retrieved from: http://www.horsesensebusiness.com/products/curricula-and-program-manuals

Kane, B. (2007). *The manual of medicine and horsemanship—Transforming the doctor-patient relationship with equine-assisted learning*, version 2.0. (2011). Bloomington, IN: AuthorHouse.

Leeds, D. (2000). *The 7 powers of questions: Secrets to successful communication in life and at work*. New York: Perigee Trade.

Rudoph, J. W., Simon, R., Dufresne, R. L., & Raemer, D. B. (2006). There's no such thing as "nonjudgmental" debriefing: A theory and method for debriefing with good judgment. *Simulation in Healthcare, 1*(1), 49–55.

☐ Equine Assisted Counseling With Deaf Families

Karen A. Tinsley and Holly Jedlicka

Introduction

Equine assisted counseling (EAC) is a treatment approach that provides experiential-based counseling services to individuals, groups, and families as they interact in the presence of one or more horses. A licensed clinician and an equine specialist cofacilitate the session and set up structured activities according to clients' established treatment goals. The activities are designed to elicit feelings, behaviors, and interactions that can then be processed therapeutically. The presence of the horse adds a unique variable into the already established family dynamic.

Horses are large prey animals that are environmentally sensitive and intuitive herd animals. When horses are introduced to a session, they join the family dynamic. As with all family members, even when they disengage by walking to the opposite side of the arena, the horse is reacting to what is happening among the client and family members. As the family struggles to work together to complete the assigned activity, family members are skillfully awakened by the therapeutic team to metaphors between arena and home, patterns of behavior and communication, and feelings within the individual and between family members. Future sessions provide the opportunity to learn, practice, and change how the family chooses to interact with one another or function as a unit.

PBJ Connections, Inc., has been providing EAC services to youth and their families since 2007. One of the populations served is the Deaf Community (the use of capitalization for the words *Deaf, Deaf Culture,* and *Hard of Hearing* is a common practice within the literature to indicate an identification and affiliation with a group of individuals that encompasses more than just the audiological presentation), including families that consist of one or more Deaf members. The number of Deaf families seeking counseling services from a nonspecialized provider would be inherently low and would create a small clinical *footprint* on the typical mental health provider. For PBJ Connections to deliberately seek out and serve this population, the programmatic impact has been profound. As they soon learned, the knowledge base required to provide accessible and culturally affirmative services to this population is rich and multidimensional, thus affording a unique opportunity for professional and personal development throughout the agency. Through a grant and collaborative efforts between PBJ Connections and St. Vincent Family Centers, EAC has been made accessible to an otherwise underserved population.

Rationale

In 2006, the National Center for Health Statistics estimated that 37 million Americans had some form of hearing loss. Half of those individuals were under age 65 (Mitchell & Karchmer, 2004). The rubella epidemic in the mid 1960s produced an estimated 20,000 infants with deafness, deaf-blindness, or other additional congenital problems. Those children are now in their mid to late 40s; approximately one-third were in supported living environments due to their multiple disabilities (O'Donnell, 1995). The latest report from the Gallaudet Research Institute indicates there are approximately 38,000 children under the age of 21 with a hearing loss. Of those children, 42% have a severe to profound level of hearing loss (60 dB or greater); 46% have additional disabilities such as mental retardation, developmental disabilities, emotional disturbances, or attention-deficit/hyperactivity disorder (ADHD); and 72% of those children do not have family members who sign regularly. Despite those sobering statistics, only 10% are receiving any counseling services (GRI, 2006).

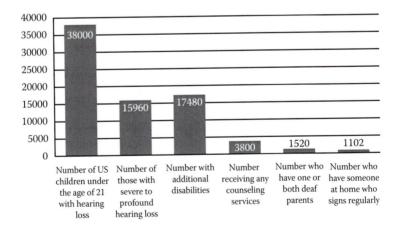

FIGURE 6.1 Demographics of youth under 21 years of age, 2005–2006.

As a low-incidence population, the National Institute on Deafness and Other Communication Disorders (NIDCD, 2006) acknowledges the difficulty in getting funding for and conducting sound clinical research on a population that is so heterogeneous, statistically small, and regionally scattered. Deaf and Hard of Hearing individuals have historically been underserved, particularly in the areas of mental health (Vernon & Leigh, 2007). In a recent report on mental health needs in Ohio, Deaf and Hard of Hearing focus group participants rated the mental health service system as *fair* in meeting their needs. They cited a combination of factors—prohibitive costs, limited support or treatment options, regional disparity, and lack of signing professionals—as major barriers to accessing mental health services (Multiethnic Advocates for Cultural Competence, 2006).

In an effort to reach this underserved population, PBJ Connections, a nonprofit organization providing EAC to youth and families, was awarded a grant to provide EAC sessions to families having one or more Deaf or Hard of Hearing members. The services took place near Columbus, Ohio, with referrals identified from St. Vincent Family Center's Deaf Services Program. Participation was voluntary and considered an adjunct to already existing mental health services. The delivery of EAC services to youth and families with one or more Deaf or Hard of Hearing members is discussed, with recommendations for creating culturally competent services.

The use of animals to facilitate therapy has been well documented (Frewin & Gardiner, 2005). Horses have a unique contribution as a herd animal; they are social beings, which interact according to an established social hierarchy. Through primarily nonverbal communication they are able to indicate a wide range of emotional states, including displeasure, fear, curiosity, anger, contentment, and playfulness. Horses have an intuitive sensitivity toward their environment, be it on the open range, in a show arena, or in their own stall. As prey animals, sight, sound, touch, taste, and smell are all sources of information for horses to maintain their primary goal—safety. What has become increasingly evident among EAC clinicians is the effective way horses sense and react to humans in a therapeutic context.

As humans, we censor our responses and even contradict ourselves between verbal and nonverbal expressions. Horses seem to sense this ambiguity, which can facilitate a more honest therapeutic dialogue between clinician and client. Horses can also serve as a blank canvas for projected thoughts and feelings. A horse may serve to represent a difficult person in clients' lives, or they may be the one "family member" who shows interest in clients. Family dynamics get recreated in the arena, where the horse's behavior serves as a catalyst for interactions. Individuals may become adept at "saying what the clinician wants to hear," but within the arena behaviors often illuminate the true dynamic of the family. It has been reported that a few EAC sessions can provide a wealth of clinical *material* that normally takes months to access in a traditional counseling session (Ewing, MacDonald, Taylor, & Bowers, 2007; Kersten, 2010; Mann & Williams, 2007; Myers, 2004).

Standards of practice require the use of a licensed clinical professional and an equine specialist (ES) who have received training in EAC (Kersten, 2007; EAGALA, 2010).* Typically, the client or family is given instructions for a task they must try to carry out successfully within the arena with one or more horses. For example, the family may have to work together to get a selected horse over a 1-foot jump. The caveat is they may not bribe the horse, touch the horse, or speak to each other. The goal is not horsemanship skills or riding. The goal is to be able to experience the activity and use events as a catalyst toward becoming aware of established patterns within the family and achieving therapeutic goals. *Who gives up? Who gets angry? How do the individuals interact? How does the horse react to their attempts?* The EAC clinician continues to practice in whatever theoretical approach they subscribe to, such as Gestalt, cognitive-behavioral, existential, or Adlerian psychotherapy. The arena session allows the EAC clinician to peel back the curtain on the family dynamics. Meanwhile, the equine specialist focuses on the horse's behavior and contributes observations that are in concert with the therapeutic goals. Although the primary focus of the ES is the safety of all participants around the horses as well as the physical and emotional wellbeing of the horse, the ES and EAC clinician should be able to work in harmony toward the therapeutic goals.

In addition to individual and family therapy sessions, EAC has been used with juvenile offenders; combat veterans; lesbian, bisexual, transgender, and gay (LBGT) youth; inpatient psychiatric and substance abuse programs; and social skills development programs (Frewin & Gardiner, 2005; Kersten, 2010). Although EAC has been used with Deaf and Hard of Hearing individuals, there has yet to be any documented study of this population receiving EAC.

Description

In an effort to provide EAC to Deaf and Hard of Hearing individuals, PBJ Connections was able to collaborate with the Deaf Services Program

---

* Editor's note: This book does not endorse any specific model. References to any treatment or therapy model or to any program, service, or treatment are solely the views and opinions of the authors.

of St. Vincent Family Centers, a community mental health center in Columbus, Ohio. The families that participated were already receiving services to address behavioral and emotional issues for one or more of their children. PBJ Connections was able to offer an adjunct service with the intent of enhancing those existing services through a cooperative effort of service delivery. The goal was to give a visually and nonverbally oriented group of individuals the chance to explore, practice, and apply more effective strategies of interpersonal communication among family members. Families were recruited voluntarily through their existing therapist or case manager at the Deaf Services Program (DSP).

Families were given the opportunity to attend 10 sessions, 1 hour per week, every other week. The session was facilitated by a licensed social worker and an equine specialist, following the EAGALA model of EAP. American Sign Language interpreters were provided by DSP or were privately contracted by PBJ Connections. The referring DSP clinician was invited to observe but not participate in sessions, with the goal of providing support and carryover outside of the sessions. Transportation assistance was provided for families in need, either through DSP staff or taxi service. PBJ Connections' EAC clinician was invited to monthly team meetings with DSP staff, to review progress, and to discuss any concerns. At the end of the program, families attended a closure event.

Families were administered the Achenbach System of Empirically Based Assessment (ASEBA) forms, including the Child Behavior Checklist (CBC), the Youth Self-Report (YSR), the Adult Self-Report (ASR), the Adult Behavior Checklist (ABC), and the Teacher Report Form (TRF) pre- and postservice delivery. The choice to use the ASEBA was based on already established practices of St. Vincent Family Center, which had previously selected this tool for agency-wide use and with consideration for their Deaf Services Program clients. St. Vincent Family Center also agreed to facilitate the scoring of data.

In an effort to promote cultural competency and forge interagency collaboration, the Deaf Services Program was invited to actively participate as a *family* in a 1-hour introductory EAC session at PBJ Connections. By experiencing EAC firsthand, DSP clinicians were better prepared to support their clients and families, and DSP interpreters were given a chance to experience and gain context for what they would later be interpreting. PBJ Connections' staff participated in a 2-hour Deaf Culture/ASL orientation to educate them on proper use of an interpreter, basic signs, and cultural norms.

A total of 12 families completed the intake process through St. Vincent Family Center, which included administration of the ASEBA facilitated by a DSP clinician or PBJ Connections' program director. Two families were included that were not receiving services from the Deaf Services Program, and they used the Ohio Youth Problem, Functioning, and Satisfaction Scales for a measurement tool. Two families delayed services for 1 month due to health issues, and two other families dropped out before beginning sessions. During the 5-month period, 12 families were seen, which included a total of 20 youth. Eight of the families had Deaf or Hard of Hearing parents with Hearing children, and four families had Hearing parents with Deaf or Hard of Hearing children.

It was not surprising that there were no families with both Deaf parents and Deaf children represented, as statistically this is found in only 4% of the Deaf Community (Mitchell & Karchmer, 2004). Ages of the children ranged from 7 to 19 years old. Four families did not complete the 10 sessions, with one of those families attending only two sessions. Two families completed more than 10 sessions. Post-program ASEBA forms proved difficult to collect, since staffing changes in the Deaf Services Program impacted the administration, collection, and scoring of data. As a result, few reports were collected; many of those had questionable validity and reliability, and ultimately there were too few to make any generalized conclusions with confidence. Anecdotally, feedback was primarily positive, despite having sessions midwinter in an unheated arena. One family reported seeing no real benefit.

Application

It was a shared assumption between PBJ Connections and St. Vincent Family Center's Deaf Services Program that EAC could be a powerful treatment approach with Deaf and Hard of Hearing individuals and their families. It is important to note that, with the exception of two participating families, all clients were already receiving support services, either through counseling, case management services, psychiatric services, or a combination of the three from St. Vincent Family Center. The families that participated are in no way a composite representation of the Deaf Community. They did, however, share some characteristics that are often seen in families of the general population who are in need of such supports.

Parent–Child Role Reversal

Eight of the families had Deaf parents and one or more hearing children. To those familiar with Deafness, these children are sometimes labeled *Children of Deaf Adults*, or CODAs. Sharing many common experiences, both good and bad, CODAs are a distinct identity among the Deaf

Community. In an ethnographic study of the CODA experience (Preston, 1994), stories shared describe pride, pain, incredulity, isolation, stoic bravery, and even mirthful humor. Preston (1994) points out the CODA experience is as varied as the individuals yet with an undercurrent of silent fraternity. One common experience reported is the child who is instructed or otherwise feels obligated to interpret a very adult situation to his or her parent and complex emotional responses resulting from such a duty (Filer & Filer, 2000).

Much of the literature, movies, and research of the past decades portray textbook examples of the term *parentified child* when addressing CODA dynamics. It would be prudent to note that much has changed in just the past 20 years to limit such dynamic shifts. With research in the 1970s finally giving American Sign Language legitimate recognition, advancements in technology were not far behind. Closed-captioning, first available on a limited basis in 1972, is now standard on televisions built since 1993. Text messaging put Deaf and Hearing on equal ground during the 9/11 attacks. TTYs have been replaced by videophones, a technology widely available to the Deaf only 5 years ago. In 2006, the U.S. Food and Drug Administration reported that cochlear implants, a hotly debated issue in the Deaf Community, have been provided to approximately 41,500 adults and 25,500 children (NIDCD, 2010). Advances in technology have now afforded many Deaf with the luxury of rapid information sharing, the impact of which is only beginning to be realized. It should be noted that the parentified child dynamic was also seen in the four families with Hearing parents, and as such this may be a clinical observation that is commonly seen in families who are seeking services not as a factor of Deaf–Hearing status.

EAC activities that promoted an identified *leader* were used with families so that the children were required to take direction from the parent who was often hesitant in her or his authority. One activity, which required the *leader* to hold onto two ropes that each child then held, had to be modified for Deaf parents so that they could communicate with their hands. By tying the rope ends to the parent's belt, signed communication could still take place. An additional insight was provided through the metaphor of how *secure* the rope was attached and how the children perceived that level of security as they resisted direction and tried to take over.

Empowerment Issues

All of the families had one or more members struggling with self-esteem, confidence, or establishing healthy boundaries in one form or another. Some were domestic violence or trauma survivors; others were being treated for clinical depression or anxiety disorders. Some were used to having those around them make all the decisions; others were always getting decisions invalidated. Whether child or adult, Deaf or Hearing, feeling comfortable enough to make and stand by a decision, even when it doesn't work, is a difficult hurdle for many.

EAC activities that were used during these sessions specifically focused on empowerment issues and often involved the act of getting a 1,000-pound equine to move to a designated area or perform a designated action at the request of the client. As clients would figure out how to communicate their request to the horse, they were naturally empowered in their own ability to communicate and feel success. Activities often involved different family members going through a process of working together toward a common goal of influencing the horse in some way. Children and parents alike experienced increased self-esteem and feelings of empowerment as they were able to communicate with each other effectively to achieve this common goal. For example, a family unit may have been asked to get a horse to stand in a *box* made of poles on the ground for 10 seconds. They had to communicate their request to the horse with predetermined caveats (i.e., rules and consequences) and work together to accomplish this goal. The celebration by family members at the successful completion of the task was filled with smiles and compliments to each other for a job well done. For some family members, this positive acknowledgment and sense of pride was a breakthrough in treatment.

Ineffective Communication Patterns

Despite the many aspects that made each family unique, a common dynamic appeared among family members regarding communication—not just whether they signed but also how they attended to, interacted with, and conveyed meaning to others who were present. Many of the children with Deaf parents had to be reminded to sign, and usually it was not the parent doing the reminding. Some children instructed the interpreter not to sign something they had just said (usually hurtful and directed toward the Deaf parent). Some Hearing parents were reluctant to acknowledge the limitations of their spoken or signed comments around their Deaf child, believing the child was simply being "difficult" when in fact the child was searching for the interpreter to get accessible communication. Some families just did not "listen" to each other at all, each going their own way, assuming they were "right." Some families felt they were being very detailed and clear, only to realize through feedback from the horse, the clinical team, and other family members that their communication was actually vague or conflicting. At times, the horses moved between the family member who was depending on a visual line of sight for communication and the interpreter, which led to a discussion process of how communication can be blocked by outside influences. This gave the EAC clinician the opportunity to comment on the horse's behavior to open the door for clients to change their situation, which then carried over into home experiences.

For example, a family may have been asked to set up an obstacle course and then get the horse through the course. During the process of setting up the obstacle course, the clinical team was able to observe and reflect back to clients as to how they were working together and if they were considering each others' needs as well as considering the horse's needs related to its size and comfort. Often discussions would arise about whether the family members felt they were working as a unit or breaking down into individual leaders as they were guided toward interacting in a healthier way to promote a more cohesive unit. Once the family was working directly with the horse on performing the obstacle course, the horse's behavior would dictate to family members the need to pay attention to each other and the horse to maintain safety and self-rated success. If clients became too self-absorbed and inconsiderate of others' safety needs or the needs of the horse, the horse would react by refusing to move, pulling its head up, backing up, or trying to walk away. This would invariably bring the attention of the family back to the equine and facilitate a need to communicate more clearly with each other and with the horse. The EAC clinician was able to guide the family through discussions about the process of setting up and getting through the course, which was then used as a metaphor to discuss other events that may have dissolved into arguments and dissatisfaction at home.

"Cultural" Differences

This section is labeled in quotations because, stereotypically, the areas mentioned have been attributed to Deafness. Some differences that did appear to be more prevalent with the Deaf clients included the lack of implicit knowledge; a tendency to be painfully blunt with family members; the need for literal, direct communication; and difficulty in applying metaphors to their everyday experiences. While a gradation of these tendencies are often acknowledged within the Deaf Community, it would be irresponsible not to reinforce that the families participating in the EAC sessions were seeking services because of dynamics that were not effective. The epistemological *lens* would need to encompass a multitude of variables in the life of a Deaf individual: etiology, age of onset, language exposure, degree of hearing loss, early developmental environment, educational placement, encounters with discrimination, social services, medical professionals, and the list goes on. For the families who participated, one possible factor could simply be limited communication access to learn about other ways of problem solving or communicating. All of the Deaf parents came from families who did not communicate effectively to them as they were growing up. Behavior is visible, and the less subtle the behavior, the easier it is recognized. Subtle communication requires an advanced level of interpersonal skills. To convey subtleties in a second language requires very proficient interpreting. Blunt, literal communication gets the job done but at an interpersonal expense.

Drawing parallels between two different events is what clinicians have been *trained* to observe and indicate clearly back to clients. Some individuals have a harder time stretching beyond their cognitive comfort zone than others. To address these issues within the sessions, the EAC clinician had to be cognizant of the need to break some instructions down and give tasks in stages. Part of this was of a practical necessity. If Deaf individuals started to search for a halter, they missed the interpreted message detailing the rest of the instructions. Some of the younger children were not able to retain complex instructions and so were assisted with role-play and modeling. Some family members struggled to come up with consequences that were appropriate if the *rules* of the task were broken and needed a list of examples to facilitate appropriate parameters. Again, Deaf individuals' experience with rules is subject to their developmental experiences. Some Deaf who attended residential schools decades ago would have probably encountered forms of corporal punishment as the norm. Some may have had overprotective parents who limited their experiences, and still others may have had rules conveyed to them through a sibling who could sign. To facilitate sessions, visual supports were often used, such as labeling, numbering, or using objects to represent abstract concepts or places. Again, these visual adaptations would not be unique to families with Deaf or Hard of Hearing members, as other families also benefit from visual cues.

Activities used that follow the EAGALA model of EAC are designed to stretch one's problem-solving skills, to promote healthy interpersonal communication, and to create self-awareness. All of the activities are designed to be modified to accommodate the appropriate level of functioning, age, athletic ability, and clinical need. Therefore, PBJ Connections' staff regularly modifies activities to promote the greatest therapeutic benefit for any particular client unit. A common practice in these sessions is to ask the clients to come up with a consequence for breaking any given rule during the activity. The process of having the clients design their own consequence leads to a wealth of clinical information on how a family views consequences (i.e., negatively or positively) and how they, as a family unit, communicate to decide on a consequence. *Do they consider each others' physical limitations, safety concerns, or individual wishes? Is one family member domineering? Does one family member focus on the degree of difficulty of the consequence (wishing to make the "punishment" fit the "crime")?* This process is consistent with all clients, Deaf and Hearing, and often creates a struggle for families before the activity even commences.

A cultural advantage of using EAC for Deaf families is that horses rarely communicate with voice. Their language is primarily nonverbal and is very conceptual, as is American Sign Language. Profoundly Deaf clients with limited experience with horses benefited from having horse *language* explained clearly to them, and children were often under the impression that horses used voice to communicate. Once they realized the horses communicated nonverbally, they were able to increase their awareness of body language in the horse as well as in family members. As clients would go through periods of frustration at not being able to clearly communicate their wishes to the horses, the situation was very representative of how Deaf individuals often feel while trying to communicate with Hearing individuals. An understanding was often achieved that learning horse communication was synonymous to a Hearing person learning ASL or a Deaf person learning English: it is not easy, but the benefit is worthwhile.

Measurement Tools

Although a clinically substantiated tool, the ASEBA proved to be an intimidating and exhausting process for most families to complete. The scales are in written English, and for the eight families with Deaf parents they needed to be explained or even transliterated. The presession administration of the ASEBAs was primarily conducted by a DSP clinician who also held credentials as a certified interpreter. Ideally, the ASEBA should have been conducted using the video version in ASL, which was not available to the DSP clinician. The fact that this same DSP clinician, or even an identified, alternative clinician, was not available to conduct the postsession administration further confounded an already compromised data collection process. Ohio scales were conducted pre- and postsession with two families. PBJ Connections has researched alternative measurement tools, which they will consider administering as common protocol for future EAC groups to protect validity, reliability, and overall integrity of the data collected.

Interpreters

The use of an interpreter, whether certified or not, has inherent complications for clinical settings. Deaf persons by and large prefer to have clinicians who are Deaf or, at second best, who are proficient enough that they can sign for themselves (Feldman & Gum, 2007; Vernon & Leigh, 2007). The linguistic and nonlinguistic nuances of communication that make for a successful therapy session are better transmitted in a one-to-one dialogue than through a third party, no matter how skilled the interpreter may be. The reality, of course, is that there are not enough clinicians who are Deaf or proficient in ASL.

Add to that a need to be experienced in EAC, and the numbers are extremely small. Most existing EAC programs will need to hire an interpreter if they are to provide services to Deaf individuals. The national certification body for this profession is the Registry of Interpreters for the Deaf (RID). Although states vary in their requirements for interpreters to practice, RID certification indicates a minimum standard of competency and skill in interpreting. It also provides a standard practice paper for mental health interpreting that explains the special skills set recommended for an interpreter in this area of practice.

More importantly, *how* the interpreter is used within the session can be a point of clinical strategy. Within a typical office setting, Harvey (1989) describes the use of an interpreter as a conscious and *conscientious* part of his systemic intervention during family therapy. The nuances of positioning, direct and indirect communications, joining and confronting, form a rich, complex clinical dance that warrants much more detail than is possible in this paper. Now add the dimension of an equine presence, in a large, open arena. Interpreters must *dance* among family members, EAC clinicians, and a horse or two as they do their job. At some point along the series of sessions, the horse invariably investigates the interpreter. As described by Harvey, this is a chance for the EAC clinician to use the interpreter's presence as *figure* or *ground* to the issue of Deafness, depending on the therapeutic goals.

Cost is a significant factor in providing interpreting services during an EAC session. Although rates vary considerably, many interpreter referral agencies have a minimum 2-hour standard and a stringent cancellation policy. Some flexibility can be found through direct contracting with an individual interpreter, but it is recommended that EAC programs new to this population investigate their state's minimum requirements to practice and ask for recommendations. The quality of the therapy session will fall to the level of the communication provided, and interpreters are providing communication for the EAC clinician as much as they are for the Deaf client.

PBJ Connections was able to share interpreter resources with the Deaf Services Program. Because families were scheduled back to back, on some days the job of interpreting proved to be overwhelming for any single interpreter, and a second interpreter was contracted at times using grant funds. The weather conditions (midwinter) proved particularly challenging for interpreters, receptively and expressively, as gloves and stiff fingers often impeded clear communication. Interpreting costs proved to be the biggest budget item, a phenomenon well known to Deaf service providers everywhere.

Service Collaboration

With the exception of two families, St. Vincent Family Center's Deaf Services Program provided the family referrals to PBJ Connections. As part of the project design, DSP clinicians were invited to observe EAC sessions so that follow-up processing would be relevant and consistent with treatment goals. Two DSP clinicians availed themselves of this opportunity regularly. Two of the families had difficulty using cab services, due either to trust issues or health reasons. Transportation was provided by the assigned DSP clinician and made observation of the session a natural benefit. Often, the ride to and from the client's home became a pre- and postsession processing opportunity. One DSP clinician, with family consent, videotaped several sessions. The taping was initially done to allow participation of a parent who had health concerns (as well as considerable resistance). Review of the session in the family's home allowed the parent to feel included and facilitated, dispelling some of the resistance to treatment to the point where both parents were able to attend sessions and the family was able to make considerable therapeutic strides. Another family was afforded transportation by a DSP clinician but attended only two sessions despite many scheduled attempts. It was felt this was actually a historically consistent pattern, representing the family's limited ability to engage in any offered treatment effectively.

The process of initiating, designing, and following through on a collaborative process between two different types of programs—an EAC program and a community mental health center—proved to be a significant learning opportunity. One is run by a few individuals able to make programmatic decisions; the other is a state-funded entity made up of many individuals, with little authority and a specific chain of command. The initial stages of the collaboration were a learning experience for all involved. However, as clients began the sessions, quality treatment became the common goal.

Recommendations from a study of Deaf adolescents with high-risk behaviors concluded that "therapy should focus on building resilience, positive thought patterns, stress management, decision making, goal-setting skills, fostering positive self-definition, and social skills" (Coll, Cutler, Thobro, Haas, & Powell, 2009, p. 34). Deaf and Hard of Hearing individuals and their families are seeking therapeutic services that are accessible and culturally sensitive to their unique and varied experiences. The nonverbal, experiential nature of equine assisted psychotherapy provides a rich opportunity for these families to reach their treatment goals.

Resources

Achenbach System for Empirically Based Assessment (ASEBA), http://www.aseba.org

ADA Information Services, http://www.ada.gov

Centers for Disease Control, http://www.cdc.gov

Gallaudet Research Institute, http://www.gri.gallaudet.edu

National Association of the Deaf, http://nad.org

National Institute on Deafness and other Communication Disorders, http://nidcd.nih.gov

Registry of Interpreters for the Deaf, http://www.rid.org

References

Center for Disease Control and Prevention. (2011). *CDC features: Make sure your child is fully immunized.* Retrieved April 2, 2010 from: http://www.cdc.gov/Features/Rubella/

Coll, K. M., Cutler, M. M., Thobro, P., Haas, R., & Powell, S. (2009). An exploratory study of psychosocial risk behaviors of adolescents who are deaf or hard of hearing: Comparisons and recommendations. *American Annals of the Deaf, 154*(1), 30–35.

Equine Assisted Growth and Learning Association. (EAGALA). (2010). *About EAGALA.* Retrieved March 12, 2010 from: http://www.EAGALA.org

Ewing, C. A., MacDonald, P. M., Taylor, M., & Bowers, M. J. (2007). Equine-facilitated learning for youths with severe emotional disorders: A quantitative and qualitative study. *Child and Youth Care Forum, 36*(1), 59–72.

Feldman, D. M., & Gum, A. (2007). Multigenerational perceptions of mental health services among deaf adults in Florida. *American Annals of the Deaf, 152*(4), 391–397.

Filer, R., & Filer, P. (2000). Practical considerations for counselors working with hearing children of deaf parents. *Journal of Counseling & Development, 78*(1), 38–43.

Frewin, K., & Gardiner, B. (2005). New age or old sage? A review of equine assisted psychotherapy. *Australian Journal of Counseling Psychology* (6), 13–17.

Gallaudet Research Institute. (GRI). (2006). *Regional and National Summary Report of Data from the 2005-2006 annual survey of deaf and hard of hearing youth.* Washington, DC: Author.

Harvey, M. A. (1989). *Psychotherapy with deaf and hard of hearing persons: A systemic model.* Hillsdale, NJ: Erlbaum.

Kersten, G. (2007). Crisis into confidence—turning bad into o.k. *Milepost Red.,* October 23–26.

Kersten, G. (2010). Equine-assisted authenticity. *Equine-Assisted Networker, 4*(4), 6.

Mann, D. S., & Williams, D. (2002). *Equine-assisted family therapy for high-risk youth: Defining a model of treatment and measuring effectiveness.* Walsenburg, CO: Journey Home, Inc.

Mitchell, R. E., & Karchmer, M. A. (2004). Chasing the mythical ten percent: Parental hearing status of deaf and hard of hearing students in the U.S. *Sign Language Studies, 42,* 138–163.

Multiethnic Advocates for Cultural Competence. (2006). *An overview of needs in Ohio. Learning your needs, cultural competence needs assessment project.*

Myers, L. (2004). *Using a horse to develop recovery skills.* Retrieved March 10, 2010 from: http://www.stonefoxfarm.net.hickball.html

National Institute on Deafness and Other Communication Disorders. (NIDCD). (2006). *Outcomes research in children with hearing loss.* Bethesda, MD. Retrieved March 12, 2010 from: http://www.nidcd.nih.gov/funding/programs/hb/outcomes/recommendations.htm

O'Donnell, N. (1995). *Congenital rubella syndrome: 30 years after the epidemic of the 1960's - Deaf-Blindness.* American Rehabilitation. Summer. Retrieved April 2, 2010 from: http://findarticles.com/p/articles/mi_m0842/is_n2_v21/ai_17986018/

Preston, P. (1994). Mother father deaf: Living between sound and silence. Cambridge, MA: Harvard University Press.

Vernon, M., & Leigh, I. W. (2007). Mental health services for people who are deaf. *American Annals of the Deaf, 152*(4), 371–381.

☐ Social Skills and Communication Shaped by Equine Baseball

Steven B. Eller

Introduction

The social skills and communication within relationships can be restructured throughout interactions in life. This restructuring should be for the benefit of those involved in the relationship, but at times these shifts may cause disruption and unhealthy involvement. Counseling can be a reasonable avenue to help correct and adjust the beliefs and behaviors among relationships. Equine assisted counseling (EAC) is an alternative approach to traditional counseling, integrating humans and horses with an experiential counseling model of learning. Horses can provide humans the interactive insight and experience, which may be useful in altering beliefs of communication, the implied meanings, and responsible reactions to promote valuable social skills to the participating community.

From the most primitive moments of life, we have been communicating with others. These early interactions are intended to be a beneficial development source. Secure mother–child attachments provide improved self-regulation and stability of biological rhythms (Izard, Porges, Simons, Haynes, Hyde, & Parisi, 1991). There is even a familiarity to both primate and human children to flourish in the milieu of consistent and caring adults (Bowlby, 1988). The existence of interaction with others provides a nurturing and developmental environment of discovering the skills of community and communication. This communication is a mutual affair between two or more individuals recognized in both human and horse interactions (Parelli, 1993).

The social and communication skills are valid objectives that may be altered and reframed through activities using EAC. The conditioned responses of humans and horses, shaped through their experience in community, may precipitate unhealthy and even dysfunctional interactions. Nichols (1987) states that the self must be looked at in context and in action, not in isolation, if it is to be understood and developed. Therefore, it is through this experiential counseling model of therapy that EAC may be used to shape relational interactions to benefit social skills and levels of communication.

Rationale

Two of the most commonly discussed and observed styles of communication are verbal and nonverbal interactions. The body language of an angry dog is easily seen as threatening and dangerous. The tone from a fearful parent is internally accepted and mirrored by other parents. The encouraging signs and applause along the marathon route are greatly appreciated and warmly accepted by a first-time runner. And the tear from the eye of a child at the grave of his dog speaks volumes to the heart of a father.

These emotions are expressed and accepted through cues across nature. As humans, our emotions can be identified through mirror neurons, where we begin imitating adults as infants by sticking out our tongue, making noises, and opening our eyes and mouth. "The most likely explanation is that imitation is central to learning and important for the coordination of group behavior" (Cozolino, 2006, p. 186). Our communication is a learned trait and can be used to improve or hinder relationships.

Biological

The neurochemicals released during moments of engagement provide an ability to regulate the human sense of safety, danger, despair, and joy. This hormonal production and availability can determine background affect, the desire to form relationships, and the ability to manage stress. Specific hormones are exchanged when these interactions take place that will reinforce and promote repetition in that same interaction. There is a physical growth occurring on the myelin sheaths of the human neural network that allows decisions to come more quickly and without much thought (Cozolino, 2006). Therefore, our brains find a way to interact, whether it is a healthy or unhealthy mode. This laziness of the brain can prove detrimental to social skills and relationships through poor communication and may need rewiring through experiences to benefit the community and self.

Another aspect of human interactions is the ability to create and live within reality. Glasser (1975) notes that humans require two basic needs: (1) to love and to be loved; and (2) to feel worthy to ourselves and others. When these needs are not met or have become distorted, individuals will create a reality in which they can feel loved and valued, despite the resultant harm or destruction of community. With that reality, every individual's sense of identity is influenced by his sense of belonging to different groups (Minuchin, 1980), thus creating a need for social skills and healthy, functioning communication.

Equine Nature

The social skills and communication among horses is also a shared human characteristic. Horses maintain an instinct of self-preservation and a need to feel safe prior to approaching a new object or environment. They base their thinking patterns on comfort, and anything that may interfere with that comfort can bring about fear and anxiety. Horses work from the mind-set of three personalities: (1) an innate personality, which is what the horse is born with and its genetic makeup; (2) a learned personality from its mother, the herd, its environment, and human interactions; and (3) its spirit, which is an innate package but has to do with the amount of life or energy given to things (Parelli, 1993).

A horse must gain your respect before you can interact with its heart and desire. If you are dealing with a horse that doesn't want to be around you, then getting its respect is a trivial or hollow thing; if a horse doesn't want to be around you, respect and performance will also be absent from your interaction (Parelli, 1993). Horses learn through interactions and patterns. The more they participate, the more they learn. There is a truth that these patterns can turn dysfunctional. For example, if a horse stops at the gate three times in a row, it begins to think this stop should happen every time. It will maintain this belief until it is made to realize this action will not occur at every instance (Dorrance, 1987). This pattern is reflective of the neural connections within the human brain.

Human and Horse

As we integrate the characteristics of human and horse, we can begin to see the benefit in using an experiential counseling model of therapy. EAC provides a way not only to bring issues to the surface to resolve but also to help people find greater fulfillment and wholeness (McCormick & McCormick, 1997). Horse and human also share the need for stable and secure community, which make available opportunities to learn, grow, and change stale interactions and skills. Horses provide humans with the insight to establish bonds within a cohesive social group and a path toward restoring humanity and healthy membership within our human-herd. "Through unconsciously identifying with the horses, individuals come to understand their own basic drives and the value of developing self-control. Working with a horse, they gain a new sense of self-mastery" (p. 42).

The learned knowledge of self-mastery can be gained from the Equine Assisted Growth and Learning Association (EAGALA) model of equine assisted psychotherapy.* This model follows four basic tenets. First, it is 100% on the ground. There is no horseback riding or horse experience needed. Second, there is a treatment team present, which includes a qualified mental health professional (MHP), equine specialist (ES), and horses. Third, the model is solution focused in orientation. And fourth, there is a code of ethics guiding the interactions between the MHP and ES team and the clients. With these four basic principles, the treatment team is able and flexible in providing a variety of interactions to engage the individual or participants with the horse and each other (EAGALA, 2010).

Social Skills

Social skills are our ability to interpret emotions into useable information concerning our relationships. There is personal responsibility in hearing and understanding what is being communicated as well as a responsibility to use that information to bring about a healthy relationship. Assertiveness is the ability to respectfully and honestly communicate to others and results in defining and refining our social roles. It prevents us from being flattened with demands and commands while providing a sense of confidence and identity. If we cannot communicate what it is we need and want from ourselves and others, we may become complacent and lost in our relationships and stripped of any social skills needed to maintain safety and community.

In our community and system of functioning, individuals can learn and teach many styles of interaction. These skills will either benefit and honor or destroy and disrespect those involved in the relationship. The advantage of working with horses is that they will not allow you to think one way and act another. According to Parelli (1993), 80% of all horse communication is nonverbal. This communication involves arms, feet, legs, voice, and facial expressions. If there is a discrepancy in your

---

* Editor's note: This book does not endorse any specific model. References to any treatment or therapy model or to any program, service, or treatment are solely the views and opinions of the authors.

actions and attitude, horses will respond immediately and let you know it will not be tolerated in their arena. The interaction with horses provides metaphors and symbols to the client and, with the guidance of the counselor, links this lesson of interpretation between verbal and nonverbal communication with others in their daily lives.

There is a notion that we deal only with images of reality and that the nature of those images determines whether our actions are effective or ineffective (Fisch, Weakland, & Segal, 1982). In the interactions with horses, it becomes obvious if the images of reality we are using to formulate our decisions are accurate or a faulty interpretation of the truth. This invites participants to reassess their communication and social skills. Glasser (1975) described that "if we do not evaluate our own behavior, or having evaluated it, we do not act to improve our conduct where it is below our standards, we will not fulfill our need to be worthwhile and we will suffer as acutely as when we fail to love or be loved" (p. 12). This unfulfilled need takes us back to operating in an environment of perceived danger and stress, with an inability to perform with respect toward others. Such a symbol and image is seen as it relates to a horse's need to feel comfortable and safe among the herd and its surroundings.

Equine Activities

EAC uses many different activities and games that invite and engage the clients' imagination. Many times these activities will remove common modes of interaction and communication to perturb normality, thus promoting creative thinking. These interruptions of normality include, but are not limited to, no talking, no touching of the horses, no lead ropes, no halters, no enticing the horses with food, and no bribing. The instructions given by the treatment team are usually simple, with a brief comment about the task and its associated guidelines. The purpose of the task is to encourage the client not just to complete the task but also to observe how the participants may go about solving problems and interacting with those present. This is a unique opportunity for the therapist to have such a concrete observation of the client, which is not usually found in most traditional therapy sessions.

Transporting therapy into an outdoor arena also removes an expectation and sometimes an implied rule to clients that they must be transparent and completely open with their emotions. This expectation in traditional therapy most often leads to clients guarding themselves and provides shadows of reality. In most therapy rooms, on the couch the therapist uses questions as the primary mode of data collection, consequently making the session about the control of the therapist (Nichols, 1987). With EAC, there is an environment created where the client begins to feel comfortable in speaking directly and symbolically about the meanings of what they are experiencing through the interactions with the horses, the involvement with the activity, and nonjudgmental acceptance from the counselor. This allows the drawing out of metaphors to be completely self-interpreted through the words and viewpoint of the client.

The role of the counselor is to help process the metaphors and symbols that arise during the EAC activities. A common phrase of "What are the horses doing?" or "Why do you think the horse is responding that way?" will direct clients to interpret the activity based on their own interactions with others. Transference that may usually take place in the traditional therapy room directed toward the therapist can now be mirrored in the arena from clients to the third party of the treatment, the horse. Clients may interpret equine emotions, the structure and placement of horses, and the reasons behind their behavior through the lens of their personal family system and community. The counselor is then able to help navigate a discussion with clients in realizing the power of implied meaning to their own lives, social skills, and communication in relationships through the observations in the arena.

Description

The following activity can be used with a small group or family, ranging in size from 4 to 10 participants. The purpose of the activity is to encourage problem solving, communication, creative thinking, and social skills needed to complete or remain involved with the task. The activity is called *Equine Baseball.*

Prior to the session the therapeutic team creates the baseball field within the arena using a plastic home plate and three orange traffic cones. The cones are positioned where first, second, and third base would normally be located. The participants are asked to divide up into two different teams. When the teams have been formed, each team is then asked to pick and catch an additional player (a horse) and reassemble their baseball team. There are two to three horses, if not more, available in the arena for the teams to make their selection. Halters and lead ropes are available on the fence; however, there are no instructions given on how to bring the new player into the group. When the task of picking the player (horse) has been completed, the treatment team may inquire of each team how they went about selecting their new player.

What qualities did they look for? Was there a group effort, or was there one leader in the group that made the decision? Was there any discussion among the existing players or difficulties in choosing the right horse? How did they go about catching the horse and bringing it to their team? Did anyone in the group know how to halter and did this affect the attitude or dynamic of the group?

If the team has not already used the halter and lead rope, the treatment team should give them the tack while they explain the guidelines of how to play Equine Baseball as the teams make their way toward the baseball field. It is useful to observe how the teams interact during these transitional moments, making note of communication, group exchanges, possible hierarchy in the team, and proximity of participants to the horse.

Guidelines of How to Play Equine Baseball

After each team has added their horse player, the treatment team explains to each group that they will be participating in a game of Equine Baseball. It is explained the purpose of the game is to see how far the team can move the horse around the bases toward home plate without using a halter or lead rope. During their turn, each team is given 90 seconds to travel around the bases. The first team in the field (home team) will keep its horse at the pitcher's mound during the inning. The first team at bat (visiting team) will commit to following three guidelines. First, the players must remain attached as a team at all times during their turn at bat. Second, during each turn, the team members may not talk with each other. It is stated that the only time they can talk is between innings. Third, they may not touch or use the halter of the horse during their turn.

It is predetermined by the treatment team that if the horse leaves the base path, roughly a 2-foot wide span, or turns around, the team at bat is called out, and it is the next team's turn. The game may continue for a predetermined set of innings or times, depending on the group's needs and time allotment. The treatment team removes the lead rope but leaves the halter on each horse. A coin is tossed to determine which team will be home and visitors. The home team will take the field with their horse while the visitors take their place at home plate. The 90-second timer is started, and the visiting team makes its way around the bases. The treatment team may allow the game to go without much comment, or they may begin to intentionally interfere with the progress of movement around the bases by repeating the instructions or asking if the visiting team is following a specific rule. The treatment team may also decide to allow turns to be cut short or even extend an at bat. The purpose for such interjections and interference by the treatment team is to promote disruption with how the team expects the game to follow the rules. There is observational learning taking place during these moments of disruption which may prompt communication among the team members. Some players may react in an angry or disgusted manner, whereas others may not be influenced by such changes in the rules. These observations become talking points with the treatment team and the participants in how they respond to external voices and criticism, changes in workflow, and unmet expectations.

Most of the processing of the game will occur after both teams have a chance at bat. There may be times during the inning where the treatment team finds it useful and beneficial to *pause* the game and process the interactions of the players and the horse. It is helpful for the treatment team to verbalize prior to the game that the postgame interviews will be the time to process. As the game concludes, the treatment team calls the players to the middle of the arena to begin processing the interactions that took place. It is at this time they can invite the teams' interpretations of how the innings went, whether the external voices were helpful or harmful, how they interacted with each other in such a unique environment, who was in charge, and how they communicated without using their voices. It is also helpful to ask the group what they would do different next time or if there would be anything they would repeat.

Case Study Observations and Insights

A specific case study with this activity was used by a group of 10 people who worked together. The group was asked to divide into teams and then select their horse player for a game of Equine Baseball. Once they selected their horse, they were to catch, halter, and bring it to the center of the arena. The treatment team introduced the game and began explaining the rules of play. The visiting team took their horse to home plate, and the home team went to the pitcher's mound.

Before the game could even start, there was already anxiety and confusion among the players about the rules of the game. They seemed to need a lengthy explanation or question and answer time to help formulate a plan of action. The teams had difficulty defining what was meant by being *attached at all times*. Some of the participants were able to abide by the three rules. However, it seemed that during the moments between innings when they were allowed to communicate with each other, team members used that time discussing the past turn rather than planning for alternatives to completing the next inning. Both teams would naturally observe and learn strategies from each other. This observation would then lead to an attempt to imitate and apply that method during their next at bat.

Between innings, as the teams were moving their player to the assigned spot, one horse made its way up the third base line as the other team came around second. The ES and MHP could tell there was some tension in the horses' behaviors, being pushed, pulled, and moved to another location. As the teams approached each other head on close to third base, with a fence on one side and people on the other, the ES stepped between the two horses to deter any possibility of equine conflict. This was done in an effort to maintain the game in a safe manner. There was not a big scene about how dangerous things were getting or what kind of threat was present to the players. It was just a small interjection of boundaries that allowed the teams to keep moving in the directions they were heading. In processing with the teams, we would address this point as becoming aware of moments of conflict, both internal and external to the teams.

Distractions during the game disrupted the teams' attempt to score. At one point, one of the horses turned around to go back to home plate. The team members, who were unable to verbally communicate with each other, seemed to be frozen in what to do next. The horse was not responding as expected, nor could they formulate a recovery plan because of the guidelines in place. However, the team did decide to break the no talking rule to bring the horse back into the group. The team was called out, and their turn was over. After the game was over, we were able to process this interference of plans and how the group reacted.

Another distraction occurred as the teams made their way around the bases. The mental health professional would randomly comment, "No touching the halter," "No talking," or "Are you staying attached to your team?" These disturbances seemed to interrupt the flow of thought for some players and to provide an evaluation of their level of involvement as well as an opportunity to observe the group reaction to external input. Even though the team maintained the guidelines, there was an internalization of the comments that seemed to influence self-esteem and confidence rather than be used as a source of information.

In observing the methods used by one group, the other team attempted to surround its horse from all sides and to push it around the bases. This method worked for the first group because its horse was able to function with those pressures. However, the other horse was a natural follower and did not appreciate the pressure from the rear. It was at this moment it decided to walk off into the outfield without the team.

Processing

There were some obvious difficulties in processing the activity with the case study group. One was the group members' inability to communicate with each other during the most critical moment of the game. As the game went on, the teams were able to maximize the *verbal* time between innings to get a game plan formulated. There was also some real-time learning and flexibility that took place in the arena as one team lost its horse between bases. As we processed with the team members, they understood the rules of play but decided to communicate verbally with each other to keep the team safe and to regroup after their plans were disrupted. We talked about how during work tasks or projects, there is a need to remain flexible when disruptions alter the expected outcomes.

We processed with the team that decided to mimic the other team's approach in pushing its horse from the rear to get it moving. Seeing what works for others soon became obvious that it doesn't always work for everyone in every situation. The horse that moved when pushed was a horse that seems to respond to pressure from the rear. However, the other team's horse was one that would follow you no matter where you were going. We processed with the team how this applies to daily work relationships and interactions with others. There are people, clients, and coworkers who may respond better in one way with certain languages and motivations, whereas others may respond and react better in different ways. We help the group understand by discovering for themselves through these interactions that maybe it's not right or wrong but just different.

We processed with the teams about the perception of the external input from the treatment team during the game. One member commented that she did not even hear the statements, whereas another mentioned she felt like she was being criticized for how the task was moving along. The team members were following the guidelines, yet the MHP continued to ask if they were following the rules. We used this metaphor to talk about how the input impacts how we may receive external voices while we are trying to perform a task. The voice is a source of information, to be deciphered, rather than a source of truth that we should always follow. There are times when the input from others is constructive, but we processed with the group that the input should be just that—input to be used to refine, change, or continue forward with the task at hand. Again, we talked about how differently each one of us will interpret comments, therefore confirming the need to be responsible for not only what we say but also what we hear.

Some of the following questions arose during the game: Was there any regret about the player (horse) they chose? Were they able to work with the human players on their team, or did they find excuses as to why the game may have not gone according to plan? How did the horse player impact the game? How has this experience shaped or changed their viewpoint of communication and social skills? In what ways did they see themselves in the horses and the task?

Some key points that may arise are imitation and learning, communicating, interpretations of nonverbal communications, external or internal locus of control, interactions with others, motivation to finish, how their motivations or competition influenced attitude and relationships, and pressure points that promote movement. Observations and explorations are a product this activity may provide to participants with images of what their interactions can look like outside the arena. As it relates to building up communication and social skills, many of the questions will promote discussion and insight to the participants long past the end of the session.

Application

This technique works best with corporations, families, and groups wanting to learn about their individual communication styles and willing to challenge normal methods of interaction. It can also be helpful for those wrestling with poor or dysfunctional social skills. I have found this technique to promote discussions about conflict resolutions, especially when tasks and expectations do not go according to plan. Key discussions that may arise during this technique include leadership styles, group discussion, goal setting, speaker–listener exercises, and assertiveness.

Clients who have interacted in this unique method have been able to improve the way they read and recognize nonverbal communications in others. They have also learned how to address challenges and struggles as a group by not blaming disruptions on individuals but by looking at the problem as something external to fight against. The externalized ability to focus as a group on a specific problem enables individuals to communicate in a constructive way, directing their needs and wants from the other group members to overcome the challenge.

References

Bowlby, J. (1988). *A secure base: Clinical application of attachment theory.* London: Routledge.

Cozolino, L. (2006). *The neuroscience of human relationships.* New York: W.W. Norton.

Dorrance, T. (1987). *True unity: Willing communication between horse and human.* Bruneau, ID: Give-it-a-go Enterprises.

Equine Assisted Growth and Learning Association. (EAGALA). (2010). *What is the EAGALA model?* Retrieved from: http://eagala.org/Information/What_Is_EAGALA_Model

Fisch, R., Weakland, J. H., & Segal, L. (1982). *The tactics of change: Doing therapy briefly.* San Francisco: Jossey-Bass.

Glasser, W. (1975). *Reality therapy: A new approach to psychiatry.* New York: Harper & Row.

Izard, C. E., Porges, S. W., Simons, R. F., Haynes, O. M., Hyde, C., & Parisi, M. (1991). Infant cardiac activity: Developmental changes and relations with attachment. *Developmental Psychology, 27,* 432–439.

McCormick, A., & McCormick, M. D. (1997). *Horse sense and the human heart.* Deerfield Beach, FL: HCI.

Minuchin, S. (1980). *Families and family therapy.* Cambridge, MA: Harvard University Press.

Nichols, M. P. (1987). *The self in the system: Expanding the limits of family therapy.* New York: Brunner.

Parelli, P. (1993). *Natural horse-man-ship.* Colorado Springs, CO: Western Horseman, Inc.

☐ Life's Obstacle Course

Deborah Goodwin-Bond

Introduction

Many equine assisted counseling (EAC) activities increase insight in clients, often enabling them to tap into their subconscious mind. This activity appears to bring the central issue to forefront while giving clients control over the issues. Clients usually have the answers to their issues in their subconscious, and as therapists we and our horses facilitate the clients uncovering those answers. This activity offers the client and the therapist an opportunity to explore the issues kinesthetically. The horse's presence adds an additional dimension to this activity. One horse used in this activity picks up cones and moves them about. How the client responds to this can tell the therapist about the client.

Rationale

Clients present with multiple issues. A good deal of the therapist and client's time is spent in locating the common element in the presenting issues. This technique allows the client to obtain control over the myriad issues in a nonthreatening way.

Description

Choose an enclosed area for the exercise, such as a round pen or small arena. Inside of the space have a variety of items such as cones, buckets, ground poles, cavalleti—whatever items are available. Ensure that the items are of different sizes, shapes, and colors. You will also need a roll of masking tape and a marker. Ask clients to spend a few minutes thinking about the issues that bring them to therapy. Tell clients they are creating an obstacle course for the horse. This can be helpful since some clients present their issues as belonging to the horse. Ask clients to write each issue on a separate strip of masking tape. After the issues are written, have clients place each piece of tape on the item of their choice to represent that specific issue. Next, ask clients to arrange the items in the round pen or small arena. Give clients several opportunities to rearrange the items, making sure they are just where clients want them to be.

The horse that the client has chosen to work with will offer nonjudgmental support and a sounding board for the client. Some clients find the horse's presence comforting, especially if they have already built a relationship with the horse. When clients are ready, the counselor initiates conversation with regard to the item choices, placements in the arena, and how the issues relate to one another. Different arrangements of the items can offer insight into how the clients solve problems. The activity allows clients to discover which of these issues relates to most, if not all, the others. The following case study will illustrate this process.

Case Study

While working with a client presenting with depression, anxiety, and low self-esteem, this activity revealed the core issue underlying the others. After writing out the issues the client wanted to address and placing each piece of tape on an object, the client rearranged the items several times. When the client was ready, the therapist and client walked through the obstacles, discussing the significance of each one. What the client noticed was that in the center, attached to the tallest cone, was an issue titled *Relationship*. Through processing, the client realized that the relationship was connected to every issue the client had identified. Different clients create different patterns. Some patterns are linear, some spiral, some like a wagon wheel with a hub and spokes. The central issue usually appears in the center of the pattern as though the subconscious is telling the client exactly what they need to know.

While the horse is a more passive observer in this particular exercise, it will respond to the emotions clients are processing as they explore their various central issues and how they interrelate. The horse provides support and stability and will frequently show interest in how clients are proceeding through the issues.

Application

This technique can be useful with clients dealing with relationship issues, addiction, abuse, self-esteem, and loss of control.

☐ Is Labeling People Really Harmless?
Using Equines to Explore Labeling Stigma

Kay Sudekum Trotter

Introduction

Countless examples of labels used to describe others can be explored and processed in counseling. One of the most common terms used by young people today to describe others is *loser*. Merriam-Webster defines a label as a descriptive or identifying word or phrase. The labels given to people are typically used to describe a particular behavior, physical characteristic, or social group. Usually these labels hold negative condemnations. When we assign a label to individuals we are at risk of making assumptions about what they think, how they feel, and what their life is like. Having made that assumption we may never then consider it necessary to explore whether it is true. This can then form the root of prejudice, stereotypes, and "permanent" views about people. When we say someone is *gay*, a *nerd*, or a *princess*, the same is true. And it also applies if we assume the label given to us by others. These social bumper-sticker stereotypes we blindly attach to others and ourselves can last forever if we're not careful. This activity is twofold and is designed to explore how and why we label people while also having fun learning the different body parts of a horse.

Rationale

We are all guilty of using stereotypes, more than we care to admit, and adults fail to realize how their sometimes seemingly casual remarks about others dramatically intermingle in the young developing brains of children and adolescents. Within social psychology theory, environmental and group factors play a role in the development of stereotyping and prejudice in children. According to Bigler and Lobliner (1997), children's cognitive skill affects their construction of social categories and meaning and explains the developmental path of social categorization and stereotyping among children. Kurcinka (1992) states that labels can be devastating for children and adolescents because negative labels directly impact children's ability to build a healthy self-esteem or self-concept.

Labeling theory (synonymous to *identifying against*) was first introduced by Howard S. Becker in 1963, and its tenets center around the tendency of majorities to negatively label minorities or those seen as deviant from norms. The theory is concerned with how the self-identity and behavior of individuals may be determined or influenced by the terms used to describe or classify them and is associated with the concept of a self-fulfilling prophecy and stereotyping. Building a healthy self-esteem can be a formable task when individuals have to overcome a negative label.

For children and adolescents, counseling can bolster hope and self-esteem, improve mastery and coping abilities, change maladaptive behavior patterns, and facilitate normal developmental processes. A major distinguishing feature of equine assisted counseling (EAC) for individuals is the role of the equine and the healing power of the animal–human bond. This type of therapy is appropriate when internal conflicts contribute significantly to individuals' problems, helping clients to express their repressed emotions and resolve their inner conflicts. According to O'Connor (2006), "...it is the horse's differences to the socialized man that brings about the successes that the traditional therapist cannot achieve" (p. 5).

In Shedler's (2010) *The Efficacy of Psychodynamic Psychotherapy*, empirical evidence supports the efficacy of psychodynamic therapy, also known as insight-oriented therapy, which focuses on unconscious processes as they are manifested in a person's present behavior. "The essence of psychodynamic therapy is exploring those aspects of self that are not fully known, especially as they are manifested and potentially influenced in the therapy relationship" (p. 98). Shedler's meta-analytic study found an "effect size"—a measure of treatment benefit—of 0.97 for psychodynamic therapy. For cognitive-behavioral therapy (CBT), 0.68 is a typical effect size. For antidepressant medication, the average effect size is 0.31. The studies also suggested that clients "who receive psychodynamic therapy maintain therapeutic gains and appear to continue to improve after treatment ends" (p. 98). These findings are especially important because EAC is an example of brief psychodynamic therapy model.

The findings of research studies on EAC programs indicate that after completing EAC programs participants had clinically significant increases in self-esteem (Brown & Alexander, 1991; Shultz, 2005; Trotter, Chandler, Goodwin-Bond, & Casey, 2008). In addition, participants reported feelings of being in control of their lives following EAC interventions. Smith-Osborne & Selby's (2010) review of literature investigating psychosocial benefits of equine-assisted activities continues to support the effectiveness of EAC on improving children and adolescents self-esteem:

> Cawley et al. (1994) found improved self-concept as a psychosocial outcome in their study of therapeutic riding with adolescents with learning disabilities and cognitive difficulties requiring special education. Kaiser et al. (2004) found that children participating in as little as a week long

program of therapeutic riding showed lower scores on anger and higher scores on quality of life and self-esteem measures. Hayden's qualitative dissertation study (2005) found perceived improvement in treatment effectiveness, as observed in coping and communication skills, behavior, and perceived self-efficacy, for adolescents involved in EFP. (p. 301)

Description

This activity is designed not only to teach clients about the different body parts of a horse, but it is also used as a springboard into a discussion on how we label people and why we resort to or accept the labeling of others. For middle school students, words, particularly labels like *skaters, jocks,* or *athletes,* the *nerds* and the *emos,* can harm their emotional vulnerability. This technique provides clients with a safe atmosphere where they can express themselves, try on different solutions, and learn more effective coping methods. Sometimes the equine is used by clients as projection for projecting things they don't want to acknowledge about themselves or find it too difficult to talk about in the first person, so they turn it around and put it on the horse (e.g., "It's not that I am alone and ridiculed for being smart, it's the herd who keep George (horse) on the outside and apart!"). In this example, instead of feeling inadequate (the client's true feeling) they suffer with the feeling that everyone is critical of them. In active therapy such as EAC, the therapist is invited to participate in the client's unconscious expression in a highly personal way. This requires some courage on the part of the therapist to enter into a client's world and for a time to be an integral part of the client's internal experience.

Before the group or individual arrives, bring a horse up from the pasture and tie its lead rope to a rail. When you are ready to begin the activity, explain to the group all the different parts of a horse. Use this opportunity to review horse safety—how to walk behind a horse by using either the "dirty shirt" method or the "elephant behind the horse" method. Then, tell the group that you want them to take turns placing the labels where they think they go by sticking the label on the horse. Have a laminated copy of a horse showing various body parts available for the group to use to determine label placement. Once all the labels are on the horse, lead the group in a discussion of how we label people and why we accept or reject the labeling of others.

Labels Used

Print on a standard label sheet the following suggested horse body parts:

Poll	Withers	Knee	Forelock
Back	Girth	Jaw	Hip
Flank	Muzzle	Tail	Barrel
Face	Heel	Throatlatch	Chest
Fetlock	Shoulder	Chestnut	Neck
Belly	Mane	Hoof	

Clinical Observations

As the group performs this task be sure to carefully watch how the horse responds to each individual and how each individual interacts with each other, the horse, and the therapist. Note the verbal and nonverbal communications such as

- How did the horse react to having labels placed on him?

- How did the horse respond to different individuals?

- Did anyone display fear? If so, how did they handle that? How did the group respond?

- What are the other group members doing while waiting their turn?

Clinical Processing

Once all the labels are on the horse, lead the group in a discussion of how we label people and why we accept or reject the labeling of others and ourselves.

- How do you think the horse feels about being labeled?

- Talk about what you observed both with the horse and the other members of the group.

Acknowledgment

I wish to thank my friend Deb Bond, who first introduced me to the concept of labeling horse body parts and linking it to a discussion on the negative impact of labeling in society.

References

Becker, H. (1963). *Outsiders: Studies in the sociology of deviance.* New York: Freedom Press.

Bigler, R., Jones, L., & Lobliner, D. (1997). Social categorization and the formation of intergroup attitudes in children. *Child Development, 68,* 530–543.

Brown, L., & Alexander, J. (1991). *Self Esteem Index examiner's manual.* Austin, TX: Pro-ed.

Kurcinka, M. (1992). *Raising your spirited child.* New York: Harper Collins.

Shedler, J. (2010). The efficacy of psychodynamic psychotherapy. *American Psychologist, 65*(2), 98–109.

Shelby, A. (2009). *A systematic review of the effects of psychotherapy involving equines.* Master's thesis. University of Texas Arlington: Arlington, TX.

Shultz, B. (2005). *The effects of equine-assisted psychotherapy on the psychosocial functioning of at-risk adolescents ages 12–18.* Unpublished master's thesis, Denver Seminary, Denver, CO.

Smith-Osborne, A., & Selby, A. (2010). Implications of the literature on equine-assisted activities for use as a complementary intervention in social work practice with children and adolescents. *Child and Adolescent Social Work Journal, 27,* 291–307.

Trotter, K., Chandler, C., Goodwin-Bond, D., & Casey, J. (2008). A comparative study of the efficacy of group equine assisted counseling with at-risk children and adolescents. *Journal of Creativity in Mental Health, 3*(3), 254–284.

☐ The Use of Mythological Themes to Elicit Socially Appropriate Behavioral Skills

Deirdre Stanton, Blair McKissock, and Robert Dailey

Introduction

The Journey, an equine assisted counseling (EAC) program, is based on Joseph Campbell's (1949) work *The Hero* and is a series of activities that provide each client with a journey or passage through specific life challenges. Each activity is flexible in structure to address clients' individual behavioral goals. Some of those goals may include problem solving, communication skills, improvement of impulse control, appropriate social interaction, and coping skills. Through the evolution of this program, it has been common for those unexpected aha moments to come from the unpredictable interaction with the horses.

The Journey is a behaviorally based program that introduces activities to elicit behavioral results. It was originally developed when clients within the mental retardation/developmental disability (MR/DD) population (dually diagnosed) did not experience empowerment within the traditional treatment model. That is, these individuals had not experienced reciprocal compassion. This program has been developed with the goal of providing opportunities for the clients to experience empowerment while subsequently working on behavioral goals for the improvement of verbal aggression, agitation, and social interactions. Moreover, group and individual problem-solving skills are also addressed.

When individuals are encouraged to move past ineffective behaviors, personal empowerment can then be promoted. The capability to process "in the moment" feelings and frustrations expressed by clients is also factored into the session curriculum. This is achieved through choice and consequence, with the horse providing support and companionship on a simulated hero's journey. Therefore, this program can also be effective experientially as well as behaviorally.

Rationale

The journey of the hero, as described by Joseph Campbell (1949) and other mythological folklore from various cultures, has been previously used as a guide for treatment by many professionals working in the mental health field. In his book *Hero With a Thousand Faces*, Campbell (1968) described 17 stages in a hero's or heroine's journey that have been applied to behavioral and psychotherapy sessions. The format for the hero's journey is considered effective as a metaphor for treatment, as it parallels the pattern of many treatment methodologies from cognitive-behavioral therapy to basic wellness behavior change. Usually, clients engaged in this therapy are prompted to begin due to a *call* to action, not unlike a tragedy, unpleasant situation, or moment of reckoning. By answering this call and thus embarking on the journey of treatment, clients will tend to follow the same behavioral or experiential pattern as the hero does during the mythological journey brought to life in many works of fiction. The goals and activities of the Journey program are loosely based on eight of these stages.

The first phase of the hero's journey can be compared to the precontemplation and contemplation phase in the Transtheoretical Model of Change (Prochaska, Velicer, DiClemente, & Fava, 1988). As one moves from the precontemplating stage of change into contemplation, there will typically be a coinciding event that causes the move, similar to hearing the call. In Gestalt therapy, it would be considered the Emergence of the Problem. It is not all that dissimilar to the Introduction phase of the animal assisted learning model (Mckissock, 2003) or the model of behavioral change (Stanton, 1998), where the animal is introduced as a stimulus to a participant to generate motivation for change.

As Joseph Campbell explored the world of ancient to present mythology, he discovered a shared structure that he called the *monomyth* (p. 23). He summarizes the monmouth as "a hero ventures forth from the world of common day into a region of supernatural wonder: Fabulous forces are there encountered and a decisive victory is won: the hero comes back from this mysterious adventure with the power to bestow boons on his fellow man" (p. 23). The shared structure can be considered the stages a hero goes through. It begins with the Call to Adventure and concludes with the Freedom to Live (Campbell, 1949).

According to Campbell, the first stage of the journey begins in the common world of suffering. The hero then hears a call to adventure when the ordinary world is no longer endurable and the hero is ready for change. As in any challenge-based program, heroes have the right to refuse the call. They might have enough feelings of fear and terror to avoid or deny the call and choose not to embark on the journey. When clients choose not to answer the call, the sessions can then be adapted into activities to fit their individual needs. If they accept the call the Journey program provides a specific stimulus to elicit a change in behavioral responses.

Why the Horse?

In the opinion of McCormick and McCormick (1997), based on their observation of case studies related to equine assisted interventions, based on that the horse creates an upheaval in a person's psyche. They report that the etiology of this finding is not clear. However, a human is a predator, and a horse is a prey animal; the relationship between the two is unique. A horse has the capacity to fight off a mountain lion and therefore has the capability to fight off a human. However, for some reason, horses work with us. They allow us to ride them, care for them, and sometimes mistreat them. This relationship has shown to be a benefit to humans in more ways than one. The relationship between the human–predator and horse–prey is different from the relationship between humans and other predator animals, such as dogs and cats. "Horses quickly anchor us, making it difficult to escape from some of the basic realities of our existence. Around them we are confronted with existential truths and with matters of life and death" (McCormick & McCormick, 1997, p. 166).

When clients are involved with an equine program, it is difficult for their attention to be anywhere but on the immediate activity. The horse will respond to clients' body language and ability to appropriately communicate wanted behaviors. Equine activity, by its very nature, prohibits complacency in action. As fear is mastered and skill is increased, working with a horse can provide a great sense of accomplishment and confidence in the ability to handle situations outside of the barn. The interaction with the horse can force the release of old habits, such as verbal aggression, while concurrently promoting innovative thought processes.

Traditionally, during therapy, the facilitator is the companion for the hero along the journey. However, it was determined that to enable the client to experience empowerment using all senses, the EAC framework would be the most effective treatment modality as the horse would become the hero's companion. But why is the horse so effective in bringing psychological and behavioral issues to the surface and easing the stress on confrontation?

Historically, horses have long been a beast of burden and a companion to humans. Traced back to the works of Xenophon (350 BC), horses were used not only for war, agriculture, and transportation but even as rehabilitation for soldiers injured in battle. Today, we face challenges due to the advent of technology that has reduced physical and verbal human interactions. In general, individuals have been exposed to violence at a young age by various mediums. This exposure has been shown to cause an increase in incidents of physical aggression in children.

There has also been evidence that an increasing number of children are born with disabilities or will develop emotional and behavioral challenges during their life. It was determined that due to a human's intrinsic attraction to nature (Kellert & Wilson, 1993), interaction with horses could be an effective treatment tool for numerous populations. There is substantial support in the growing body of research that the horse can be effective in treatment for more populations than any one drug or single intervention. Therefore, the Journey program determined that the horse would be the most effective source for successful achievement of behavioral and psychological goals. The physical advantages that can be gained from the experience of movement while riding a horse are many.

The horse's movement creates a simultaneously forward–back, side to side, and rotational response in the rider, which causes an off-balance effect that has to be continuously corrected. This in turn will cause the rider's muscles to contract and relax in an attempt to regain balance. The contraction and relaxation can reach deep muscles not typically accessible in regular physical therapy. The rhythmical movement of the horse is similar to the human motion of walking and therefore will teach rhythmical patterns to the muscles of the legs and trunk in the rider. "Since horseback riding is enjoyable the rider has an increased tolerance and motivation to lengthen the period of exercise. The increased use of muscles strengthens them" (NARHA, 1997).

Moreover, leg muscles are also stretched when sitting on a horse, whether riding with or without stirrups. This movement will stimulate the nerves and muscles in the body, improving head and trunk stability and upper extremity function. A study from Washington University (Shurtleff & Engsberg, 2010) suggests that, within a population of children with cerebral palsy, not only can the horse's movement improve functioning but also the positive outcomes are still present several months after the participants have stopped riding. The study also indicated that the motion and heat of the horse not only can aid a rider's blood circulation and reflexes but also will gently exercise the rider's spinal column, joints, and muscles. Therefore, the horse's three-dimensional movement can provide a combination of sensory and neurological input that can be used to address a variety of disabilities. Currently, the horse's movement has not been duplicated by traditional exercise or by exercise machines, which typically work on only one muscle group at a time and cannot produce body movements in a natural, rhythmic, and progressive way.

Cognitive Functioning and EAC

The diagnosis of developmental disabilities has steadily grown over the years. That every 1 in 150 children is diagnosed with autism, is one example. Additionally, the variability of disabilities has grown. According to Barkley (1990), 1 to 3 children in every classroom has been diagnosed with attention-deficit/hyperactivity disorder (ADHD). He has also found that upwards of 4% of the total adult population also exhibits ADHD symptoms. Therefore, due to such high rates of dysfunction, it is imperative to find treatment interventions that will improve cognitive functioning. Due to the enjoyable nature of horse-related activities, attention to task and learning can be improved as the participant is involved in continued engagement with the horse. In an article by Doolittle (1997), mental functioning is not transmitted verbatim from teacher to student, but it is the result of a social experience. Vygotsky (1978) believed that individuals' immediate potential for cognitive growth is limited by what they can accomplish independently. Higher degrees of functioning can be accomplished with the assistance of a partner.

Paired with the experiential nature of EAC, horses can help bridge gaps in learning. The activities experienced in EAC can affect cognitive functioning in many ways. For example, during the simple act of brushing a horse, the midline of the body is crossed activating the corpus-callosum in the brain, which will stimulate the centers for learning. Riding stimulates the tactile senses both through touch and environmental stimuli. The movement of the horse, with changes in direction and speed, stimulates the vestibular region of the brain. The olfactory system will respond to the many smells surrounding a stable and ranch environment. Vision is stimulated during control of the horse. The many sounds of the ranch help to involve the auditory system. All of these senses work together and are integrated in the act of riding and horse-related activities. In addition, proprioceptors are activated, resulting in improved spatial awareness. It is because of this factor that horses can be extremely effective for children and adults with sensory processing disorders.

Emotional Functioning and EAC

Dewey (1938) hypothesized that putting a person in an unfamiliar environment will result in a psychological shift creating an opening for learning. Interacting with animals in general can create a greater sense of well-being by decreasing blood pressure and increasing endorphins (Katcher & Beck, 1983). The sense of achievement experienced while riding can increase self-esteem. Additionally, the bond created between the horse and person can improve functioning in people with emotional challenges.

It can be said that in an era where technology prevails, in a country considered the world power, a large percentage of people do not possess the interpersonal skills to succeed in life. Recent work supports the value of horse interaction as being dramatic in the healing process (Irwin & Weber, 2001). Through their study of horses they believe that horses need us to be honest and consistent. Because horses are so sensitive to our emotions, through their behavior they force us to see what lies beneath the surface. Levinson (1969) contends that animals can act as transitional objects that act as a defense against anxiety, thus reducing emotional tension. The emotional attachments between the clients and the horses were considered in the development of the Journey program activities.

Description

The Journey program activities follow a preset pattern as described in Campbell's (1949) monmouth, from answering the call through the initiation of trials and eventually to the return journey home. Every hero hears a call to begin a quest. That call accompanies adversity or tribulation demanding action. Hearing the call is the recognition that action needs to be taken; it is up to heroes whether they will answer the call of a task to be undertaken. To hear the call, one must have the communication skills to hear what is being said. They must have the courage to step into the unknown and pay the cost of an adventure that will change their life.

Since the program is designed to be 10 weeks long, there are many opportunities for exploration, growth, and the practice of appropriate behaviors and interactions. Typically, each session is 45 minutes to 1 hour long. The sessions include several phases; the first phase is an introduction to the task or experience for that session. During the second phase, clients plan out strategy and problem solve what they will need to do to accomplish or complete the task. The third phase is action oriented with the implementation of activities. Debriefing takes place during the last phase.

Each week's activities build on the previous week and consist of ground exercises, mounted exercises, or a combination of both. The activities for the program have been based on mythical themes and present the client with challenges that may come in the form of obstacle courses, puzzle solving, or metaphoric exercise that will advance the client along the journey. For example, the concept of a detour is presented to clients and gives them an opportunity to address a challenging behavior by choosing to engage in a battle or avoid confrontation by choosing an easier challenge.

Within the construct of the session, the facilitator can make adjustments to fit the client's current situation or overall treatment goal. The format for the program allows accommodation for the imagination and style of any mental health professional. Some of the set up is elaborate; however, the program activities use basic equine center equipment.

Within the session format, processing time is allotted for explora-tion of similarities between the hero's journey and the life journey of clients. Thus, clients can apply what is learned in the session to everyday life. The program format addresses all styles of learning and cognitive functioning levels. The authentic experience elicited between the *hero* and the horse partner can lead to feelings and behaviors that can and should be addressed and processed in the moment. This essay contains a case example and two 10-week examples; more session examples are available at http://www.ehorseeducation.com.

Model Stages

At this stage participants choose their companion in the form of a horse to share their fear and to provide support to motivate them to answer the call. Clients are assessed for program appropriateness by use of established behavioral tools such as Functional Analysis Screening Tool (FAST), Questions About Behavioral Function (QABF), and Taxomomy of Problem Situations questionnaire (Dodge, McClasky, & Feldman, 1985), which can be used to determine the function of the maladaptive behavior. Indices of Happiness can also be used to determine Evaluation of a Multiple-Stimulus Presentation Format for Assessing Reinforcer Preference (DeLeon & Iwata, 1996). The Beck Depression Inventory (BDI) and the Beck Anxiety Inventory (BAI) are also useful assessment tools.

Based on the function of the behavior and the functioning level of the client, the activities are then developed ranging from difficult to easy as necessary to meet the client's needs. According to Joseph Campbell (1949), the first stage of the journey is the Ordinary World of the hero with its suffering, boredom, and neurotic anguish. At this stage, clients choose their companion in the form of a horse to share their fear and provide support to motivate them to answer the call. The second stage is the Call to Adventure when the ordinary world is no longer endurable and the hero is ripe for a change. The hero then has the opportunity for Refusal of the Call when the hero is scared, even terrified at first, and avoids the challenge. Most people who come to the Journey program are somewhere between the second and third stages. The facilitators then assist them to take the plunge into the fourth stage and continue to acknowledge, encourage, and support them through the later stages.

To follow Joseph Campbell's subsequent stages, the Journey EAC program has developed activities to promote a mentor relationship. Therefore, participants meet a mentor who acknowledges, supports, and spurs the hero onward. The mentor assists the participant to Cross the First Threshold when the hero begins to feel peculiar and becomes very scared. In the Allies and Enemies stage, the hero feels greater stress and anxiety than ever before, and is tempted to not continue. However, the hero finds people who can help and sometimes a few dangerous ones who can hurt.

Approach to the Inmost Cave is where heroes glimpse the dark side of their true, hidden self—the side they have always denied for most of their life. Heroes can also experience the supreme ordeal, in which parts of the true self are used that have caused previous shame and fear. During the final stages, heroes can experience reward for seizing the sword, as the discovery for new passion begins with self-empowerment from harnessing the power of their true self.

In the Journey EAC Program, the goal for clients is to leave maladaptive behavior behind. The maladaptive behavior is represented by carrying a ring throughout the program. The ring represents the specific behavior that is to be left behind. At the end of the program, as new skills were developed and old behaviors extinguished, clients participate in a "ring-burning" ceremony, where they throw the ring in a fire, representing leaving the old habits behind and starting fresh with the new skills. Last, heroes must find the road back when their newfound passion is adjusted to the demands of the ordinary world. This can be a trying time for imaginative heroes impatient with bureaucracies and the tedious people who inhabit them.

The last of the 12 stages are implemented according to the functioning level of the client. It has been found that clients with traumatic brain injury were very engaged in the last two stages and made great steps to continue with their lives, as opposed to being caught in a time warp between the time of the brain injury and the present. In particular, after the program, one client fulfilled a long-time goal of giving a presentation in front of 75 people to discuss his brain injury. In the inspiring and emotional address, he described what he experienced and how he is now able to move forward.

Post-Journey

The post-Journey experience mirrors the rebirth or resurrection part of the story, when heroes glimpse their impending death and ask, "What have I done with my life?" This is the time heroes reexamine their past choices and determine how those choices conflict with the present and future self. Having participants speak of their experience and offer to return as mentors is the final stage Campbell describes as the Return with the Elixir, when heroes share what they have learned with younger heroes and heroines in the ordinary world scenario (Campbell, 1949).

Sample Activities

Week 1: The Call

Background

Below are two sample activities from the ten-week curriculum. Weeks 1 and 7 are offered for demonstration. The complete curriculum is available at www.horseeducation.com.

"A hero ventures forth from the world of common day into a region of supernatural wonder: fabulous forces are there encountered and a decisive victory is won: the hero comes back from this mysterious adventure with the power to bestow boons on his fellow man" (Campbell, 1949, p. 23). Every hero hears a call to begin a quest. That call accompanies an adverse situation or major life event demanding action to prevent a potentially negative outcome. Hearing the call is the recognition that action needs to be taken. However, it is up to heroes whether they will answer the call of a task to be undertaken. This is the choice given to each client up front during the first session after the instructions and explanations have been given. Given the challenge by choice philosophy they can choose not to participate if they are not ready or unsure. If they choose not to participate it is up to individual facilitators and counselors how they wish to proceed or what alternative they wish to present. Clients must have courage to step into the unknown and accept the horse as their companion for the Journey. If they choose to go forward, they are asked to engage in a discussion about behaviors they wish to change during the journey. The behavior they choose is then represented by an object that they will carry with them.

We all carry things around that follow us and that we wish would leave us alone, such as thoughts that will not go away, impulses that are difficult to overcome, and issues that have occurred long ago. Each client decides on the behavior to address and is given a token to represent that behavior. A necklace or ring that becomes the burden they must overcome and leave behind at the conclusion of the program. This is a journey to "conquer" these issues and leave them behind. Let clients determine what will be their particular journey to overcome, such as lack of problem-solving skills that result in the inability to form social relationships.

The Set Up

No physical set up for this activity. Take the client to an arena or pasture where he or she can observe a herd or group of horses to choose a companion from.

Discussion

- Explain to the client why communication is important; for example, if you have difficulty getting your ideas across to others, miscommunication and arguments can occur. So why is communication important?

- Relate to why communication is important for horses. Horses communicate for survival.

- Discuss the predator–prey relationship and where humans fall within this relationship. We are predators and must take care to not have our communications with our horses reflect our predator status.

- Horses need to be able to discern who is friend or foe. How does the client think horses communicate with each other?

- Describe how horses see, hear, and smell and how that helps them to identify predators.

- Discuss how the client can communicate with the horse, so that the horse knows that the client is a friend, based on predator–prey behaviors. For example, the client should approach to the horse's shoulder.

- Discuss the need for support along the journey and whom they will call upon for help and the horse's role in the journey as a helpmate.

Activity: Choosing Their Companion

- Observation of horse herd:

    Explain that the client is going to observe a horse herd for 15 to 20 minutes in silence.

    The object is just to see how the horses interact and what they are "communicating to each other."

    Ask the client about what they observed. How are the horses interacting, and what might their stories be?

The client will then choose a horse to accompany them on the journey.

- Processing questions to ask:

Review session for today.

Discuss what will happen next week.

Any questions.

Week 7: The Gate of Fear

Review the session for the day. Which horse did they choose and why? How is the horse similiar or different from the client?

Background

"Artists are magical helpers. Evoking symbols and motifs that connect us to our deeper selves, they can help us along the heroic journey of our own lives..." (Campbell, 2004, pp. 132–133). Along any journey, help is needed to complete the final task. To obtain these keys, the hero must pass a test or overcome an obstacle. In this session the hero must obtain a key by solving a puzzle. The puzzle, when assembled, is typically a picture of a power animal, such as a Phoenix. Only after overcoming an obstacle is a piece of the puzzle given. Once clients have overcome all of the obstacles and have received all of the puzzle pieces, they have to correctly assemble the puzzle. When the puzzle is successfully assembled, the key is given. The key can then open a chest containing a reward or the key is a symbol that must be carried to complete another task down the road.

This exercise can be made as difficult or elaborate as your situation allows. It is assumed that facilitators will change the vernacular used in the description to fit their client and that they will take into consideration issues the horse companion has related to props. However, this activity is more powerful if there is real obstacle navigation difficulty that will require clients to recognize that assistance is required and that the assistance has to be solicited before successful completion of the task can be accomplished. This will allow for the exploration of seeking assistance. Once the puzzle is assembled, clients are considered to have arrived at the gates of the "enemy." To enter the gate, clients must present the key that was earned from the puzzle completion. This activity can be done mounted or unmounted and is designed to address problem-solving techniques.

The Setup

- Arrange series of four (or more) obstacles using standard equipment—can be set up as an obstacle course.

- Set a jigsaw puzzle piece made from any available material (e.g., cardboard) at each obstacle. When all jigsaw pieces are assembled, the picture should represent a power animal of some kind, for example, a Phoenix.

- Place four power animal pictures along the sides of the arena in plain sight. One of the pictures will be the replica of the completed puzzle of the Phoenix. Behind the picture of the Phoenix will be the key to open the gate of the enemy.

Discussion

Discuss what symbols are powerful in their life. What does the ring symbolize? How has that changed while on the journey?

Activity: The Quest for the Key

- The client will be instructed to navigate a series of obstacles and obtain a puzzle piece upon successful completion of each obstacle.

- The puzzle piece will then be taken to an area of the client's choosing to be a staging area to assemble the puzzle. This process will be repeated for each piece of the puzzle.

- When all of the pieces have been collected, the client will assemble the puzzle. Have the client identify the picture on the completed puzzle.

- The client must then determine which picture along the side of the arena matches the picture on the puzzle. The client must then go to the picture and obtain the key.

- The client is now ready to enter the domain of the named enemy and complete the final task set in the first lesson.

Processing Questions to Ask

- Do you know what picture was on the puzzle?

- Do you know the story of the Phoenix?

- Relate the story of the Phoenix, rising from the ashes and beginning anew.

- Do you think that by burning your ring of things that have been troubling you that you might have something in common with the Phoenix?

Case Study

Donna,[*] one of the clients in the Journey program, suffered from cerebral palsy and mild mental retardation; she was a young woman in her mid-20s. She and her mother had what could be described as a combative relationship where power struggles prevailed throughout the day. The house was filled with tension, and the mother never smiled. The interaction between Donna and her mother became progressively worse until physical aggression was the form of communication between the two. The behavior consultant (BC) implemented many varied protocols that resulted in no reduction of inappropriate behavior or improvement of social interactions. It was evident that the dynamic of the relationship would require drastic change that could not occur in the home. The BC consulted with a recreational therapist, and together they developed a program to facilitate improved social interactions. The behavior consultant and the recreational therapist were the facilitators for the program where the goal was to have Donna and her mother work as a team for task completion. This would hopefully improve their interactions and, specifically, their problem-solving skills.

At the program onset, Donna and her mother had tense body language and would not make eye contact with each other. They did not ask or confer with each other for task completion. The latency between being given a task and verbal interactive problem solving was 5 minutes or more. They did not engage in any spontaneous or casual conversation, nor did they work together. They would both make physical contact with the horse but at separate times. As the program progressed and they practiced talking to each other and the horse, they started to relax. Their interactions became more spontaneous, and their eye contact with each other improved from not at all to periods of 3 to 5 minutes. The latency for problem solving was 30 seconds. They began to develop a common bond around the horse, which became a subject of conversation between them outside of the arena.

---

[*] Names have been changed to protect identities.

During the course of the program, as they worked on problem-solving skills and effective social interaction to accomplish the tasks, it was not apparent to them that their interactions were improving. The facilitators also observed that as Donna and her mother bonded more closely with the horse, bonding behaviors between Donna and her mother concurrently occurred. The two women stood closer to each other; they looked at each other. Donna would laugh, and her mother would smile. The facilitator would hear them say, "You know, I love you." They would say that "things" were just getting easier. Throughout the program, as they worked to meet the needs of the horse for task completion, they verbalized their own needs and how their needs could be met. A nonthreatening atmosphere that was present during the sessions was necessary to encourage the improvement in interactions.

Donna exhibited physical improvements as well. She became stronger and was able to move more easily. She stated how strong she felt as she bravely rode her horse into battle to defeat the enemy. For the first time, Donna felt empowered.

At the conclusion of the program, as they engaged in the fire-burning ceremony as described in the stages of the Journey, Donna and her mother were able to leave the confrontation between them behind. It was observed during the closing ceremony that they were smiling, hugging, standing next to each other, and looking into each other's eyes. Postprogram, these behaviors were also observed in the home setting. Donna and her mother both noted that they now had something positive to talk about. They stated how happy they felt when reminiscing about their shared time with the horse. The Journey changed the dynamic of their relationship from strained and hateful to a relationship that found love and care.

Case Study Note

Three weeks after the conclusion of the program, Donna was diagnosed with stage 4 breast cancer. She fought bravely, just as bravely as she fought riding her horse into battle. Sadly, Donna succumbed to her last battle 9 months later. Throughout the last months of her life, Donna and her mother stood by each other; they looked into each other's eyes and smiled. They said, "I love you." After Donna was gone, her mother stated that the time they spent with Whinnie, their horse, was the happiest time in their life. Her mother discussed how grateful she was for the Journey, as it brought her back to Donna just in time to let her go.

Conclusion

Through the interaction with the horse and the treatment team clients meet along their journey, the hero often comes face to face with fears or feelings that have never been processed. In Campbell's (1949) work this is known as the Innermost Cave where heroes glimpse the dark side of their true, hidden self—the side they have denied for most of their life. Due to people's relationship to the natural world and their subsequent attraction to it (Wilson, 1984), the atmosphere of the barn and the horse as their companion can help clients feel empowered and supported to venture into that cave. The hero can also experience the "Supreme Ordeal," which is the climax of the journey and sometimes the greatest challenge. The activities in this curriculum are progressive in that each challenge becomes more difficult. This progression has the effect of challenging clients to use knowledge and experience gained from previous activities to complete the next activity or stage.

The activities can be frustrating, which will allow clients to honestly express and process verbal aggression. The sensitive and sometimes exaggerated prey response of the horse during times of frustration gives rise to opportunities to process in the moment. Parts of the hero's true self that previously caused shame and fear are used.

Postclimax, participants experience the aftermath of the Supreme Ordeal or reward for Seizing the Sword as the discovery for new passion begins with a steady, daily glow from harnessing the power of their true self (Campbell, 1949). When the celebration is over, the newly minted heroes must face the long road home, where they must confront realities of everyday life and struggle. They must now integrate their new behavior and newfound passion within the demands of the ordinary world. This can be a difficult time for all heroes as they try to resist falling into old patterns when faced with the people in their life who have not changed.

During the Journey program, the clients expressed delight at riding a horse. They stated that it was scary at first but that as experience was gained the treatment team observed confidence in the clients' riding abilities. As the clients encouraged their horses through the activities, the treatment team also observed that social interactions as well as problem-solving abilities were improved. As the clients continued to gain experience with the horses, they expressed empathy for the horses' experience and welfare.

The treatment team also observed behaviors and heard comments from clients that indicated the formulation of bonding or empathetic relationships beginning to form with the horses. The clients, who had previously been assessed to have difficulty with verbal or emotional interactions with others, began to be concerned about the horse's welfare during activities. They wondered if the horse was comfortable or if they observed that the horse was nervous, they corrected their interaction to soothe the horse before continuing the activity. If the activity was challenging, they took into consideration the horse's feelings in their approach for task accomplishment. These behaviors were also observed between the clients and the humans in the arena. Postprogram, these interactions were observed to occur within clients' social network.

Historically, every culture has had its hero. Humans have spun wild tales of countless battles won by the great hero who, along with a great companion, overcame all odds to win a great victory. Those stories continue to serve an as inspiration and moral guide to preserve an ever diminishing heritage. Those stories have reminded us to aspire to be greater than we are and always to move forward in our lives. They tell us that life is never easy and that we will all face tragedy or oppression at some point. The stories give us hope that each of us can overcome life's obstacles. The quest or the journey is as important, if not more so, than the final goal or destination because of what is learned along the way. When we look out at the green pastures filled with grazing horses, we are somehow connected with those stories of glorious battles and heroic feats. By their power and effortless beauty we are inspired and humbled with awe. The heroic epics remind us that we are never alone on our journey and that they will carry us through our darkest hours of night. As facilitators we were transformed and became witnesses to the clients' journey, just as they were transformed by living it.

Application

This program was developed for use with people with MR/DD, who have maladaptive behavioral challenges. However, it can be adapted for use with a variety of client groups. These activities have also been effective in programs with absentee fathers as well as for teenage girls with self-esteem issues. Horses in these programs become a bridge upon which a new foundation for bonding can be built. In an age when children spend up to 7 hours a day playing video games and watching TV, the ability to interact socially becomes diminished. Horses can be a way to facilitate attachments that may result in successful social relationships. This program is also impactful for clients suffering from posttraumatic stress disorder. Again, the horse becomes the stimulus and motivating factor that can assist someone in overcoming trauma-induced anxiety. The motivation gained from the interaction with the horse can illicit a desire to connect. This is accomplished because connection with the horse occurs in a quiet peaceful environment that is less threatening than a traditional counseling environment, thus allowing the client to feel safe and supported. Thereby, maladaptive behaviors resulting from the trauma can be addressed. Moreover, when clients choose a horse that mirrors their emotional state, a powerful metaphor for them can be established that will allow the horse to carry the burden during the journey.

Animal assisted therapies in general can be so powerful. From a very basic and primitive place, humans want to connect with nature. There is a natural driving force to return and seek solace in nature. It is this desire to connect that is the foundation for all our work in this field. It creates powerful and motivating experiences that bring about life change. The development of a program that uses a broad concept and then addresses each client's needs specifically can give a practitioner greater flexibility in application. Ponder generally about opportunities to connect and that perfect moment will come.

Acknowledgment

This essay is dedicated to Donna's bravery: her bravery with disability, her bravery to change, her bravery to face death. This essay is dedicated to all who bravely embark on the Journey.

References

Barkley, R. (1990). *Attention deficit hyperactivity disorder: A handbook for diagnosis and treatment.* New York: Guilford.

Campbell, J. (1968). *The hero with a thousand faces.* Princeton: Princeton University Press, Novato, California: New World Library.

Campbell, J. (1990). *The hero's journey: Joseph Campbell on his life and work.* New York: Harper and Row.

DeLeon, I. G., & Iwata, B. A. (1996). Evaluation of a multiple-stimulus presentation format for assessing reinforcer preferences. *Journal of Applied Behavior Analysis, 29,* 519–533.

Dewey, J. (1938). *Experience and education.* New York: Simon and Schuster.

Dodge, K. A., McClaskey, C. L., & Feldman, E. (1985). A situational approach to the assessment of social competence in children. *Journal of Consulting and Clinical Psychology.*

Doolittle, P. E. (1997). Vygotsky's zone of proximal development as a theoretic foundation for cooperative learning. *Journal on Excellence in College Teaching, 8*(1), 83–103.

Irwin, C., & Weber, B. (2001). *Horses don't lie: What horses teach us about our natural capacity for awareness, confidence, courage, and trust.* New York: Marlowe.

Katcher, A. H., & Beck, A. M. (1983). *New perspectives on our lives with companion animals.* Philadelphia: University of Pennsylvania Press.

Kellert, S. R. (1993). The biological basis for human valves of nature. In S. R. Kellert & E. O. Wilson (Eds), *The biophilia hypothesis.* Washington, DC: Island Press.

Levinson, B. M. (1969). *Pet-oriented child psychotherapy.* Springfield, IL: Charles C. Thomas.

Mckissock, H. B. (2003). *A model for using interaction with horses to increase reading motivation of first grade urban students.* Lafayette, IN: Purdue University.

McCormick, A., & McCormick, M. (1997). *Horse sense and the human heart.* Deerfield Beach, FL: Health Communications, Inc.

North American Riding for the Handicapped Association. (NARHA). (1997). *What is therapeutic riding?* Retrieved from: www.narha.org/narha1.html

Prochaska, O., Velicer, F., DiClemente, C., & Fava, L. (1988). Measuring processes of change: Applications to the cessation of smoking. *Journal of Consulting and Clinical Psychology, 56,* 520–528.

Shurtleff, T. L., & Engsberg, J. R. (2010). Changes in trunk and head stability after hippotherapy, a pilot study. *Physical and Occupational Therapy in Pediatrics, 30*(2), 150–163.

Stanton, D. D. (1998). *Effects of animal assisted therapy on the behavior of children in a therapeutic day school.* Chicago, IL: Roosevelt University.

Vygotsky, L. S. (1978*). Mind in society.* Cambridge, MA: MIT Press.

Wilson, E.O. (1984). *Biophilia: The human bond with other species.* Cambridge, MA: Harvard University Press.

CHAPTER 7

Techniques That Improve Self-Esteem and Self-Worth

☐ **Improvement of Self-Efficacy and Social Skills Through Participation in Great and Small, a Therapeutic Horseback Riding Program**

Patricia Westerman, Holly A. Hargreaves, Delores Westerman, and Melissa Verge

Introduction

This chapter illustrates, through the use of two case studies, that horses and humans can develop important relationships that can enhance social skills and psychosocial issues, including self-efficacy. The case studies were assessed in the context of a therapeutic riding program called Great and Small in the state of Maryland. The mission of this program is to bring together horses and humans to allow them to support each other. Every horse who works in the program is an animal whose life has taken a turn of some type. In most cases, the horse led a "productive" life as an athlete and competitor or a school horse, only to outlive its perceived usefulness in that role. In each case, however, the horse proves to be very capable of offering a great deal to the riders, whose needs involve primarily unconditional love and patience.

The horses in the program also receive immeasurable benefits from their participation. Whether rescued from unfortunate situations or retired by loving, nurturing owners, the horses find renewed energy and pride while contributing to the rehabilitation of the riders. People who know horses are aware that most horses thrive when given a combination of loving care and a true purpose. The sense of dignity and self-respect that the program's horses demonstrate is testament to the fact that their involvement produces positive consequences for them as well as the riders whom they help.

The riders in the program are persons with a variety of special needs: Some of them have been victims of physical and sexual abuse, some have medical issues such as autism or cerebral palsy, some have mental retardation, some have behavioral issues, and many have a combination of these conditions. The program brings caring, noble horses together with brave, determined people and allows the horses and people to heal each other in a number of profound ways.

Rationale

Humans and animals have been inherently connected since the beginning of our existence (Hargreaves, Westerman, Westerman, & Verge, 2007). Since that time the human–animal bond has continued to develop, and for many centuries now animal assisted therapy has existed in some manner (Hargreaves et al., 2007). Numerous historical accounts document ways animals have helped people in a multitude of contexts (Burch, 1996; Chandler, 2005; Eggiman, 2006; Taylor, 2001).

Currently horses are recognized worldwide as having both physical and emotional benefits for children (Maello, 2003). There is a decrease in heart rates and blood pressure as well as improved respiration for people while they brush horses (Sentoo, 2003). Research also shows that children who participate in therapeutic riding programs demonstrate greater self-confidence, self-esteem, and motivation to learn (Bizub, Joy, & Davidson, 2003).

The emergence of equine assisted counseling (EAC) has developed as an outgrowth of the healing bond that can develop between animals and humans, and research indicates that this type of counseling provides a safe and secure environment that nurtures inner healing and encourages optimal growth and development (Chandler, 2005; Trotter, Chandler, Goodwin-Bond, & Casey, 2008). There is a growing body of evidence that animal assisted activities and, specifically, equine assisted activities are efficacious for children with a wide variety of special needs such as autism, attention-deficit disorder, sensory integration problems, conduct disorders, and other behaviors. Equine facilitated activities (EFAs) occur within an emerging field with effective and beneficial therapeutic interventions for a wide variety of populations that are in need of alternative forms of therapy (Chandler, 2005; Eggiman, 2006; Mühlhausen & Nickel, 2005; Nathanson, 1989; Pace, 1996; Reichert, 1994; Taylor, 2001).

Description of First Case Study

The first case to be described here involves Jenna.* Jenna is a competent, bright, generous woman in her 50s who has multiple sclerosis (MS). The horse with whom she has a special relationship is Goldie, a very large draft horse whom Jenna describes as a goddess.

Jenna was diagnosed with relapsing remitting MS 20 years ago at the age of 38. Prior to this diagnosis, she was an extremely active woman who enjoyed many outdoor activities, such as skiing, hiking, biking, camping, backpacking, and cross-country skiing. In fact, at the time of her diagnosis, Jenna owned and operated an outdoor adventure business that involved taking clients on backpacking and hiking trips that covered many miles per day. Before her diagnosis, Jenna typically hiked about 10 miles a day with pack on her back. Then she and her clients would set up camp, and she would go out later and walk after dinner. Several months after being diagnosed with MS, Jenna noticed that her ability to take long hikes was already diminishing.

Jenna's physical capabilities have gradually decreased so much that she began using canes periodically to help her walk beginning 13 years ago. Soon she could ambulate only by using an electric wheelchair when she was outside of her house. Her current diagnosis is *secondary progressive MS*, for which she says there is no prescribed medical therapy that has been especially helpful to her.

Jenna describes MS as a disease of loss. She described her loss of two activities that she loved—riding a bike and skiing—as devastating to her. She soon also lost the ability to drive a car without adaptive equipment.

---

* The names of the riders described in this essay have been changed. In addition, portions of this essay have appeared in print in the social work journal *Reflections*.

She was afraid that she had also lost the ability to ride horses, but she was heartened when one of her medical doctors, several years ago, offered her some profound words, saying that she should "use somebody else's feet." Jenna thought, "How am I going to do that?"

Then, in 2007, Jenna watched a television program on therapeutic riding. She was especially interested in a story about a couple with a young daughter who could not walk. The workers at the riding program put the 3-year-old girl on a horse, and, after a short while, she began walking. After seeing this show, Jenna started calling therapeutic riding programs in her area but found that they were all full and had long waiting lists. A staff person of another therapeutic riding program referred Jenna to Great and Small.

When Jenna arrived at Great and Small, she had her first lesson with Huck. Jenna describes her first lesson as illustrative of the strengths of the program and of the collaboration that can take place between a person and a horse. Jenna drove to the program in her adaptive van and was very excited to see the horse she was to ride. She also saw a group of volunteers who had assembled to help her. Jenna drove her wheelchair up the mounting ramp and prepared to mount Huck for the first time. As she did so, the instructor and the other volunteers asked her how she would like to mount the horse. The instructor described three or four possibilities but left the decision up to Jenna. She believes that this was done to include her and to allow her to play a significant role in the therapy. Jenna decided how she would like to mount, and the six volunteers helped her up on the horse. In recalling this event, Jenna said, "Sitting on this horse, I thought I'd died and gone to heaven."

She then described how the lesson progressed as well as the support she received from the person leading the horse, the two side walkers, the person behind her, the person on the ramp "overseeing everything," and the one teaching her. She was amazed that the program pulled together this team of six people "just to get one person on a horse." She described Huck as very patient and steady. At that first lesson, Jenna went around the ring only twice because she had so little strength in her legs. When it came time to dismount, Jenna wondered how she would get off the horse, but the team just took the event in stride and made her feel very confident.

Jenna went on to ride Huck one more time and then rode Murphy a few times. Jenna made good progress in her riding, eventually mounting from the ramp from a standing position instead of from the wheelchair. Ultimately, Jenna started riding Goldie, whom Jenna described as a very large, unflappable, businesslike horse, and has continued to ride her for many months.

When asked what Goldie has given Jenna, she answered in this way:

What she's given me is that I can move through space. I'm not in a wheelchair. I have the experience of moving forward not in a mechanical way. She gives me the ability to 'walk,' to go places where I couldn't go without her. I used to hike in a national park because it allowed me to go places I couldn't go in a car. Goldie allows me to go places I couldn't go without her. On my first trail ride on Goldie, we just went around the barn, but we were outside; we were in the air. I couldn't ride by myself—I didn't have enough strength—so two volunteers had to go with me.

But Jenna describes this as a very freeing experience. MS had taken away all of the outdoor activities that Jenna loved, but Goldie brought back one of the activities for Jenna. "Now I'm riding again. And I love doing this. I get to do something I love two or three times a week."

Similar to the model employed by Equine Assisted Growth and Learning Association (EAGALA, 2010) our model at Great and Small involves various therapeutic and learning activities designed to apply particular skills:

1. Assertiveness

2. Nonverbal communication

3. Leadership

4. Creative thinking and problem solving

5. Accountability or responsibility

6. Confidence and self-esteem

7. Teamwork and building relationships

The formal goal of our program is to provide quality therapeutic riding that will instill positive self-esteem, a sense of self-worth, and empowerment within clients, will establish or reestablish trust within clients, and will help clients gain an understanding of unconditional love with another being (the horse; Hargreaves et al., 2007). Through achieving these goals with the horse it is the hope that the clients will then transfer these same goals to their relationships with other people.

The informal goals of our program are to help clients improve interpersonal relationships; to increase self-esteem and coping skills; increase confidence, assertiveness, and patience; develop a sense of self-worth;

develop teamwork and cooperation skills; reconnect with the children with lost feelings; bring back or initiate a sense of a sense of the feeling of good touch and love for people through the loving relationship with the horse; learn appropriate social skills; learn about themselves and what they fear; increase awareness of the outside world; increase self-awareness; increase self-control; reduce stress; learn to follow directions and ways to solve problems; and learn about the importance of nurturing reconnecting with lost feelings (Hargreaves et al., 2007). These activities assist clients in finding their own solutions as to how to best cope and address the various therapeutic issues that they face in their daily lives (Project Horse, 2010). Thus, they are empowered to persevere through adversity first in the safe therapeutic environment and then to apply their new life skills to the real world (Project Horse).

In the case of Jenna, she was able to overcome the profound loss of her physical movement and freedom as well as the depression from such an experience through her therapeutic riding experience with Goldie and the staff at Great and Small. Great and Small also employs transference theory as it serves as one of the primary theories behind animal assisted therapy and equine assisted counseling (Hargreaves et al., 2007). In accordance with the belief that animals are useful aids in therapy for humans, the use of the theory of transference in such therapeutic interactions came about as a means of understanding some underlying mechanisms at work in animal assisted therapy. It is also believed that the animals can act as a bridge (Reichert, 1994; Sentoo, 2003) between the client and other people through the process of transference (Sentoo, 2003). The concept of transference originated with Sigmund Freud (Patterson, 1959) and is used in animal assisted therapy through the therapeutic interchange.

The therapeutic interchange generally occurs in three steps (Sentoo, 2003):

1. Transference is first completed by the introduction of an attentive animal that should elicit a positive response from the client.

2. It is believed that the "warming effect" of the positive interaction between the client and the animal will elicit another positive response from the person.

3. Clients will then transfer their positive feeling from the interaction with the animal onto another person, such as the therapist, within the environment.

Furthermore, through the therapists modeling kind behavior with animals, it is theorized that clients will also demonstrate kind and assertive behavior with the animal as well as the therapist (Taylor, 2001).

Jenna successfully completed the process of transference as she was able to transfer her positive feelings, coping skills, life skills, and overall positive growth experience gained by her therapeutic riding experience at Great and Small to other aspects of her life, including but not limited to improvements in her physical and mental well-being. Jenna describes some improvements that she has noticed in her physical abilities. She says, MS colors absolutely everything in my life. It is chronic, capricious, and incurable." Yet, after riding for only 6 months, Jenna noticed:

> "...[G]reat improvement—I have better ankle flexibility. My feet feel better. I can keep my heels down and my toes up. I have better posture. I have enough strength in my legs to get Goldie to weave in and out of poles using only my legs. I have more core stability. In my last lesson, I was able to stand up in the stirrups all the way around the indoor ring twice. These may seem like little things, but they're huge."

Jenna's ability to reach the aforementioned goals was a major therapeutic milestone that reflected not only Jenna's hard work and dedication to increasing her physical strength but also the significant improvement in her mental health and well-being, especially as it pertains to her increased self-esteem, self-efficacy, and feelings of empowerment.

Jenna explains that it is not just the relationship with the horse that has helped her but also the caring of the people who work in the program. Jenna explains that she needs only two people to help her now instead of the six she needed when she first started, but they are always completely devoted to her and to Goldie. She describes the volunteers and teachers as very emotionally supportive. Jenna says that every lesson is positive, with instructors and volunteers always focusing on her accomplishments, however small, for the day.

What is fascinating is Jenna's reflection on the intangible things that the interactions with the horses seem to bring the riders in this program. She says,

> I see children with autism with so little control over their environment. The world is just huge for them. And they get on a horse and they get this really big animal to respond to them. They can control it. It's the same with me and MS. I can't control it. But the riding is empowering. And it's

a two-way street. I am empowered because the horse responds to me. But I also respond to the horse, listening to her, to what she needs from me. The relationship is important. Goldie lets me ride her, but I'm very clear that when she's done, I respect her and I stop riding. She's good to me. She has all the spirit and ego that a goddess has.

Jenna also describes the sense of community and celebration at the barn. She tells a story about a day when another rider was just finishing his lesson as she arrived for hers. The teacher told her about the wonderful things that the previous rider had done. Thus, all riders can revel in each other's successes.

Horses act as mirrors to humans and, in so doing, act as sources of inner reflection. Clay (2004) notes that animals act as mirrors to humans because they see "what," or more specifically "who," is really there instead of "what" or "who" one perceives oneself to be. Taylor (2001) poignantly describes this concept especially as it pertains to equine facilitated therapy as follows:

> With a philosophy of horse as mirror and projective object, the work is rich for analysis (Rector, 2001). There would be an emphasis on the development of relationship with the horse when designing a session. The horse is "honest" in responses and interactions. The task of separating a horse from the herd for the purpose of catching and haltering will present material about how the client interacts in the world. The horse may respond by running away, pinning his ears back as a sign of aggression or irritation, or may simply wait to be caught. The assumption is that the horse will imitate the patient's energy and/or that the client will unconsciously gravitate toward a horse that will mirror the client's inner process. The outcome may provide an expanded sense of self and a desire on the part of the patient to take personal responsibility for his or her behavior. (p. 42)

Horses have a direct and almost automatic response to a way a person approaches them. This concept is very powerful and effective as a therapeutic tool because horses do not lie, use manipulative behavior, or operate under *hidden agendas* as humans often do. As a result, they are in a unique position to offer humans great insight into their behavior toward others and, perhaps more importantly, toward themselves (Hargreaves et al., 2007). By working with the horses and the staff at Great and Small, people such as Jenna have been able to gain greater insight into their own conscious and subconscious behavioral patterns and then work on achieving more effective and healthy behavioral patterns and attitudes.

Some healthy behavioral patterns and attitudes that we have seen clients gain from their participation in the therapeutic riding program at Great and Small include the following (Hargreaves et al., 2007):

- Healthy attachment behaviors in abused children who used to have attachment problems

- The horse as a self-esteem booster partly because having successfully commanded a horse, a very large animal, makes the clients very proud of themselves and gives them increased self-esteem

- Clients' ability to empathize with a horse because it is nonjudgmental

- Clients' capacity to transfer the feelings of trust and love that they have with the horse to other people

As one adolescent (a survivor of extreme abuse and trauma) in the program at Great and Small who has been participating in the program since childhood stated, "My horse is the only one who understands me" (Hargreaves et al., 2007, p. 9). This poignant statement demonstrates how powerful the human–animal bond, particularly in animal assisted therapy, can be for clients. The adolescent had been working with this specific horse for a long period of time and created a bond with the horse that surpassed all others from the participant's perspective. Furthermore, one Washington, DC, social worker stated that "going to horseback riding at Great and Small has been the only activity that has reached her," speaking of an 11-year old abuse victim (Hargreaves et al., 2007, p. 9).

Description of Second Case Study

Another inspiring story about the impact of a relationship with a special horse involves Katrice. Through interviews with Katrice as well as her mother, the broad and deep effects that a relationship with a horse and a number of caring people can have on a person became evident.

Katrice is a 17-year-old girl who has developmental delays and learning issues. Her disabilities stem from an abnormality on chromosome 18Q, resulting in cognitive and social skills deficiencies as well as motor coordination problems. Katrice grooms and rides "her" horse, Bear, once a week. She has been riding for several years, but riding Bear and working at Great and Small as a volunteer over the last year have played a strong role in her emotional maturation.

We believe that Katrice's emotional maturation resulted from the impact of the horses serving as social facilitators. Horses possess the innate ability to facilitate or serve as a catalyst for interaction between clients and counselors or therapists. Gene Myers describes this concept by referring to animals as "optimally discrepant social others" (Kruger, Trachtenberg, & Serpell, 2004, p. 9) in that because animals are similar to humans they can "elicit pro-social behavior and positive affect." Also, because they are simultaneously dissimilar, they do not threaten humans; therefore, animals are able to "mediate interactions in otherwise awkward or uncomfortable therapeutic contexts" (p. 9).

Fine (2006), a licensed psychologist, also suggests that animals can work as facilitators of social interaction as well as catalysts for emotion and adjuncts to clinicians. Fine recently conducted a patient survey at her practice. The results of Fine's study suggest:

> That the presence of animals made the therapeutic environment seem more friendly and the therapy itself less threatening. Respondents also reported that the animals made them feel more relaxed and open, and made them feel more comfortable in general. These findings suggest that animals can ease the stress inherent in the initial phase of therapy, and may help to expedite the trust the trust and rapport-building process between therapist and patient. (p. 16)

The results from Fine's (2006) survey suggest that animals may also be helpful in initiating therapy and rapport building with resistant or shy clients such as children who are survivors of abuse. With the aforementioned research findings in mind, it is quite apparent how Katrice's social maturation was facilitated by her therapeutic riding experience at Great and Small. Katrice volunteers as a leader and side walker every Saturday. She is so devoted to Bear and to her work that she wanted to stay home from her family vacation last summer because she didn't want to miss Bear or miss her work. Katrice's attachment to Bear further supports another theoretical foundation in animal assisted therapy that is employed at Great and Small, which is the concept that animals act as sources of social support (Hargreaves et al., 2007). The unconditional love and support that animals such as Bear provide to people enable them to become "confidantes" for clients, particularly children and adolescents such as Katrice. Melson and Fogel (1996) found that 76% of children and adolescents (ages 7–15) felt that an unfamiliar dog knew what they were feeling after only 5 minutes of interaction. Melson and Fogel determined that 84% of those children would feel comfortable confiding secrets to the dog (Kruger et al., 2004).

Animal assisted therapy is particularly beneficial for children and adolescents. The unconditional positive regard that the animal provides allows the children to feel safe in sharing their stories with the animal. Additionally, the nonverbal nature of the animal helps children because they know that the animals will not tell their stories to anyone else. Further, the therapy animal can serve as both a transitional object in healing as well as a symbol of hope within recovery (Hargreaves et al., 2007).

Bear was most definitely Katrice's symbol of hope during her therapeutic riding experience at Great and Small. In addition to the emotional support that Katrice feels from Bear, Katrice's participation in the program has improved her physical coordination, her academic achievement, and her maturity level. Only several years ago, Katrice, according to her mother, often exhibited inappropriate social behaviors, but this has been minimized dramatically. She has matured in her communication skills, her poise, her manners, and her eye contact. The responsibilities of caring for Bear and working in the program have contributed to a dramatic increase in her initiative as well. Katrice's mother also reports that she has seen major improvements in Katrice's academic ability: "Her reading level has improved two grade levels in one year; her math ability has improved several grade levels in one year." Her mother believes that this is because Katrice has found something she loves (Bear) and a place "where she doesn't feel different." Katrice's mother believes that the improvements she has seen in her daughter stem from a number of factors, including the "very positive feedback from teachers" and volunteers as well as the encouragement that the riders give each other. The improvement may also be due to the theory that animals can assist in learning when clients are participating in animal assisted therapy. This type of therapy has been shown to be efficacious with a variety of populations, particularly children. Nathanson (1989) demonstrated this in his animal assisted therapy study using Atlantic bottlenose dolphins with children with special needs. Nathanson found that animals can increase attention in children and, in so doing, improve cognitive processing. Nathanson states that the results indicated that the participants learned 2 to 10 times faster when they were interacting with dolphins. It is very probable that Katrice's participation in the therapeutic riding programs improved her cognitive processing skills, among other factors, resulting in her academic improvement. She also has noticed that "the riders and teachers and volunteers show respect for the horses and for the riders," and she believes that this is a very important element of the program.

After hearing from Katrice's mother, Katrice had her chance to describe her relationship with Bear and her work at Great and Small. She articulates in a very mature manner the work she does as a mentor for new volunteers. She exhibits a sense of pride in her ability to teach others what she knows about horses and riders. When asked how she feels when she is mentoring and assisting in the riding lessons, Katrice said, "I feel proud that I teach the kids who don't know how to ride how to sit in the saddle straight. I help them if they're off balance. It's a great feeling to do that because I'm helping someone who's never had that experience." She explained further, "Some of the riders have autism, but they're very able to ride and I know they can. But sometimes they don't want to try."

When asked why, Katrice said, "I think they don't want to try because they're having a bad day or they're sad about something. But I'll tell them, 'Come on, you can do it.' I'll put a happy face on and tell them what to do." When asked for an example, Katrice reported, "One day, one little girl didn't want to mount. I was on the other side of the horse and we were on the ramp. I kept saying, 'Come on, you can do it,' but she wouldn't get on. The trainers got her on the horse and she started crying. I think she was a little bit afraid. But then when she was on the horse, she stopped crying and smiled." When asked how she responded when the little girl cried, Katrice said, "I put on a happy face because she's gonna see it and feel stronger."

Application

In attempting to analyze how this healing takes place, it is necessary to know the theoretical basis for the therapeutic riding program. The program employs Bandura's (1977) self-efficacy model in the training of teachers and volunteers. Self-efficacy refers to the confidence that one has in one's ability to achieve a task. The model asserts that one can help people to develop self-efficacy through the combination of specific strategies, including mastery experiences, vicarious experiences, and verbal persuasion.

The mastery experience component of the model refers to placing people in situations in which they cannot fail. This component is implemented by asking riders to make very small, incremental steps in their riding rather than asking them to attempt huge leaps of progress from one lesson to the next. The vicarious experience aspect of the model is implemented by offering, when needed, a model of the new behavior that the instructors ask the riders to perform. The verbal persuasion component refers to offering only positive feedback to the riders at all times. Every attempt that the rider makes is responded to in a positive manner by the instructor and the volunteers. Even when making corrections to the rider's form, the volunteer is careful to point out something positive that the rider is doing.

The program trains all volunteers and teachers to implement the concepts of this model, and the volunteers and teachers, including very new volunteers with significant disabilities, employ the methods consistently. The trainers believe that this takes place because the teachers and long-term volunteers use the methods in the presence of the newer volunteers, so there is constant observation and imitation of the self-efficacy enhancing strategies employed in the program.

In addition to the theoretical model that underlies the training and teaching that occur in this program, the relationships that the people and horses forge effortlessly through their mutual participation are very powerful. The horses, without any overt knowledge of doing so, provide positive feedback simply by sensing what the riders need and giving it to them. The riders, therefore, experience the feeling of trusting the horses because the horses make the riders feel safe and nurtured.

Interestingly, many of the riders, instructors, and volunteers report that they are initially drawn to Great and Small because they want to be with horses. What they find once they arrive is that they benefit greatly from the interactions they have with the other people as well. The ability to build relationships based on trust, dependability, empathy, and empowerment is a beautiful product of a number of people and horses being brought together under extraordinary conditions to heal each other.

References

Bandura, A. (1977). Self-efficacy: Toward a unifying theory of behavioral change. *Psychological Review, 84*, 191–215.

Bizub, A. L., Joy, A., & Davidson, L. (2003). "It's like being in another world": Demonstrating the benefits of therapeutic horseback riding for individuals with psychiatric disability. *Psychiatric Rehabilitation Journal, 26*(4), 377–384.

Burch, M. R. (1996). *Volunteering with your pet: How to get involved in animal-assisted therapy*. New York: Macmillan.

Chandler, C. K. (2005). *Animal assisted therapy in counseling*. Boca Raton, FL: Taylor & Francis.

Clay, A. (2004, May). Discover your inner equine. *Horse Illustrated*, 114–122.

Project Horse. (2010). An overview of equine assisted psychotherapy and equine assisted learning. Retrieved from: http://projecthorse.org/ProjectHORSE_EAP_EAL.html

EAGALA. (2010). What is EAP and EAL? Retrieved from http://eagala.org/Information/What_is_EAP_EAP

Eggiman, J. (2006). Cognitive-behavioral therapy: A case report—Animal-assisted therapy. *Topics in Advanced Practice Nursing E-Journal, 6*(3). Retrieved from: http://www.medscape.com/viewarticle/545439_1

Fine, A. (2006). *Handbook on animal-assisted therapy, third edition: Theoretical foundations and guidelines for practice.* Philadelphia, PA: Elsevier Science.

Hargreaves, H., Westerman, P., Westerman, D., & Verge, M. (2007). The benefits of animal assisted therapy with children that are survivors of abuse. In: *CSA sociological abstracts database.*

Kruger, K. A., Trachtenberg, S. W., & Serpell, J. A. (2004). *Can animals help humans heal? Animal assisted interventions in adolescent mental health.* Center for the Interaction of Animals and Society University of Pennsylvania School of Veterinary Medicine. Retrieved from: http://www2.vet.upenn.edu/research/centers/cias/pdf/CIAS_AAI_white_paper.pdf

Maello, N. (2003). Will Rogers saw it. *Exceptional Child, 33*(11), 1–2.

Melson, G. F., & Fogel, A. (1996). Parental perceptions of their children's involvement with house-hold pets: A test of a specificity model of nurturance. *Anthrozoos, 9,* 95–106.

Mühlhausen, R., & Nickel, C. (2005). TTEAM as an intervention in the therapy: I.) Of patients with dementia, and II.) Of chronic alcohol addicts. Unpublished master's thesis, University of Cologne, Germany.

Nathanson, D. E. (1989). Using Atlantic bottlenose dolphins to increase cognition of mentally retarded children. *Clinical and Abnormal Psychology, 233–242.*

Pace, K. N. (1996). The impact of animal assisted therapy with an adolescent substance abuse population. Unpublished master's thesis, Rush University.

Patterson, C. H. (1959). *Counseling and psychotherapy: Theory and practice.* New York: Harper & Row.

Reichert, E. (1994). Play and animal-assisted therapy: A group treatment model for sexually abused girls ages 9–13. *Family Therapy, 21*(1), 55–62.

Sentoo, G. S. (2003). The influence of animal-assisted play therapy on the self-esteem of adolescents with special needs. Unpublished master's thesis, University of Pretoria.

Taylor, S. M. (2001). Equine facilitated psychotherapy: An emerging field. Unpublished master's thesis, St. Michael's College, Colchester, VT.

Trotter, K. S., Chandler, C. K., Goodwin-Bond, D., & Casey, J. (2008). A comparative study of the efficacy of group equine assisted counseling with at-risk children and adolescents. *Journal of Creativity in Mental Health, 3*(3), 254–284.

☐ Using Equine Assisted Counseling With Psychotherapists in a Group Setting

Judy Weston-Thompson

Introduction

Working with horses and humans as a Certified Equine Facilitator Interactive Professional-Mental Health (CEFIP-MH) along with being a Licensed Marriage and Family Therapist (LMFT) for more than 20 years has led to my creation of an equine program designed to foster the ongoing psychological health of those who do healing work. Knowing full well the intuitive and healing capacities of horses, I embarked on a pilot *consultation* group for psychotherapists with the intent of creating interest in the field and possible referrals. However, by the second or third meeting of this pilot group, six therapist clients and I were deeply involved in the process. And, as with any process, one gets involved by personally experiencing it.

My intention was threefold: (1) to promote professional develop-ment; (2) to enhance personal growth; and (3) to provide my therapist clients with an overview of equine assisted counseling (EAC). I imme-diately knew that psychotherapists and horses would be a perfect fit, because horses naturally model and reflect the very qualities which we therapists, in our many years of training, work so hard to achieve: pres-ence, empathy, intuitive skills, connectedness, and increased somatic awareness. Horses are also ideal models for inner harmony, balance, and insight—the goals toward which we humans strive. Because my deep association with horses has so significantly increased my own inner knowing, I was completely confident that the therapists who were drawn to my group would be seeking much more than didactic consultation.

Rationale

Both my personal and professional experiences have proven to me the healing and psychological benefits of EAC. My years of working with horses have taught me that there is a level of opening and honesty that occurs in their very presence. Horses are archetypal in that they evoke powerful emotional sensations in human beings (Hargreaves, Westerman, Westerman, & Verge, 2007). EAC involves a beneficial, effective integra-tion of the horse's innate healing ability with psychotherapeutic work (Bizub, Joy, and Davidson, 2003; Chandler, 2005; Maello, 2003; Trotter, Chandler, Goodwin-Bond, & Casey, 2008).

Upon deciding to facilitate EAC groups for psychotherapists, I had to give thorough consideration to the issues therapists face on a daily basis, both with our clients and within our own psyches. The ability to be present with one's client and with one's self may be considered a therapist's guiding light. Horses innately know and instantly reflect one's level of presence. The ability to be in relationship and one's capacity for connectedness are essential for doing healing work with clients. Horses pull you into relationship if you're willing and walk away from you if you are not. The ability to realize one's own true inner nature is at the foundation of therapeutic work. Horses have an astounding ability to cut through the outer layers and quickly draw us into a deeper relationship with ourselves.

There are numerous ways I've experienced my equine cofacilitators teaching and modeling these qualities that are so essential to both personal growth and professional development. One member of my therapist group, Jean, had a strong connection with her horse but felt she came up short in her willingness to "take charge" and be the leader. I noted the connection between Jean and her horse but also remarked that she made eye contact with the animal more often while leading him instead of watching where she wanted him to go. In our second working session, Jean shared her awareness of feeling challenged to take charge in her life.

Psychotherapists also find EAC to be particularly helpful because our work requires us to keep constantly abreast of our countertransference issues (the therapist's emotional reactions to the patient based on the therapist's unconscious needs or feelings; Sentoo, 2003). The therapist, for example, may feel helpless with a client. These deep feelings of helplessness will be brought into the foreground in one's work with a horse. Or a therapist may feel disconnected in relationship to a client; this inability to connect will manifest immediately in the presence of a horse (Reichert, 1994; Sentoo, 2003). In our second pilot group meeting at my barn office, two women broke into tears, noting the vulnerability that came forth in relationship to their horse partners.

Description

Overview

The group, composed of up to six members, meets with me for six consecutive weeks. The first group session includes the required paper work, logistics, group rules, my introduction to the class, and introductions by individual members. All other group meetings begin with a check-in and segue into horse work and debriefing.

During the very first check-in, members disclose their reasons for attending as well as their personal and professional goals.

In subsequent check-ins (groups two through six), members describe how the previous group may have affected their personal or professional work. The purpose of the check-in is to ground the members in being present in the group, to increase group safety and cohesion, and to reflect on any personal or professional process that has occurred since the last meeting.

The second part of each group is experiential and involves partnering each member with a horse and engaging in various EAC activities. I have designed these activities specifically for therapists to enhance the personal and professional qualities referenced in my introduction (presence, empathy, intuitive skills, connectedness, and increased somatic awareness).

The third part of the group—debriefing—includes feedback as well as self-observation and facilitator observation of group members. As with any group therapy, participants are striving toward insight. The debriefings are focused on the here-and-now (presence), what is happening (process rather than content), and interpersonal–interspecies relationship (self and horse). The debriefing segment serves as an integration of what has taken place with each participant through personal process and experiential.

Human–Horse Relationship

Being in relationship with a horse requires that one be fully present—without agenda, as agendas don't lend support to interspecies friendship. Thus, the all-encompassing goal of my group exercises is to support my clients in being truly present without expectations. Horses respond to a human's competency, need for control, and expectations. When one of my horse cofacilitators, in this case Caesar, isn't compliant, the participants have a difficult time because they feel incompetent. In this way, Caesar has become the therapist.

Caesar has a way of letting me know when a client has an agenda with him, and I have learned to intuitively interpret the horse's response to his human partner. My relationship with Caesar alone evokes transference in people who sense my protectiveness of him and worry about my feelings even after I've assured them that I would stop a session if human or horse safety was at stake.

Exercises

Safe Horse Practices

Besides being an ethical necessity, I'm continually tying safety issues—such as clear and appropriate boundaries with horses—back to safety issues with each therapist's own clients. Although I interject safety practices throughout all the sessions, our first exercise is specifically devoted to demonstrating and using safe horse practices around the barn and with horses. I explain what we are doing and why. I'll show the clients how to approach a horse, how to stand behind a horse, and how to interpret a horse's ear and head signals, such as jerking the head or twitching the ears upon being inappropriately approached. The clients further integrate these practices as we move on to the grooming exercise.

Grooming

The grooming exercise may evoke a great deal of emotion for clients. Through grooming in pairs, members learn how horses regulate our emotions as we regulate theirs. They calm down as we calm down, and vice versa, in a synergistic manner. For example, in one grooming exercise when Jean and Adele were working on Caesar together, Caesar kept moving toward his connection with Jean and away from Adele. We had already debriefed some on Adele's family of origin issues with regard to feeling excluded and not being allowed to have a voice. During this exercise, I could clearly witness her attempt to have a perfect technique, which disallowed her ability to be fully present for Caesar. Her feelings also rippled through our dynamic as a group.

Also, clients often rush through the brushing exercise. To the horse, intentional brushing by a person is a glorious experience in somatic connection. Thus, a horse's response to one's hurry may be another reminder for clients to be present, to get into their own somatic experience, and to let go of their agenda.

Leading Horse With Halter and Lead Rope

The goal of this exercise is leadership with connection. Horses, like therapy clients, are more comfortable when they know who is in charge. The issue of taking charge while remaining connected is an ongoing struggle for therapists with their clients, and thus this exercise continually evokes feelings in the group. Participants' goal is to take charge while staying connected to and present with the horse by showing intention of where they want to go. Just as the therapist is challenged to maintain the perfect balance of leadership, presence, and connection with clients, the therapist, now as client, must communicate this balance with the horse.

Personal communication issues will most certainly surface for the group participants as they commonly look at the horse rather than looking at where they want to go, as in the example of Jean. I emphasize walking shoulder to neck with the horse to demonstrate this dilemma, which is especially common with women who are not so encouraged to take charge in our culture. With this exercise, each member of the pilot group was able to tie in leadership and communication issues in both their personal and professional relationships. The exercise had a lasting effect on the participants because it is such a great metaphor for relationship.

Awkward Exercise

The awkward exercise involves creating a situation that tests the participants' flexibility as well as their feelings about the unknown, and rules and questions of professional competency. Without ever compromising human or horse safety or creating any humiliation, I lead participants through a series of exercises. For example, I ask the members as a group to move Caesar around without words, without touch or a lead rope, while I observe who takes charge and who stays behind. In another exercise, I snap off the lead rope and see if the horse continues to follow the group member. I observe at what place the horse breaks connection with the human, why this may have happened, and question how this may be happening in the client's life or work. Most often the participants are intent on performing the task rather than truly being present with the horse. The goal is to match energies with the horse and step outside the box in the ways we connect.

Horse Observation

Clients need to notice how horses are responding to us, so this exercise is about our projections and observations about horses' behavior with each other as well as their responses to our energy. Often I will have group members observe horse behavior in a herd. I also encourage them to watch the horse's behavior when we're processing material as a group. Their observations frequently elicit our projections, such as, "That horse is really angry at the other one." We seem to want to project emotions onto horses.

I also have them observe Caesar as he watches us from his stall. When we enter the barn as a group, I encourage each person to notice which horse they feel drawn to. Sally, for example, who followed my directives with great intention, slowly moved down the barn aisle, meeting and greeting each horse. She clearly understood our effect on the horses as she took time to allow each to feel her energy.

Bareback Riding

Bareback riding as a therapeutic exercise is intensely evocative for clients. Control issues arise, and clients find it challenging to communicate the correct signals to the horse to keep it moving on its own and not returning to me as a reference.

Jean, for example, was very successful in establishing a strong connection with Caesar during the grooming and other exercises and had left the fourth session feeling very positive. But her control issues surfaced when she took the reins and had to do the steering, and Caesar began moving in my direction. As we processed Jean's frustration, Caesar didn't move a muscle. He was responding to what he was feeling from the client, so he came to me. A horse doesn't just do what humans want because they want it. Intention and anxiety are transmitted through one's body—thus the somatic experience plays a part.

Generally speaking, the seasoned riders will have more difficulty with the exercises because they are expecting to feel in control. Jean had show riding in her background. During the riding session, she took a show posture when she mounted Caesar, but he didn't feel her authenticity or her clear intention. She held the reins like a show jumper, and her body wouldn't quite relax into Caesar. In our debriefing, we learned that it was difficult for her to take charge. She led Caesar with communication but with unclear intention.

Inquiry Exercise

In the sixth group session I ask the members, one at a time, to lead the horse of their choice to a private area. Here they are encouraged to ask a question on anything for which they desire insight. Out of this private time, all members of my pilot group reported receiving powerful images, profound feedback, and guidance from their horses. Jean felt reassured that her decision to end her current relationship was correct. Sally felt guided not to join the next group and said her good-bye to Caesar. Adele received feedback that the path she had chosen to ignite her career was accurate. While speaking to Caesar, Adele imagined her process taking flight, like a bird. While the other members and I observed, a bird came to rest on the railing next to them. Not one member reported being self-conscious, as all of us watched this magic unfold.

Riding With a Surcingle

While writing this essay I discovered a way to integrate Star, my other horse facilitator, into the group. Sally and Jean were becoming impatient to begin their riding lessons outside the group structure, and, wanting to continue the therapeutic nature of our work, I created a new exercise that would fulfill many of our common goals.

A surcingle, a strap that fastens around a horse's girth area, is used for ground training and vaulting on a horse. It allows riders to have a bareback experience with the safety of handles on the side. It also allows them to work on their balance and somatic experience while holding them in position without reins for steering.

In this exercise I stand in the center of the ring holding Star on a lunge line while the rider sits on Star with the surcingle. As I move Star through the three gaits—walk, trot, and canter—in a circle approximately 20 meters in diameter, the client experiences the physical positioning of riding. It was a pivotal moment when I told Sally, the least experienced rider, that I had the reins, because it allowed her to surrender to the motion in all three gaits. She closed her eyes and let go into her experience, exceeding our expectations.

Jean, who most desired the riding lesson, continued to want to *think* her position. Since her therapeutic issue was about letting go of control and allowing herself to be carried in life, I had her close her eyes and enter into her body. I felt so empowered and grateful to Star for his role in the work. He and I were truly a team working together to carry these women.

Conclusion

Although these exercises were designed to use with psychotherapists, they would be relevant in working with anyone seeking EAC to bring their desire to connect and be present into alignment with their behavior and emotions. Horses are the most unique of all healers. They can smell if a person is afraid. They can smell if one is authentic. The greatest gift of all that the horse can bring to psychotherapists is the gift of authenticity. Above and beyond everything, isn't this what therapists are required to be?

References

Bizub, A. L., Joy, A., & Davidson, L. (2003). "It's like being in another world": Demonstrating the benefits of therapeutic horseback riding for individuals with psychiatric disability. *Psychiatric Rehabilitation Journal, 26*(4), 377–384.

Chandler, C. K. (2005). *Animal assisted therapy in counseling.* Boca Raton, FL: Taylor & Francis.

Hargreaves, H., Westerman, P., Westerman, D., & Verge, M. (2007). The benefits of animal assisted therapy with children that are survivors of abuse. In: *CSA sociological abstracts database.*

Maello, N. (2003). Will Rogers saw it. *Exceptional Child, 33*(11), 1–2.

Reichert, E. (1994). Play and animal-assisted therapy: A group treatment model for sexually abused girls ages 9–13. *Family Therapy, 21*(1), 55–62.

Sentoo, G. S. (2003). The influence of animal-assisted play therapy on the self-esteem of adolescents with special needs. Unpublished master's thesis, University of Pretoria.

Trotter, K. S., Chandler, C. K., Goodwin-Bond, D., & Casey, J. (2008). A comparative study of the efficacy of group equine assisted counseling with at-risk children and adolescents. *Journal of Creativity in Mental Health, 3*(3), 254–284.

☐ EASEL: Equine Assisted Social–Emotional Learning

Mari Louhi-Lehtiö

Introduction

Emotional intelligence (EI or EQ) is used to describe our ability, capacity, skill, or a self-perceived ability to recognize and manage our own emotions and our inner potential for positive relationships. This includes the ability to recognize and understand how others feel. There are different definitions of EQ, and some disagreement exists as to how the term should be used (Mayer, Salovey, & Caruso, 2008). Linked closely to EQ are, for example, resilience, self-confidence, stress management, and problem-solving skills needed to cope with the demands and challenges of one's environment. Social intelligence is a related term with the focus on self in relation to others (Goleman, 2006).

In 1994, Daniel Goleman and Eileen Rockefeller Growald formed the Collaborative for Academic, Social, and Emotional Learning (CASEL) to advance the science and evidence-based practice of social and emotional learning (SEL), particularly with school-aged children and teens. The term *social–emotional learning* is defined by CASEL as a process in which children and adults develop the fundamental skills we all need to manage self and to handle our relationships and our work effectively and ethically (www.casel.org)—in other words, self-awareness, self-management, social awareness, social skills, and responsible decision making.

Equine Assisted Social Emotional Learning (EASEL®) is Cavesson's experiential facilitation method used since the mid 1990s to enhance education, mental health therapy, and coaching processes. The general process description can be tailored for different client groups and facilitated from each facilitator's own theoretical framework. While working toward individual developmental or therapeutic goals, EASEL allows clients to simultaneously strengthen and fine-tune their own social emotional skills to better match the demands of their daily lives. The facilitation method and the progressive set of relational activities with horses make it possible to have individual facilitation even in a group program and to tailor the facilitation according to criteria for clients' personal needs and goals, temperament, developmental stage, personal history, and culture. Nature and the EASEL horses reduce stress and support the building of a milieu that feels both safe and challenging. The facilitation style, tools, and experiential exercises activate clients' thinking and challenge their beliefs and attitudes. But there are also feelings of happiness caused by the aesthetic and powerful experiences (Lazarus & Lazarus, 1994). EASEL is a particularly suitable experiential facilitation method with clients who feel that they don't want to "just talk."

Rationale

Social–Emotional Skills Cannot Be Taught but They Can Be Learned

Scientific research provides strong evidence that people's social and emotional skills are shaped by both social influences throughout life and their biological makeup (Ridley, 2003). Our social–emotional development begins with attachment formation as a baby and continues to be shaped in all the different relationships we have or lack. But over 100 studies have also shown the efficacy of social–emotional learning programs with school-age children and adolescents (Payton et al., 2008; Zins, Weissberg, Wang, & Walberg, 2004). According to the reviews, effective SEL programs tend to use active forms of learning and a sequenced set of activities to achieve skill objectives, and they focus on developing personal or social skills and explicitly target particular skills for development.

Adding professionally facilitated experiential animal assisted counseling to social–emotional learning programs enhances results. Working with horses has been shown to strengthen in school-age children more areas of social–emotional skills than an award-winning SEL program at school (Trotter, Chandler, Goodwin-Bond, & Casey, 2008). In another study with behaviorally challenging school-age children and teens with ADHD, an animal assisted program was shown to be more effective and motivating for the participants than an Outward-Bound program (Katcher & Wilkins, 2002). The results were so good in the animal assisted program that after the first 6 months the researchers decided on ethical grounds to allow changing from the Outward-Bound program to the Animal Assisted Therapy program.

Effective training principles for adults are well established, but, based on a review of 12 studies (McEnruem, Groves, & Shen, 2010), there is limited evidence of the efficacy of training programs aimed at specifically developing EQ in adults. However, programs that combined psychoeducation, group discussions, and private individual feedback, along with experiential learning methods, demonstrated significant results in the EQ areas that were measured.

Social–Emotional Skills Are Linked to Health

Social–emotional skills are profoundly important. Research results from the past 2 decades have shown a strong link between physical and mental health and beliefs, emotion regulation, and social connectivity (Goleman, 2006). We now know that continuously stressful levels of emotions affect us all the way to the level of gene expression in the immune cells vital for healing wounds and fighting infections and that even a relatively small amount of social isolation is as great a health risk as is cigarette smoking or high blood pressure (Cacioppo, Berntson, Taylor, & Schacter, 2002). Social rejection shows as increased activity in the same brain areas as physical pain (Rock, 2009).

The influence of thoughts and beliefs on health is equally well established. In just one study, spanning over 20 years and involving over 650 research subjects, the scientists found that those who viewed aging more positively lived, on average, 7.5 years longer than those who held negative thoughts and beliefs (Levy, Slade, Kasl, & Kunkel, 2002). As a reference, lowering blood pressure and cholesterol are calculated to improve life span by 4 years and exercise and not smoking by 1 to 3 years (Levy et al.).

The Need for Powerful Experiences

Large changes in emotional reactions and behavior require making large-scale changes in thinking and challenging the underlying irrational beliefs and attitudes. Our attitudes and beliefs color our thinking and perception of situations and influence how we feel about things. Emotions are chemical cocktails in our body, and we have individual refractor periods, the time it takes our bodies to return to baseline (Ekman, 2003). It is even possible to become accustomed to an emotion to the extent of an addiction where we try to arrange social situations to result in that feeling (Dispenza, 2007). To change thinking with training or therapy, we need some kind of event or experience that allows us to change our attitudes and expectations more quickly and dramatically than we normally would.

It is generally thought in all therapy and education models that the most effective learning and growth happens when people find their own solutions through experiential learning, even if only in the mind, and active processing. The activities with EASEL horses place people in a state of active problem solving. The activities are designed to produce a natural process that can be investigated rather than to complete any particular task with a horse. The objective of EASEL is not to teach equestrian skills. As in life and relationships in general, the activities are open and shaped by the horse and the client in that moment. The facilitators' job is to individually guide clients' exercise so that they can safely and productively investigate alternative ways of being, thinking, and doing. The learning arising from this is profound and revealing.

If we want to help children, we need to also work with the adults around them. Not only do emotions influence both what people think and how they think, but they also have a profound effect on what occurs at work and elsewhere in daily life. There is mounting evidence demonstrating how social emotional competence, and not just knowing about it, is essential for leaders. Employee well-being and productivity are strongly linked to the leader's EQ (Goleman, 2006; McEnruem et al., 2010). Similarly, adults model to and reinforce in children their own social–emotional strategies, not only the family's or classroom's social codes but also how to manage emotions. A Finnish study on the emotion regulation of two generations showed that the emotion regulation strategies used by children between ages 7 and 13 were largely the same as those used by their 38- to 40-year-old parents (Tirkkonen, Kokkonen, & Pulkkinen, 2004).

Goals and the Theoretical Framework of EASEL Facilitation

In addition to the individual goals of clients, the general facilitation goals of EASEL are as follows:

- Self-awareness: Knowing what we are feeling in the moment; having a realistic assessment of our own abilities and a well-grounded sense of self-confidence

- Self-management: Handling our own emotions so they facilitate rather than interfere with the task at hand; being conscientious and delaying gratification to pursue goals; persevering in the face of setbacks and frustrations

- Social awareness and empathy: Understanding what others are feeling; being able to take their perspective; appreciating and interacting positively with diverse groups

- Relationship skills: Handling emotions in relationships effectively; establishing and maintaining healthy and rewarding relationships based on cooperation, resistance to inappropriate social pressure, negotiating solutions to conflict, and seeking help when needed

- Responsible decision making: Making decisions based on accurate consideration of all relevant factors and the likely consequences of alternative courses of action, respecting others, and taking responsibility for one's decisions. The ability to make decisions and solve problems does not guarantee that people will use these skills to do good. Therefore, it is important that training in decision making also focuses on building a sense of responsibility and respect for others.

- Effective and emotionally intelligent parenting and leadership

- Play and joy

- Happiness caused by aesthetic and powerful experiences and compassion

The facilitation principles of EASEL draw from solution-focused coaching and brief-therapy, experiential learning and Montessori pedagogy, sociodynamic counseling, dialectic behavior therapy skills training, mindfulness, family therapy, and dyadic developmental psychotherapy. Noncompetitive games, team-building activities, adventure, and arts are other experiential elements of EASEL programs. The training facility and surrounding nature form the learning environment.

The progressive steps of relational activities with horses follow Erik Erikson's and Daniel Levinson's psychosocial stages of development and developmental tasks. Clients make friends with horses in authentic relationship-building processes. Such a process also serves as a metaphoric journey of growing up and the psychosocial stages. Clients can revisit their own history and reflect on the developmental tasks of each stage. EASEL activities create novel challenges for practicing being safe and managing stress, regulating emotions, communicating nonverbally, and earning leadership. Furthermore, EASEL offers these opportunities to experiment and practice away from their own real-life situations. New skills can then be used also in daily life.

Creating Optimal Milieu for Change and Personal Growth

Change is unavoidable in life; growth is optional. Facilitators strive to create an environment that is challenging enough to create the need for problem solving and learning yet safe enough to allow clients to let go of unproductive defenses and to find the courage to try something new. Repeated, purposeful, and focused attention builds new neural highways in the brain; old ones can be modified at any age, but it requires mindful attention. Mindfulness requires both concentration and serenity.

Feeling threatened physically or socially causes our attention to divert to the potential danger. EASEL facilitators build mutually respectful, affectionate, and caring relationships with the program horses for ethical and safety reasons but also to model relationships based on trust and care. Horses have the tendency to draw people's attention. Seeing the horses calm and content and enjoying being around the facilitators helps clients relax and feel safer.

Cognitive scientists have known for 2 decades that the brain is capable of significant internal change in response to environmental changes. It is now also known that the brain changes as a function of where individuals puts their attention. EASEL facilitators create and modify the physical environment to influence the outcome, like a Montessori teacher sets the classroom ready for the next day thinking what elements the children in that stage of development might be drawn to and benefit from. The selected elements in the physical environment may vary according to the EASEL facilitator's framework, but clients are always welcomed with tea and snacks, wrapped in blankets when cold, and generally treated with respect and care.

The Chemistry of Bonding

In an interaction, depending on the emotional content, either the level of the stress hormone cortisol or the bonding and care hormone oxytocin may rise. Stress disturbs learning. Oxytocin acts as a stress hormone down-regulator. It is released in emotionally safe situations and seems to require bonding first (Elsevier, 2010), hence the friendship-based relational activities in EASEL. In addition to increasing self-awareness and emotion regulation and stimulating social interaction and social competence, human–animal interactions have been shown to induce lowering of cortisol level, to cause a significant rise in oxytocin level, and to decrease blood pressure (Uvnäs-Moberg, 2010). The levels of oxytocin, dopamine, endorphin, and prolactin have been shown to rise significantly also in therapy dogs during interactions with people (Odendaal, 2000; Uvnäs-Moberg, 2010). This indicates that voluntary interactions between clients and therapy dogs can be mutually beneficial. As oxytocin has the same roles and chemical structure in all mammals, we can work from the hypothesis that the same mutual joy is possible with horses as with dogs. The extra challenge with horses, which are sensitive prey animals, is that the threat-based flight–fight response is even more easily activated than with dogs.

In humans the oxytocin levels are higher when being touched than when touching (Uvnäs-Moberg, 2010). In EASEL the horses are always at liberty and free to interact or walk away. Clients learn to build a relationship based on mutual respect, trust, and care. As with people, both take responsibility of their own 50% in the relationship. Patting and scratching the horse to make the horse feel good, without wanting anything for self, is often an important learning experience for clients. To then have the horse gently groom back and voluntarily join in free play is even more powerful.

EASEL Horsemanship

As EASEL's equine activities are about making friends with a horse and learning social emotional skills in the process, interactions with horses cannot include attitudes and behaviors that would not be acceptable with people either. Clients interact with horses at liberty in a working arena or pasture, and EASEL horsemanship follows the model of the lead mare. There are some important differences from the stallion's natural behavior. The stallion steals mares from other stallions and needs to establish leadership first to be able to keep its mares and keep them safe. The stallion then builds an affectionate relationship with the mares over time. A mare, however, starts by setting mutually respectful boundaries, builds communication and basic trust, and then accepts the newcomer and possibly proceeds to making friends. Horses bond for life if allowed to stay together. The mare's style is what horses use with people, too, unless people out of their own fear and busy schedule try to build a relationship through domination. Leadership is earned from EASEL horses by becoming such a safe, fun, and wise friend that they want to follow and play.

Free Play, Happiness, and Emotion Regulation

All mammals learn the social codes of their species in free play (Bekoff, 2007). In EASEL, the ultimate goal of making friends is to be able to play with the horse at liberty. EASEL horses are trained to learn different reciprocal games. They "specialize" in the ones they enjoy most and often engage clients by behaviors such as taking turns rolling a ball. The process of making friends gives the clients experiences of the seven types of happiness defined by Ekman (2003):

- Amusement

- Fiero (the delight of meeting a challenge)

- Relief

- Excitement, novelty

- Awe, wonder

- Sensory pleasures

- Calm peacefulness

The progressive set of relational activities with horses gives clients opportunities to experience, regulate, and process thoughts and emotions in authentic situations but outside the challenges in their everyday lives. With the guidance of the facilitator, clients can modulate the level of challenge in the activities, thereby regulating the intensity of their experience and emotions so that they can be recognized but also handled and processed with the psychoeducative tools and the facilitator's guidance.

Equine Activities Are Short in Duration

Each EASEL session is a minimum of 90 minutes for an individual and 3 hours for a family or a small group. However, the activities with horses don't last long. Our brain works on autopilot in familiar situations. The brain saves energy by making us think and do what we have always done in similar situations. Novel situations require conscious thinking and working memory and activate the prefrontal cortex. Learning and creativity become possible but take more energy. The work of Rock and Schwartz (2006) on how the brain processes information, how it accepts or adapts it, and how that is connected with changes in behavior suggests that regular short high-attention activities are more effective than long ones. Also, the reduction of cortisol levels and the increases in the levels of oxytocin, prolactine, endorphin, and dopamine were seen in people and dogs within 5 to 24 minutes after they met and started interacting with one another (Odendaal, 2000). Interestingly, interactions between clients and horses in EASEL activities rarely last longer than 15 minutes, if the clients and horses themselves decide what feels enough.

Description

The process descriptions of different programs depend on the clients' overall needs and goals. The horse activities, however, always follow the same progressive steps of making friends. Each session starts with clarifying what clients want to investigate that day and defining what they already know and what already works. Scale questions are often used to define goals for the session. This also allows the facilitators to assess the emotional state of clients and if horse activities are possible. Horses are never "used" to help clients calm down because of ethical reasons and because the horses will not be with them all the time in daily life. Instead, facilitators teach mindfulness techniques and share general psychoeducative information and SEL tools. Sometimes clients don't feel calm enough to work with horses and choose other options. Sessions end with a closing discussion.

In the horse activities, clients start from the first step, regardless of their past experience with horses. They start by observing a herd of horses and proceed to getting acquainted with one. The process of making friends eventually leads to free play. The arena holds various possibilities selected by the facilitator, and the horse and the client together choose what they want to do. The instructions are usually to just go to the arena and "hang out" with the horse and see what happens. The various elements placed around the arena help to activate clients and horses. Facilitators can influence the depth and direction of sessions by removing or adding elements.

The client and the horse may progress to investigating consensual leadership and challenge courses. The horse is always at liberty to walk away if the game is not fun. Obstacles are negotiated together and at a speed that feels comfortable to both. Depending on the client, these activities may involve metaphors and symbolism. Clients design metaphoric agility courses that may symbolize problem solving or learning a new skill needed at school or work. Other themes might be boundaries, a narrative, intention versus behavior, buckets of needs, mapping own strengths, visioning own future, and leading self to lead others. Psychoeducation and EASEL tools are given in all sessions to support the process.

All steps of the program have several alternative open-ended activities to choose from, and clients may stay on one step for several sessions. This repetition makes it possible to reinforce something while processing what is happening in the moment. Like in life in general, we never know what is going to happen. The challenge is to discover ways to communicate and develop an adequate level of mutual trust, respect, and care to match the demands of the task at hand. We process what happens. In longer processes some clients may eventually proceed to drive or ride their new equine friends but many find the free play and agility courses at liberty even more rewarding.

The General Process for Clients

The personal process of change and growth can be described with Richard Boyatzis's (2001) model of self-directed learning:

1. My ideal self: Who do I want to be?

2. My real self: Who am I? What are my strengths and gaps?

3. My learning agenda: How can I build on my strengths and reduce gaps?

4. Experimenting with and practicing new behavior, thoughts, and feelings to the point of mastery. In EASEL this stage follows the cycle of experiential learning by Kolb (1984).

5. Developing supportive and trusting relationships that make change possible. This is the role of the EASEL facilitators and horses but also the whole group or family. We work with children and teens and the whole family. In our coaching and counseling programs, we encourage our adult clients to bring to some sessions anyone they feel is important for their own well-being and the process.

Application

EASEL can be used equally well in education, in coaching, and with various patient groups in therapy. The experiential activities with trained EASEL horses form a progressive program that can serve both clients' goals and those of SEL. The experiential exercises of an EASEL program can be used equally well with school-age children and youth, families, corporate clients, and professionals wanting experiential coaching.

According to Chandler (2005), in animal assisted counseling the key to the success of a program is in the skill of the facilitator to guide the processing after an animal assisted activity directed toward clients' goals. The EASEL facilitator training program is a 1-year process training of 30 continuing education credit points for professionals in the fields of education, social work, mental health, and supervision and coaching. The training is composed of 20 days over a 1-year period, with home assignments, literature, and practice using the methodology in one's own work in the weeks between experiential workshops. It is a process training where participants experience the basic EASEL program as clients.

The training is also tailored to each participant's professional needs and interests with individual and group coaching. The participants are taught how to train EASEL horses, and we test their training skills and relationship with their horse companion. In their final written paper the students need to show logical integration of EASEL into their own professional framework both in theory and in practice. EASEL facilitator training programs are offered in Finnish, Swedish, English, French, and German. In Finland, the training is arranged in collaboration with the university of Jyväskylä's center of continuing professional education, Educluster, Finland.

References

Bekoff, M. (2007). *The emotional lives of animals: A leading scientist explores animal joy, sorrow, and empathy—and why they matter.* Novato, CA: New World Library.

Boyatzis, R. (2001). *Unleashing the power of self-directed learning.* Retrieved from: http://stemrc.aihec.org/NASASRE/SREFACULTY/Shared%20Documents/self_directed_learning.pdf

Cacioppo, J. T., Berntson, G. G., Taylor, S. E., & Schacter, D. L. (Eds.). (2002). *Foundations in social neuroscience.* Cambridge, MA: MIT Press.

Collaborative for Academic, Social, and Emotional Learning. (CASEL). (2010). *About CASEL.* Retrieved from: http://www.casel.org

Chandler, C. (2005). *Animal assisted therapy and counseling.* New York: Routledge.

Dispenza, J. (2007). *Evolve your brain: The science of changing your mind.* Deerfield Beach, FL: Health Communications.

Ekman, P. (2003). *Emotions revealed: Recognizing faces and feelings to improve communication and emotional life.* New York, NY: Times Books.

Elsevier. (2010). Oxytocin: It's a Mom and Pop thing. *ScienceDaily.* Retrieved from: http://www.sciencedaily.com/releases/2010/08/100820101207.htm

Goleman, D. (2006). *Social intelligence: The new science of human relationships.* London, UK: Hutchinson.

Katcher, A. H., & Wilkins, G. (2002). *The centaur's lessons: The companionable zoo method of therapeutic education based upon contact with animals and nature study.* Animal Therapy Association and People, Animals, Nature, Inc. Retrieved from: http://www.ourfarmschool.org/evaluation/clinic_trial.php

Kolb, D. A. (1984). *Experiential learning: Experience as the source of learning and development.* Englewood Cliffs, NJ: Prentice-Hall.

Lazarus, R. S., & Lazarus, B. N. (1994). *Passion and reason—making sense of our emotions.* London: Oxford University Press.

Lehtinen, E., & Kuusinen, J. (2001). *Kasvatuspsykologia.* Helsinki: WSOY.

Levy, B. R., Slade, M. D., Kasl, S. V., & Kunkel, S. R. (2002). Longevity increased by positive self-perception of aging. *Journal of Personality and Social Psychology, 88*(2), 261–270.

Mayer, J. D., Salovey, P., & Caruso, D. R. (2008). Emotional intelligence: New ability or eclectic traits. *American Psychologist, 63*(6), 503–517.

McEnruem, M. P., Groves, K. S., & Shen, W. (2010). Emotional intelligence training: Evidence regarding its efficacy for developing leaders. *Leadership Review, 10*, Winter, 3–26.

Odendaal, J. S. J. (2000). Animal-assisted therapy—magic or medicine? *Journal of Psychosomatic Research, 49*(4), 275–280.

Payton, J., Weissberg, R. P., Durlak, J. A., Dymnicki, A. B., Taylor, R. D., Schellinger, K. B. et al. (2008). The positive impact of social and emotional learning for kindergarten to eighth-grade students: Findings from three scientific reviews. In: *Collaborative for Academic, Social, and Emotional Learning.* Chicago, IL. Retrieved from: www.lpfch.org/sel/casel-fullreport.pdf

Ridley, M. (2003). *Nature via nurture: Genes, experience, and what makes us human.* Oxford, UK: Harper Collins.

Rock, D., & Schwartz, J. (2006). The neuroscience of leadership. *Strategy + Business, 43.* Retrieved from: http://www.strategy-business.com

Rock, D. (2009). Managing with the brain in mind. *Strategy + Business, 56.* Retrieved from: http://www.strategy-business.com/article/09306?pg=all

Tirkkonen, A., Kokkonen, M., & Pulkkinen, L. (2004). Tunteiden säätelyn siirtyminen vanhemmilta lapsille lapsilähtöisen vanhemmuuden välityksellä [Transfer of emotion regulation strategies from parents to children through child-centered parenting]. *Psykologia, 1,* 46–58.

Trotter, K., Chandler, C., Goodwin-Bond, D., & Casey, J. (2008). A comparative study of the efficacy of group equine assisted counseling with at-risk children and adolescents. *Journal of Creativity in Mental Health, 3*(3), 254–284.

Uvnäs-Moberg, K. (2010). Coordinating role of oxytocin. A plenary session at the IAHAIO congress in Stockholm, Sweden.

Zins, J. E., Weissberg, R. P., Wang, M. C., & Walberg, H. J. (2004). *Building academic success on social and emotional learning: What does the research say?* New York: Teachers College Press.

☐ Grounded Strategies That Improve Self-Efficacy

Mary Looman

Introduction

Beginning in the early 1900s, social scientists began developing many respected theories and models of ways humans evolve into autonomous individuals capable of sustaining life and living purposefully among others. The breakthrough in our understanding came with Abraham Maslow's work, *Motivation and Personality*, published in 1954. Considered the father of humanistic psychology, Maslow suggested that beyond survival, humans need self-esteem to exist. He believed that humans have an innate desire to realize their full potential and do not simply react to situations but develop insights that push them toward accomplishing greater ways of living.

In agreement with Maslow, Nathan Branden (1994), the definitive expert on self-esteem, believed that adequate self-esteem is essential to our survival because "it is a motivator. It inspires behavior" (p. 4). His two-component definition of self-esteem—competency and worthiness—has provided researchers a practical way of studying self-esteem, which today is viewed by most "as one of the few dimensions of behavior that stretches across the full spectrum of human existence" (Mruk, 2006, p. 2).

Our sense of value and purposefulness derives from the knowledge that we have the ability to cope with the problems presented by living (competence) and that we have the right to happiness and success (worthiness). This knowledge, however, does not stem from our cognitive abilities but from our abilities to feel. Emotions form the bridge between our subjectivity to the objectivity of the larger world (Greenspan, 1997). While our cognitive system evaluates factual information important for survival, our emotional system evaluates significance and meaning, which is important for the survival of our humanness. "Muting emotions causes problems such as doubt, indecision, weakened judgment, and an over- or underestimation of the significance of events or actions" (Looman, 2003, p. 218).

Humans learn to mute their emotions when they grow up in shame-based families (Bradshaw, 1988). Shame is internalized when one is abandoned and one experiences the loss of the authentic self and psychological existence. The authentic self evolves as the child's inner reality is matched by the child's relationship with others—thus the critical need for appropriate emotional interaction between the parent and the pre-verbal child, ages birth to 3 years. In shame-based families, babies and toddlers learn to ignore their emotions as an aspect of problem solving.

Rationale

For many who come to counseling or therapeutic growth and learning programs, they have lost, or never had, the ability to use their emotions as cues to direct their actions towards survival-oriented behavior and existential problem solving. They have been unable to develop a meta-cognitive or mindfulness process that involves two internal systems: (1) an organizational system that sorts and categorizes stimuli at an emotional level; and (2) an evaluation system that tests and refines stimuli in terms of its adaptive qualities. Mindfulness connects affect and reason, which allows individuals to step back and contemplate on the level of significance an event or idea has rather than immediately reacting to any given stimuli (Bennett-Goleman, 2001).

Horses, on the other hand, must develop metacognition as quickly as possible to survive. A horse's very survival depends on how success-fully it can learn to live constantly in the present moment, totally aware of itself and its surroundings and relentlessly focused (Hallberg, 2008). Horses, just as babies, innately develop affective processing skills quickly. The only difference between foals and babies is their parents. A mare aligns and reflects matching emotional cues with its foal, whereas the shame-based mother often ignores the baby's emotional cues or reflects opposite emotions (e.g., the baby cries because of hunger feelings and the mother yells at the baby).

In the nonverbal environment of the arena, then, the horse meta-phorically reparents clients. The horse provides a present moment—no past, no future—where clients can examine internal needs, motivations, and patterns of behaviors. Without words, clients find themselves, once again, infants, in a world where learning takes place by observation, imi-tation, and trial and error. Social learning theory (Bandura, 1977) comes to life as clients' lack of awareness and control-or-be-controlled expec-tations clash with the horse's empathic awareness and herd-survival expectations. As a result of a 1,200-pound horse's patient nonchalance, clients must reevaluate themselves. To do this, they must draw heavily on their emotional system where intuition and empathy have been lying dormant or, at best, rarely used. As clients change approaches to their relationship with the horse, they begin to form expectations about the consequences that future behaviors and decisions will likely bring. The brilliance of equine assisted counseling (EAC) is the fact that the horse always reacts immediately, consistently, and without judgment, therefore consistently and immediately reinforcing appropriate behavior in the client. Inherently, EAC techniques provide the four critical components of social learning: attention, retention, experience, and self-efficacy.

Self-Efficacy

Self-efficacy is the outward sign of self-esteem. It is the desire to engage in behavior that one believes capable of executing successfully. It is demonstrated by individuals' joy in activities they feel they will be successful in doing and in persistence and effort that they are willing to put into activities they consider worthwhile and capable of learning from. Self-efficacy is the observable characteristic of self-esteem when clients, in the arena, complete the task and a smile crosses their face as they lean their head against the horse and lovingly give it acknowledgment of success.

Research (Chandler, 2005; Leblanc & Ritchie, 2001; Neil, 2003; Rubin, 2001) on outcomes in any type of learning or therapeutic endeavor (e.g., cognitive, art, play, experiential) suggests that regardless of clients' presenting issues, the increase of self-esteem is a basic goal because it is so essential to human survival. However, self-esteem is not the means but the end; it is a "consequence of internally generated practices" (Branden, 1994, p. 66). EAC techniques, then, are the independent variables that affect self-esteem, the dependent variable. Research (Branden, 1994; Mruk, 2006) has identified three components that contribute to individuals' level of self-esteem (items 1, 3, 5) and three corresponding components that contribute to individuals' level of self-efficacy (items 2, 4, 6):

1. *Awareness* is the way individuals are actively conscious of all that is going on around them and ways to adapt to their environment in a manner that is affirming and protective. Individuals' level of awareness is demonstrated by the ability to be mindful of their perceptions, thoughts, and feelings and understand the way these processes affect behavior and, ultimately, survival.

2. *Acceptance* is the way people value themselves as unique individuals with both strengths and flaws. Individuals' level of acceptance is demonstrated by their willingness to fully engage with others in a positive and affirming manner.

3. *Accountability* is the way individuals take responsibility for their own emotions, actions, and achievements. Individuals' level of

accountability is demonstrated by the ability to acknowledge their choices, actions, and consequences as well as deserved praise and success.

4. *Assertiveness* is the way individuals are able to effectively accomplish goals that have a personal significance by overcoming challenges or obstacles. Individuals' level of assertiveness is demonstrated by acts of determination and self-control.

5. *Achievement* is the way individuals transform their dreams and thoughts into productive tasks and relationships. Individuals' level of achievement is demonstrated by the ability to plan and organize in ways that lead to purposeful living.

6. *Admirability* is the way individuals feel connected to humanity through the adherence to values or standards of behavior that are universal. When individuals fail to live up to universal truths and expectations, they experience guilt, shame, or disgrace. Individuals' level of admirability is demonstrated by altruistic and ethical and moral behavior.

Description

EAC techniques are directed interventions that create a metaphorical relationship between horse and human from which participants can focus on a specific problem and become acutely aware of their cognitive entanglements, psychological rigidity, and avoidance of affective processing and then can gain introspective insights that transform them toward healthier living. To engage with a horse that cannot talk back requires clients to learn to perceive and accept their thoughts, images, emotions, and memories as they are; to relate to the horse with openness, interest, and receptiveness (much like they did as an innocent child who encountered the world with curiosity and fearlessness); to value their own true experience; and to establish their own goals according to their own values and then carry them out responsibly.

Although many research projects in the last decade have demonstrated the success of EAC in specific populations and for specific syndromes in initiating positive change in clients (Froeschle, 2009; Kakacek, 2007; Kohanov, 2001; Klontz, Bivens, Leinart, & Klonta, 2007; Trotter, Chandler, Goodwin-Bond, & Casey, 2008), there is a need to understand the overall effect that EAC has on self-esteem and self-efficacy. This concept is similar to the impact Carl Rogers' (1951) client-centered therapy had on creating the fundamental techniques used in most psychothera-peutic sessions: unconditional positive regard, genuineness, and empa-thy. The following EAC strategic categories, with related EAC techniques, propose a methodological way to provide fundamental techniques to increase clients' level of self-esteem and self-efficacy. They are presented in procedural order for organizations that provide a therapeutic program that offers daily or weekly EAC sessions from which clients can build on previous experiences and insights.

Treatment Outcome: Increase in Awareness

Strategic Treatment Category: Grazing

Techniques that fall within the grazing strategy encourage clients to observe and reflect on their perceptions and emotions. Postactivity dis-cussion guides clients in becoming aware that everything in the envi-ronment, consciously or unconsciously, bears on our actions, purposes, values, and goals and that our perceptions and emotions regarding our interpretation of the environment may or may not be adaptive and healthy. Techniques include activities such as

- Clients observe a small group of horses and give them names that characterize their perceived attributes and discuss the thoughts and feelings the horses were having.

- Clients enter the arena with a group of 3–5 horses and walk among them, with or without touching, and then discuss different aspects of the relationships, horse characteristics, and emotions.

- Clients observe other clients in horse activities and discuss their own perceptions and emotions.

Treatment Outcome: Increase in Acceptance

Strategic Treatment Category: Lateral Softness

Techniques that fall within the lateral softness strategy encourage clients to feel accepted through acts of caring and nurturance. Postactivity dis-cussion guides clients in reflecting on their relationships with the horse and the horse with clients and insight they had regarding the power and size differentiation between them and horses. Techniques include activi-ties such as:

- Clients each select a horse from the herd, halter with lead rope, tie horse to pole, groom, and then walk with horse around the arena.

- Clients clean the horses' hooves.

- A client and horse are in large circle made by a rope on the arena floor. The client keeps the horse in the circle while rubbing or petting all over the horse.

Treatment Outcome: Increase in Accountability

Strategic Treatment Category: Gathered Up

Techniques that fall within the gathered up strategy encourage clients to recognize their thoughts, emotions, and behaviors that affect their ability to achieve desired results. Postactivity discussion guides clients in scrutinizing their own reactions and involvement in the task and working with others. Techniques include activities such as

- Client picks a horse in the arena and tries to get the horse in a small pen (in the arena made from poles) without touching it, coaxing it with food, or using any handling tool (halter/rope).

- Clients are in teams of 2–3 people. During technique, team members must always be in contact with each other. Team must select a horse from 3–4 horses, halter it, and bring it back to facilitators without holding onto the halter.

- Clients, as a group, must select a horse from 3–4 horses and direct it through an obstacle course with only one client at a time being in charge. (Equine specialist announces when the next client is to be in charge.)

Treatment Outcome: Increase in Assertiveness

Strategic Treatment Category: Nose-to-Nose

Techniques that fall within the nose-to-nose strategy encourage clients to experience a range of emotions from anxiety to courage and to develop thought processes and strategies that empower them to overcome their timidity. Postactivity discussion guides clients in analyzing their thoughts, feelings, and behaviors and identifying strengths, biggest challenges, and shifts. Techniques include activities such as

- Client stands in a rope circle made on the arena floor. There are 2–4 buckets of alpha cubes around the client. The client is to keep the horses from eating the cubes.

- Client must select a horse, bring it to a Hula-Hoop on the ground, and keep the two back feet of the horse in the hoop for 5 minutes.

- Clients are divided into teams. There are two parallel lines of PVC poles about 10 feet from each other that create an alley (create a metaphorical label, such as river, valley, black hole of depression), and on one side of the alley are various objects (buckets, cones, saddle blankets, exercise balls, grooming tools). One team is the enemy, and one team is the hero (create metaphorical labels that would be meaningful to the group). The goal is for the hero team to get the horses and objects across to the other side of the alley while the enemy team tries to prevent them from getting there. Various rules can be set up to make the experience more challenging.

Treatment Outcome: Increase Achievement

Strategic Treatment Outcome: Easy or Hard

Techniques that fall within the easy or hard strategy encourage clients to accomplish tasks that require planning, organizational, and creative problem-solving skills. When working with clients who will be returning for several sessions or have time to complete several assignments, each assignment should have greater and greater challenges. Postactivity discussion guides clients in analyzing their thought process from beginning to end, any cognitive or affect shifts that have taken place, and any behavioral changes that occurred during the exercise. Techniques include activities such as

- Client guides a horse to weave through three poles with the ability only to touch the horse with hands.

- Clients create an obstacle course that has both obstacles and temptations for the horse. Then select a horse to go through obstacle course; various rules can be established to create different metaphorical meanings.

- Clients play horse hockey by setting up goals at each end of the arena, dividing into teams and choosing a horse to use as a puck. There are 4–5 horses in the arena. Each team tries to get the horse past its goal.

Treatment Outcome: Increase Admirability

Strategic Treatment Outcome: Alpha

Techniques that fall within the alpha strategy encourage clients to establish their own standards for accomplishing tasks. Postactivity discussion guides clients in accessing their own internal wisdom and ethical and moral beliefs. Techniques include activities such as

- Client catches and halters a horse, brings the horse to a designated spot in the arena, ground ties and grooms the horse, and must walk several feet from the horse to get each grooming tool (a different brush must be used for each side of the horse, mane, and tail); the horse is not to go anywhere while ground tied.

- Clients each pick a horse and stay beside their horse while it wanders around the arena. As the horse nears another horse, clients speak for the horse in giving the other horse a compliment. The second horse's "voice" responds back. Each horse voice must say three positive comments before moving on. Clients must encourage their horse to move on after the three comments have been spoken.

- Clients have a haltered horse on a lead rope and an egg in a spoon which is held in their nondominant hand. The egg represents the trait clients most want to keep safe. They must lead the horse, carrying the egg, through an obstacle course that involves twists and turns and a jump (representing life's challenges).

Summary

In summary, self-esteem is as important to life as food, clothing, and shelter. We live better with it, and our lives are filled with despair without it. Self-esteem develops as we find our worth in the world and our ability to live in the moment assured that we have the competence to manage life as it comes. For centuries, horses have demonstrated a way to live in balance between life's extreme pains and extreme joys that so often negatively affect our levels of self-esteem. "Horses appear to have the ability to envision and act upon the 'bigger picture' of herd survival, rather than on individual needs, emotions, desires, or wants, and in doing so seem to act 'outside of self,' an art that we humans may not always recognize or feel comfortable with" (Hallberg, 2008, p. 20). Through the metaphorical relationship participants have with horses during EAC activities, they have an opportunity to experience ways to live more balanced and congruent lives. Within the experience, they can remember what it is to trust in their own inner voice again, the voice that speaks of the universal vision of humanity.

Application

The EAC techniques discussed in this essay can be used with clients of all ages. However, they are especially useful for clients with mood disorders as might occur as a result of trauma, divorce, natural disaster, child maltreatment, and domestic violence. These clients tend to have emotional numbing, or they overreact to environmental cues. They have generally lost their ability to use emotions as cues for present-moment survival and within social constructs and interpersonal relationships. These techniques, especially for the internal alpha components (awareness, accountability, admirability), will assist clients in comprehending their emotions, gaining insights into current maladaptive behaviors, and practice progressively adaptive processes that lead to increased self-efficacy.

Second, these EAC techniques are useful for clients with personality disorders, especially Cluster B and Cluster C, as the general goal of therapy with these clients is to rectify their pathological system of insidious strategies and mechanisms that they have developed to cope with life that developed from their misunderstanding and unawareness of the emotions underlying their thoughts and behaviors. The EAC techniques that focus on the three internal alpha components—awareness, accountable, admirability—assist clients in practicing integration of internal cognitive and affective processes. The three external components—acceptance, assertiveness, and achievement—assist clients in connecting action with meaning, which in turn develops a healthy network of problem-solving and interpersonal relationships strategies and mechanisms.

Finally, these EAC techniques can provide a basic foundation to construct growth and development courses, such as marriage enrichment, youth leadership, team building, and corporate leadership programs. The purpose of most growth and development courses is to assist participants in becoming more aware of their own unique personality traits, problem-solving, and learning styles and to develop metacognitive abilities—the ability to integrate affect and reason—which then generates reflective and value-driven responses to environmental cues. Value-driven responses, based on congruency between internal affective and cognitive processes, create self-actualizing environments for individuals and organizations. These techniques, when completed in order, assist clients in progressively building metacognitive abilities.

Author's Note

In the future, research should be focused on two areas: (1) correlating EAC strategies with each component of self-esteem; and (2) correlating specific EAC techniques (setup, rules, debrief discussion) with the EAC outcome strategies. There are several valid psychological instruments currently available for pre–post assessment: Basis-A Inventory (TRT Associates, Inc.), Cognitive Distortion Scales (Psychological Assessment Resources, Inc.), Coopersmith Self-Esteem Inventory (Mindgarden, Inc), Multidimensional Self-Esteem Inventory (Psychological Assessment Resources, Inc.), and Tennessee Self-Concept Scales (Western Psychological Services, Inc.). Empirically based strategies, techniques, and outcomes will provide solid ground for advancing the benefits and professionalism of equine assisted counseling.

References

Bandura, A. (1977). *Social learning theory.* New York: General Learning Press.
Bennett-Goleman, T. (2001). *Emotional alchemy: How the mind can heal the heart.* New York: Random House.
Bradshaw, J. (1988). *Healing the shame that binds you.* Deerfield Beach, FL: Health Communications, Inc.
Branden, N. (1994). *The six pillars of self-esteem.* New York: Bantam.
Chandler, C. K. (2005). *Animal assisted therapy in counseling.* New York: Routledge.
Froeschle, J. (2009). Empowering abused women through equine assisted career therapy. *Journal of Creativity and Mental Health, 4,* 180–190.
Greenspan, S. (1997). *The growth of the mind.* New York: Addison-Wesley.
Hallberg, L. (2008). *Walking the way of the horse: Exploring the power of the horse–human relationship.* New York: Universe, Inc.
Kakacek, S. L. (2007). *An arena for success: Metaphor utilization in equine-assisted psychotherapy.* Paper based on a program presented at the Association of Counselor Education and Supervision Conference, Columbus, OH.

Kohanov, L. (2001). *The tao of equus: A woman's journey of healing and transformation through the way of the horse.* Novato, CA: New world Library.

Klontz, B. T., Bivens, A., Leinart, D., & Klonta, T. (2007). The effectiveness of equine-assisted experiential therapy: Results of an open clinical trial. *Society and Animals, 15,* 257–267.

Leblanc, M., & Ritchie, M. (2001). A meta-analysis of play therapy outcomes. *Counseling Psychology Quarterly, 144,* 149–163.

Looman, M. D. (2003). Reflective leadership: Strategic planning from the heart and soul. *Consulting Psychology Journal: Practice and Research, 55,* 215–221.

Maslow, A. (1954). *Motivation and personality.* New York: Harper.

Mruk, C. J. (2006). *Self-esteem research, theory, and practice: Toward a positive psychology of self-esteem.* New York: Springer.

Neil, J. (2003). Reviewing and benchmarking adventure therapy outcomes: Applications of meta-analysis. *Journal of Experimental Education, 25,* 316–21.

Rogers, C. (1951). *Client-centered therapy: Its current practice, implications and theory.* London: Constable.

Rubin, J. A. (2001). *Approaches to art therapy: Theory and technique,* 2nd ed. New York: Brunner-Routledge.

Trotter, K. S., Chandler, C. K., Goodwin-Bond, D., & Casey, J. (2008). A comparative study of the efficacy of group equine assisted counseling with at-risk children and adolescents. *Journal of Creativity in Mental Health, 3,* 254–284.

☐ Soft Eyes

Deborah Goodwin-Bond

Introduction

Equine assisted counseling (EAC) relies on clients having an awareness of their surroundings to be safe. Clients are usually unfamiliar with the horses being used in the therapeutic process and in fact are often unfamiliar with horses of any kind and their behavior. For clients to maintain their personal safety, they must be aware of their surroundings. The Soft Eyes activity introduces new skills and awareness of the individual's behavior and how it influences visual awareness.

Rationale

Becoming too focused can be problematic for individuals in most areas of their lives. That focus can block out awareness of anything but the object being focused on. Creating awareness of external factors in clients is important not just for safety but personal insight as well. Horses respond much like humans respond to each other, though without the personal baggage that humans bring to the interaction. Horses physiologically can change their focus only by changing head position or distance to the object.

Description

Often clients become so focused on one task or event that they become blind to their surroundings. This exercise aids participants in thinking outside the box. There are several variations to this activity, and it is equally effective with groups or individuals. Learning to soften and open themselves to new experiences aids clients in opening themselves up to the experiences of the therapeutic process.

What Is Needed?

Choose an item or a particular spot on a tree or building. Orange plastic cones work well, as does a brightly colored bucket or cloth. Ask the clients to locate the focal point. When you're ready to begin the exercise, ask the clients to close their eyes. After a few seconds, ask them to focus on the focal point for 10–15 seconds. When the time has passed, ask clients to relax and talk about what they saw. If necessary, ask them to relax using deep breathing or any other relaxation technique you wish. Have clients look in the direction of the focal point and ask what they see now. Usually participants note that while relaxed and less focused they have seen more of what is around the focal point.

This technique leads to discussion of seeing more than just the focal point. Most participants note that while they are relaxed their surroundings actually become clearer. Translating this activity to real-world experience is easily done—for example, "Have you ever been so angry about something that you fail to see how other events created the situation?" Once the bigger picture emerges, the anger lessens. Clients gain a different perspective. Not only does relaxation allow participants to see the broader perspective, but also stress is often lessened. Clients with excessive stress, or with problems of becoming overwhelmed, respond well to this activity because it provides tools for decreasing anxiety and stress while allowing them to mentally step back from a disquieting situation.

Application

This activity can be used with most clients. In group settings clients can share their experiences. It is interesting having clients share how the activity feels—before and after. Clients often are surprised at how this technique can be applied to other areas of their lives.

INDEX